CREATIVE LEARNING IN HIGHER EDUCATION

This book provides higher education faculty and administrators a scholarly resource on the most salient aspects and emerging trends in creative learning in higher education today. International contributors explore ways to foster creativity in any student, regardless of academic discipline or demographic characteristics, and demonstrate that creativity is a skill all students can and should learn. Chapters analyze how different countries and cultures implement creative learning, exploring issues of instruction, assessment, and ultimately how these practices are transforming learning. This important book helps higher education professionals understand and cultivate creative learning across disciplines in any college or university setting.

Linda S. Watts is Professor of American Studies and Co-Director of the Project for Interdisciplinary Pedagogy at the University of Washington Bothell, USA.

Patrick Blessinger is Founder and Executive Director of the International Higher Education Teaching and Learning Association (HETL), USA.

CREATIVE LEARNING IN HIGHER EDUCATION

International Perspectives and Approaches

*Edited by Linda S. Watts
and Patrick Blessinger*

Routledge
Taylor & Francis Group

NEW YORK AND LONDON

First published 2017
by Routledge
711 Third Avenue, New York, NY 10017

and by Routledge
2 Park Square, Milton Park, Abingdon, Oxon, OX14 4RN

Routledge is an imprint of the Taylor & Francis Group, an informa business

Library of Congress Cataloging-in-Publication Data
Names: Watts, Linda S., editor. | Blessinger, Patrick, editor.
Title: Creative learning in higher education : international perspectives
    and approaches / edited by Linda S. Watts and Patrick Blessinger.
Description: New York, NY : Routledge is an imprint of the Taylor &
    Francis Group, an Informa Business, [2017] | Includes bibliographical
    references and index.
Identifiers: LCCN 2016009880 | ISBN 9781138962354 (hardback) |
    ISBN 9781138962361 (pbk.) | ISBN 9781315659473 (ebook)
Subjects: LCSH: Creative thinking—Study and teaching (Higher) |
    Creative thinking—Study and teaching (Higher)—Case studies. |
    Creative ability—Study and teaching (Higher) | Creative ability—
    Study and teaching (Higher)—Case studies.
Classification: LCC LB2395.35 .C72 2017 | DDC 378.1/7—dc23
LC record available at https://lccn.loc.gov/2016009880

ISBN: 978-1-138-96235-4 (hbk)
ISBN: 978-1-138-96236-1 (pbk)
ISBN: 978-1-315-65947-3 (ebk)

Typeset in Bembo
by Apex CoVantage, LLC

Printed and bound in the United States of America by Publishers Graphics,
LLC on sustainably sourced paper.

DEDICATION

This book is dedicated to educators all over the world and to the members of the International Higher Education Teaching and Learning Association whose passion for teaching, learning, research, and service are helping to transform the academy in many positive ways.

Vision, Mission, and Values Statement

The long-term vision of HETL is to improve educational outcomes in higher education by creating new knowledge and advancing the scholarship and practice of teaching and learning.

To bring that vision to reality, the present mission of HETL is to develop a global community of higher education professionals who come together to share their knowledge and expertise in teaching and learning.

To effectively fulfill that mission, HETL adheres to the values of academic integrity, collegiality, and diversity. As such, HETL supports academic and pedagogical pluralism, diversity of learning, as well as practices that promote sustainable learning and peace.

Membership, Conference, Publishing, and Research Information

For information about HETL, please see http://www.hetl.org

Patrick Blessinger
Founder and Executive Director
The HETL Association
patrickblessinger@gmail.com

Lorraine Stefani
President
The HETL Association
lorraine.stefani@auckland.ac.nz

Linda S. Watts
Secretary
The HETL Association
lswatts@uw.edu

CONTENTS

FOREWORD

This book adopts the educational view that everyone is creative and has the potential to develop their creativity. In fact being creative is an essential part of being a person and without it none of us would be the person we are. While this fundamental view of creativity might be shared by the majority of people who teach and support students' learning and development in higher education, it does not always translate into course experiences and teaching practices that actually do enable learners to develop and use their creativity. This is the 'problem' that this book attempts to address by showing academics and faculty possible ways in which students' creative development can be achieved, and it sends the very important message that there are many possible ways of achieving this goal. The fundamental premise is that creative learning—learning to be creative—is an orientation and capability that all students *could*, and most importantly *should*, develop while they are studying in higher education: a premise with which I wholeheartedly agree.

I am of the generation that has spanned the transition from an Industrial Age of design and production to an Information Age in which knowledge resources and what we are able to do with that knowledge are as crucial to economic success as our material resources. Every 'Age' requires people to be creative, but as the world gets ever more complex and disrupted (just watch the news tonight!), so does the need for human creativity grow.

We are entering a new era of social learning known as the Social Age (Stodd 2014). Foresight studies that try to imagine the future have created a new vision of future learning in which personalisation, collaboration and informal learning will be at the core of our learning projects and the central learning paradigm will be characterised by a *lifelong and lifewide [commitment to] learning*, shaped by the ubiquity of information and communication technologies (ICT) (Redecker et al. 2011).

The Social Age is founded on a rapidly growing digital networked infrastructure which amplifies our ability to access and use almost limitless knowledge resources and a rapidly growing number of tools to aid learning and analysis, and connect us to people who have the personal knowledge we need to do the jobs we need to do. Web 2.0 and 3.0 provide new affordance for everyone to participate in new forms of individual or collaborative creative enterprise to make their world a better place. 'We are on the cusp of an unprecedented opportunity. Powerful social and technological change mean that we can realistically commit to the aspiration that everyone can live a creative life' (Taylor 2015). With such optimism for the future, the timing of this book is perfect!

However, much of the learning that is going on in the Social Age is so very different to the kinds of learning normally found in higher education that it is essentially invisible. This new type of learning is a cultural phenomenon. It takes place without books, without teachers and without classrooms, and it requires environments that are bounded yet provide complete freedom of action within those boundaries (Thomas and Seely Brown 2011).

The Social Age provides higher education with a new context in which to tackle the perpetual problem which confronts all universities, regardless of their geographic location, and all disciplines regardless of their historical or institutional context—namely, 'How do we prepare learners and enable them to develop themselves for a lifetime of learning and adapting to the continuous stream of situations they create or encounter in their lives?' This is both a developmental challenge and a challenge for individual and collective creativity.

For higher education teachers it's associated with a question like, 'How do we prepare our students for an ever more complex world?' This does not just mean preparing them for their first job when they leave university. It also means preparing them so that they can deal with the many challenges, uncertainties, disruptions and emergent opportunities they will encounter over a lifetime of working, learning and living. From the students' perspective the same challenge is embodied in questions like, 'How do I develop myself so I'm better prepared for the rest of my life? What sorts of things do I need to learn, what sorts of skills, qualities, dispositions and values do I need to develop, and what sorts of experiences do I need to have in order to develop these things?' Personal and professional development needs to be so much more than the development of academic capability. The challenge for institutional leaders is embodied in the question, 'How do we change our university and enable our teaching staff to meet the challenge of preparing learners for a very complex, uncertain and ever-changing future world?' How do we move from what is still a predominantly industrial provider-designed and provider-directed model of higher education, to a more ecological, social, learner-designed and learner-managed model of learning that is more appropriate for the complex world our students will inhabit when they leave university? The idea of creative learning, when individuals motivated by their interests, passions and purposes discover for themselves the problems that they want to solve and work out how to do them, is very much part of the solution.

Teachers, educational developers and others who encourage and support students' learning and development need to harness their individual and collective creativity to address this problem, to imagine the infinite number of possible solutions, choose and develop the most useful ideas, and bring into existence new and innovative practices that have potential to enable students to develop and use their imaginations and creative capabilities. It sounds simple but my own experience has taught me that bringing about such a change in many universities is a struggle.

So we need people, like the editors of this book, to bring people together with the ability to stimulate our imaginations and share their ideas and practices, so that we might learn and expand our own thinking, and through this see the affordances in our own professional lives for creating new opportunities and practices for creative learning. This is the purpose of 'Creative Learning in Higher Education: International Perspectives and Approaches,' and the editors are to be commended for deliberately searching for and finding writer practitioners who can offer perspectives on the meanings of creative learning from many different cultural and practice settings. This is the unique contribution that this book makes to the growing body of scholarly literature on creativity in higher education teaching and learning practices.

Every reader will take away something different from this book. For myself I particularly like the emphasis on 'creative learning' and the many different interpretations that are offered. Vygotsky argued that

> any human act that gives rise to something new is . . . a creative act, regardless of whether what was created is a physical object or some mental or emotional construct that lives within the person who created it and is known only to him.
>
> *(2004: 7)*

His interpretation of creativity locates it firmly in the act of learning and personal experience and through this places creativity at the heart of the higher education teaching and learning enterprise.

How we visualise and conceptualise creativity shapes how we value and recognise it in the different domains we inhabit every day of our life. Fortunately, there are many conceptualisations from which to choose, and having the freedom to choose a concept for a particular circumstance or make one based on our experience, is important. For example, the editors of this book might justifiably have chosen the formulation of Dellas and Gaier (1970)—'creativity is the desire and ability to use imagination, insight, intellect, feeling and emotion to move an idea from one state to an alternative, previously unexplored state'—as the mission for their own creative enterprise. As I have explored the idea of creativity over the last fifteen years, I have come increasingly to appreciate and respect the way Carl Rogers (1961) framed the idea of creativity as 'the emergence in action of a novel relational product growing out of the uniqueness of the individual on the one hand, and the materials, events, people, or circumstances of his life' (p. 350), where the product includes our own learning and development. The grounding of an individual's creativity in the circumstances of their lives is entirely appropriate for the formal teaching and learning environment and places huge responsibility on the teachers who shape and influence learners' everyday circumstances. The concept is also appropriate for learners living their lives outside the formal educational environment, and so it provides us with a unifying concept of creativity that both teachers and students can act and reflect upon. For me, trying to understand our own creativity in the particular circumstances of our life is a metacognitive process. We have to be mindful of our circumstances and our responses to them—thinking, feeling and acting—if we are to become more aware of our own creativity.

Rogers's view of personal creativity and how it emerges from the circumstances of our life is an ecological concept. The ecological metaphor affords us the most freedom and flexibility to explore and appreciate the ways in which we and our purposes are connected to our experiences and the world we inhabit. Applying the idea of ecology to learning, personal development and achievement is an attempt to view a person, their purposes, ambitions, goals, interests, needs and circumstances, and their social and physical relationships with the world they inhabit, as inseparable and interdependent (Jackson 2016). The idea of ecology encourages us to think more holistically and more dynamically about the way we inhabit and relate to the world. Growing out of this idea is a belief that our ecologies for learning embrace all the physical and virtual places and spaces we inhabit in our everyday lives and the learning and the meaning we gain from the contexts and situations that constitute our lives. They are the product of both imagination and reason, and they are enacted using all our capability and ingenuity. They are therefore one of our most important sites for creativity and they enable us to develop ourselves personally and professionally in all aspects of our lives. From my perspective it is the ecologies we create to learn and achieve something in which our creative learning resides and it emerges from our involvement in the circumstances of our lives in the manner Rogers (1961) describes. The challenge for higher education then is, 'How might we accommodate ecological principles into our designs for students' learning and development?' The ideas offered in this book contribute to our understanding of how this might be achieved.

If Gregory Bateson is right, that the complexities of the world can only really be understood in terms of 'an ecology of ideas' (Bateson 1972: xxiii)—an ecology that comprehends the way people and society interact with the world and the way all sorts of things, both anticipated and unanticipated, emerge from these interactions—then perhaps the most important task for a university is to help and enable learners to think with sufficient complexity to understand the complex web of relationships that connect phenomena, causes and effects. Such ways of thinking integrate the imaginative, associative and synthetic ways of thinking with the critical and analytical ways of thinking. They are creative, generative ways of thinking insofar as they will lead to connections that have not been thought of before, and from such connections new solutions can be brought into existence.

There is, however, a danger in focusing too much of our attention on the academic world and neglecting the other worlds beyond higher education. These worlds are not bound by academic normative cultures, procedures and criteria that limit and inhibit the imaginations or stifle the enthusiasm and emotions of learners in response to something that they find interesting and inspiring. These other worlds invite people to piggyback on and play with the ideas of others in the search for many potential answers to problems and opportunities that individuals find interesting and worthy of attention. These worlds encourage people to take risks and put themselves into situations where they might fail—something higher education is loath to do. But in taking risks, either by accident or design, people connect ideas, objects, tools and practices in entirely new ways, and in doing so create entirely new futures for themselves and others. In the interests of 'creative learning,' the real challenge for higher education is to embrace these sorts of circumstances that give birth to insights that change the course of a life.

One thing is certain: integrative thinking within which our creativity resides is not enough. It must be nurtured alongside that package of dispositions, qualities and capabilities necessary for success when tackling difficult problems and the knowledge and understanding that comes from disciplined study and immersion in the problems of the field. Ron Barnett (2007: 15) was right when he said, ' "Will" is the most important concept in education. Without a will nothing is possible.' Being creative is a matter of personal choice and circumstance. If we want learners to try to be creative, we have to foster their will to be creative and help them develop the confidence, knowledge and capabilities to be creative in circumstances that challenge them and require or inspire them to be creative. Imagine inventing an education system that has the will to be creative as its core educational value and purpose. But it's one thing to imagine and quite another to develop such a system. To achieve such a goal requires enough people to care about the problem to do something about it. We need leaders, people who have the courage and are prepared to advocate, persuade and exemplify through their own practice and behaviours, at all levels of the higher education system. This book makes a valuable contribution to this noble goal by providing the opportunity for individuals who lead campus-level or field-inclusive efforts to improve teaching and learning, by providing them with a vehicle for their voices to be heard beyond the particular environments they inhabit. These authors offer a wide range of perspectives from many parts of the world, and the editors have done well to create an anthology with the potential to influence thinking and practice across higher education.

It's a privilege to be invited to write this foreword, and I appreciate greatly the opportunity to make a small contribution to this anthology. I commend the book as an important contribution to our understanding of creative learning and learning to be creative.

Norman Jackson
Emeritus Professor, University of Surrey; Fellow of
the Royal Society of Arts; Founder, 'Lifewide
Education' and 'Creative Academic'

Bibliography

Barnett, R. (2007) *A Will to Learn: Being a Student in an Age of Uncertainty*. Maidenhead: McGrawHill/Open University Press.

Bateson, G. (1972) *Steps to an Ecology of Mind: Collected Essays in Anthropology, Psychiatry, Evolution, and Epistemology*. Chicago: University of Chicago Press.

Dellas, M. and Gaier, E. L. (1970) Identification of Creativity in the Individual. *Psychological Bulletin*, vol. 73, pp. 55–73.

Jackson, N. J. (2016) *Exploring Learning Ecologies*. Available at: https://www.lulu.com/

Redecker, C., Leis, M., Leendertse, M., Punie, Y., Gijsbers, G., Kirschner, P., Stoyanov, S. and Hoogveld, B. (2011) *The Future of Learning: Preparing for Change*. European Commission Joint Research Centre Institute for Prospective Technological Studies EUR 24960 EN Luxembourg: Publications Office of the European Union. Available at: http://ipts.jrc.ec.europa.eu/publications/pub.cfm?id=4719

Rogers, C. R. (1961) *On Becoming a Person*. Boston: Houghton Mifflin.

Stodd, J. (2014) *Exploring the World of Social Learning*. Smashwords. Available at: https://www.smashwords.com/books/view/204432

Taylor, M. (2015) The Power to Create. *Creative Academic Magazine*, Issue 1 p. 9 http://www.creativeacademic.uk/uploads/1/3/5/4/13542890/ca_issue_1.pdf. Also available as an RSA Animate: https://www.youtube.com/watch?v=lZgjpuFGb_8

Thomas, D. and Seely Brown, J. (2011) *A New Culture of Learning: Cultivating the Imagination for a World of Constant Change*. Lexington, KY: CreateSpace.

Vygotsky, L. S. (2004) Imagination and Creativity in Childhood. *Journal of Russian and East European Psychology*, vol. 42, no. 1, January–February 2004, pp. 7–97.

PREFACE

The Book

Higher education throughout the world is undergoing seismic shifts that are fundamentally altering what the higher education landscape looks like and how the higher education ecosystem behaves. Part of this shift is a broadening of the concept of teaching and learning. Many important questions have emerged from this context such as, what does learning mean in the modern era and how can creativity be used to enhance learning? This book aims to address this central question by examining the intersection of creativity and learning, that is, creative learning.

Creativity may be considered by many as the province of those lucky few people who are gifted and happen to have an innate ability for creativity. In addition, some people associate creativity mainly with the arts and humanities (e.g., music, painting, performing arts, writing, poetry) and perhaps less so with fields such as the social sciences, the natural sciences, and the professional fields (e.g., engineering, medicine, law, business). However, findings in this book support the view that creativity is a process that can be learned by anyone in any discipline.

Within this broad context, this book explores how different models and approaches to creative learning are being implemented across disciplines and across national cultures in higher education. In their contributions, authors examine the following core elements:

* The need and rationale for creative learning;
* Definitions, theories, models, principles, and concepts of creative learning;
* Successful practices and strategies for cultivating creative learning environments;

- Teaching and curriculum approaches to facilitate creative learning;
- Standards and assessment of creative learning;
- Constraints (e.g., cultural, organizational) to creative learning in higher education.

Main Thesis

The main thesis of the *Creative Learning* book may run counter to the current notion that (1) creativity is an innate talent that only a lucky few are born with (e.g., the gifted), (2) that creativity is the sole province of the artistic fields, and (3) that creativity is understood and expressed in the same way across all cultures. Csikszentmihalyi, Sawyer et al. argue that creativity includes three key characteristics: (1) it is process and outcome oriented; (2) it is domain and field specific—the knowledge/symbols/rules and the domain's experts/gatekeepers, respectively; and (3) it is connected to and embedded within the creative person's culture (i.e., the specific disciplinary culture (domain and field) as well as the broader socio-culture and environment). In short, creativity is the process of creating (or discovering) something novel and valuable that changes the domain—the new creation is viewed as novel and valuable by the field and is accepted for inclusion in the domain by the field. Thus, before one can become truly creative, one must first master the knowledge/symbols/rules of the respective domain (Armstrong, 2006; Beghetto & Kaufman, 2010; Blessinger & Carfora, 2014, 2015a, 2015b; Blessinger & Wankel, 2013; Cropley, 2001; Csikszentmihalyi, 1996; Davis & Arend, 2013; Fleith, Bruno-Faria & Alancar, 2014; Heist, 1967; Jackson, 2008; Jackson, Oliver, Shaw & Wisdom, 2006; Kaufman, Plucker & Baer, 2008; Kaufman & Sternberg, 2010; Kovbasyuk & Blessinger, 2013; Kuh, 2008; McIntosh & Warren, 2013; Nygaard, Courtney & Holtham, 2012; Piirto, 2004; Robinson, 2011; Sawyer, 2012; Sweet & Carpenter, 2013; Treffinger, Young, Selby & Shepardson, 2002; Vartanian, Bristol & Kaufman, 2013).

Viewpoints

This book presents different international and interdisciplinary viewpoints of creative learning in higher education by analyzing case studies and scholarly essays of how creative learning is being implemented in higher education systems in different countries. One cannot assume that creativity is understood in the same terms across cultures. In fact, the cultural context may influence greatly how creativity is viewed and practiced. Therefore, the different international contexts presented in this book allow the analysis, we hope, to provide a more complete view on where higher education is currently at and where it is heading with respect to creative learning. By utilizing both scholarly essays and case studies, we hope this book also approaches the topic in a more interdisciplinary and multidisciplinary way. The intent of the book is to show how creative learning is being implemented across higher education systems and how creative learning can be used to create more effective learning environments and improved learning outcomes.

Purpose

The main purpose of the *Creative Learning* book is to provide higher education professionals (e.g., faculty and administration) a scholarly resource on the most salient aspects of creative learning in higher education as well as the emerging trends in creative learning occurring in higher education today. A central theme of the *Creative Learning* book is that academic creativity can be fostered in any student, regardless of academic discipline or grade level, and that creativity is not the exclusive province of any one discipline or any one mode of inquiry. In short, this book starts with the main premise that creative learning is a process that all students can and should learn and develop. The main thesis of this book is that creative learning is the pinnacle and essence of higher order thinking (as depicted, for example, in Bloom's taxonomy of learning objectives) and that creative thinking is a set of cognitive, affective, and behavioral qualities (i.e., knowledge, skills, attitudes, practices) that can and should be fostered in all students. The *Creative Learning* book provides a coherent body of evidence together with a plausible rationale to show how creative learning is the pinnacle of higher order learning.

Focal Points of Inquiry

Each chapter included within the book speaks to the central question that the book is intended to address:

- If we proceed from the premise that creative learning is a set of knowledge, skills, strategies, and practices that all students can and should learn, how do/can educators optimally engage students in that enterprise?

Two kindred questions inform the responses to that central query:

- If creative learning is to be understood as an intentional practice, how does it distinctively enhance students' abilities as autonomous, self-regulated learners whose personal agency is developed through the learning process, as collaborative learners, and as agents of social or educational change?
- Within this context, if creative learning is to be regarded as an essential component of higher order thinking, how might educators best understand the distinction/interplay between critical thinking and creative thinking?

Throughout the book, the authors also address other key questions and issues pertinent to fostering creative learning in higher education:

- What conditions favor or complicate creative learning in the higher education context?
- How do we promote creative practices through instruction (both faculty instruction and student peer-to-peer instruction)?
- How do we prompt learners through creative learning activities and assignments?
- How do we enhance and facilitate unconventional student products/artifacts as evidence of creative learning?
- How do we assess and document student progress in terms of creative learning?
- How might creative learning inform/reform/transform our understanding of best practices in higher education?
- How do definitions of creativity, as well as its importance, differ across international contexts?
- What is gained and lost in bringing a greater emphasis on creativity to higher education?
- How is growth in creativity related to student persistence, student success, and student achievement of learning outcomes?
- How does creative learning connect to, advance, or contest Kuh's notion of high impact practices in higher education? See http://www.aacu.org/leap/hips and http://www.aacu.org/sites/default/files/files/LEAP/HIP_tables.pdf.
- To what extent is creative learning aligned with the needs identified by admissions bodies for graduate/professional education and/or employers?
- How is creativity vital to a model of 21st-century outlooks, sensibilities, skills, and capacities necessary within higher learning?

Chapter Overviews

This book is arranged in four units and thirteen chapters. The first section of the book directs attention to the governing principles and concepts at work within the anthology. In the introductory chapter, titled "History and Nature of Creative Learning," Blessinger and Watts explore the nature and origins of creative learning, particularly as it has been understood within higher education during the past fifty years.

The book's second section features eight case studies in successful practices in creative learning. These cases examine different disciplinary and national contexts in order to address a wide range of topics within, and settings for, creative learning in higher education.

In "Promoting Creative Learners Through Innovative Pedagogy" (Chapter 2), Fredricka Reisman examines creative learning within graduate education. Specifically, this case study considers how students in the Drexel online

Creativity and Innovation master's and EdD degree programs apply their course-work to lived-world situations. Her work focuses on how these students, mostly employed in education or other professions, assist their colleagues in industry or educational worksites to come together as communities of inquiry. Using a variety of techniques associated with innovative pedagogy, these individuals strive to engage groups in creative problem solving. Also discussed is the Reisman Diagnostic Creativity Assessment, a free tool available as an Apple app that supports students in metacognition and in particular helps learners develop a sense of their own resources as creative beings.

Kanta Kochhar-Lindgren's contribution, "Participatory Choreographies, Our Future Cities, and the Place of Creative Learning in International Arts Exchanges" (Chapter 3), offers insights into collaborations between campuses and communities, among higher education institutions, and across artistic interventions to benefit urban environments and global landscapes. These translocal partnerships, informed by the fields of performance studies, cultural theory, and Laban movement analysis, help students engage complex contemporary issues such as migration, terror, and natural disasters. The example at the center of this chapter features interactive and immersive pedagogy as used to produce rich dialogues about community change and cultural heritage. Further, such participatory choreographies promote student engagement with arts diplomacy and global citizenship. Through arts-making conducted via workshops, site-based projects, and performance, participants open literal and figurative doors to deepened cross-cultural understanding. Such embodied practice builds empathy, forges new relationships, and helps learners see their own perspectives through fresh eyes.

"Configuring Interdisciplinarity: The Common Core at the University of Hong Kong" (Chapter 4), by Gray Kochhar-Lindgren, documents and reflects upon the power of interstices, or thresholds, joining traditionally separated areas of knowledge (whether demarcated as disciplines or departments) within the undergraduate curriculum. In this instance, he recounts what happened when eight public universities in Hong Kong shifted from a three-year to a four-year general education for undergraduates. They opted for a combination of training and sense-making in which interdisciplinarity remained a touchstone, a decision that opened new possibilities for both reflexivity and creativity in learning. An important element of this case was its premise that entering students will be entrusted with the challenges and rewards of thinking across disciplinary paradigms; they need not wait to qualify for their encounter with the liminal space of the *inter-*.

With "Creating Meaningful Learning Spaces Through Phenomenological Strategies" (Chapter 5), David Giles and Clare McCarty reexamine assumptions within higher education about the nature and nuance of the student-teacher relationship. They posit that through appreciative inquiry and phenomenological activities, students (and their teachers) can move beyond the binary separating theory and practice. Such learning opens up spaces in which students and teachers may invoke playful and improvisational strategies for creating knowledge. As co-constructors of meaning, students and teachers embrace their shared uncertainty and together explore innovative alternatives to dilemmas. Along the way, students develop their ability to narrate experience, listen actively, and connect with colleagues through exchange of such narratives.

Nives Dolšak and Cinnamon Hillyard's chapter, "Creative Learning Strategies: Learning How to Cooperate" (Chapter 6), probes the possibilities for helping students cultivate cooperation both as a value and a skill. Despite messages from educational thinkers since John Dewey about the importance of teaching students to make informed decisions about social capital and civic engagement, a host of challenges face teachers who attempt to build such abilities. Through applied strategies in higher education classrooms, these two educators helped undergraduates explore optimal approaches to social choice dilemmas. As groups of learners came together to devise plans that bring forward the most mutually advantageous response to scenarios in which payoffs may be maximized through strategic collaborations, they demonstrated their capacities not only for creativity, but also for cooperation.

In "Toward Mindful Assessment in Higher Education: A Case Study in Contemplative Commentary on Student Work to Promote Creative Learning" (Chapter 7), Linda S. Watts asks what instructor responses to student assignments might contribute to a discussion of creative learning pedagogy. Within a course dedicated to the mindful study of social observation as a contemplative practice in the helping professions, students were asked to complete a variety of assignments, including meditation, contemplative photography, and thoughtful essays to make connections among disparate literary selections. In this sense, student success required a suite of abilities related to critical, creative, and contemplative inquiry. Such work proceeded from the notion that deep engagement with these three realms would facilitate student growth in six key areas crucial throughout the helping professions: observation, description, narrative, commentary, advocacy, and intervention. Watts shares ten principles for responding to student artifacts in which they attempt to synthesize diverse material and articulate understandings of the interplay among, and implications of, these complex cultural statements.

In "Play and 3D Enquiry for Stimulating Creative Learning" (Chapter 8), Alison James poses that creative learning requires more than a reconsideration of instructional techniques; it may also demand a different turn of mind than that which characterizes conventional learning models within higher education. This orientation involves playfulness along with a willingness to take on intellectual risks. Using the example of LEGO SERIOUS PLAY as employed in higher education settings, James contends that such sessions prove instrumental to fostering creative learning for students and maintaining a climate for creative learning.

Gina Rae Foster's "The Dynamics of Creative Learning: A Case Study in Best Practices in Public Urban Higher Education" (Chapter 9) asks how higher education might best employ principles of human resilience (such as stability, capacity, flexibility, and community) to extend creative learning opportunities for students. This work is informed by research on topics such as trauma and recovery from change as it might be applied to teaching problem-solving methods. Resiliency, both for the individual and the collective, prove apt to higher educational settings, particularly as students face difficult decisions and seek to weather adversities. With the benefit of instruction, coaching, and peer mentoring, students enhance their ability to persevere as students and make creative choices as global citizens.

In the third section of the book, three chapters point the way toward identifying effective strategies for creative learning in higher education.

Stephen Brookfield's "Creative Approaches to Stimulate Classroom Discussions" (Chapter 10) notes that educators may underestimate the degree to which in-class discussions are teacher-centered rather than student-centered activities. In an effort to provide more participatory experiences for students (particularly for introverts, English language learners, or those who wish time to formulate their contributions), Brookfield shares nine techniques for broadening the base of a discussion, and in so doing establishing a more democratic learning environment. These techniques feature the novel and strategic use of visual, spatial, and performative approaches. Even social media becomes a part of enriching the classroom dialogue.

In "Developing Creative Competencies Through Improvisation—Living Musically" (Chapter 11), Robert Kaplan sets out a procedure by which the notion of ensemble play as it exists within music may infuse creative learning across the curriculum. By emphasizing principles of collaboration and improvisation, such a pedagogical model helps students develop self-awareness, forge productive relationships with others, and pursue creative interactions. Kaplan then offers exercises designed to elicit such results for learners. Through "Living Musically," students develop their ability to build responsive and reciprocal awareness needed across the lifespan.

Lorraine Stefani's chapter, "Realizing the Potential for Creativity in Teaching and Learning" (Chapter 12), moves the discussion toward a sense of the necessity for teachers and students to bring a venturesome outlook to learning. Such an attitude requires participants, particularly instructors, to relinquish some measure of control over the classroom process. Only then will it be possible to connect higher education in meaningful ways to social problems such as climate change or global conflicts. Stefani explores what barriers impede colleges and universities from engaging in creative learning of this kind, including pressures for conformity with other workplaces, accountability for resource allocation, and allegiance to traditional institutional practices, such as narrowly configured models for assessing student learning.

Finally, in the fourth section of this book, in the concluding chapter titled "The Future of Creative Learning," Blessinger and Watts explore possible future directions for creative learning in higher education and they propose a theory and model for creative learning.

Conclusion

This book combines scholarly chapters with case studies including empirical data to serve as exemplars of how creative learning has been implemented in authentic academic settings. The contributors to this collection present their work as points of reference and resource in the quest to promote creative learning, especially at colleges and universities. They draw from a range of experiences at a variety of higher education institutions. In doing so, they share their aspirations and findings, their values and their visions about what an optimal creative learning environment might be for students, faculty, and staff alike. As you will see, they approach this scholarship of teaching and learning with a focus on the experiences researcher George Kuh (2008) has identified as high impact practices in higher education.

Perhaps it is not surprising that the instructional contexts that prove most significant for college-level learners, in terms of both achievement and retention, are characterized by high degrees of engagement, autonomy, meaning-making, and self-direction—all elements strongly associated with creative learning. Taken together, these chapters coalesce around a shared concern: *how can creative learning be cultivated in students in higher education across different disciplines and domains to make the learning process and outcomes more meaningful and more effective?*

Bibliography

Armstrong, L. (2006). "The Creative University in a Flat World." 11/6/2006, USC Templeton Lectures.

Beghetto, R., & Kaufman, J. (2010). *Nurturing Creativity in the Classroom.* Cambridge: Cambridge University Press.

Blessinger, P., & Carfora, J.M. (2014). *Inquiry-Based Learning for the Arts, Humanities, and Social Sciences: A Conceptual and Practical Resource for Educators.* Bingley, UK: Emerald Group.

Blessinger, P., & Carfora, J.M. (2015a). *Inquiry-Based Learning for Multidisciplinary Programs: A Conceptual and Practical Resource for Educators.* Bingley, UK: Emerald Group.

Blessinger, P., & Carfora, J.M. (2015b). *Inquiry-Based Learning for Science, Technology, Engineering, and Math (STEM) Programs: A Conceptual and Practical Resource for Educators.* Bingley, UK: Emerald Group.

Blessinger, P., & Wankel, C. (2013). Creative approaches in higher education: An introduction to using classroom-mediated discourse technologies (pp. 3–16). In C. Wankel & P. Blessinger (Eds.), *Increasing Student Engagement and Retention Using Classroom Technologies: Classroom Response Systems and Mediated Discourse Technologies.* Bingley, UK: Emerald Group.

Cropley, A. J. (2001). *Creativity in Education and Learning: A Guide for Teachers and Educators.* London: Kegan Paul.

Csikszentmihalyi, M. (1996). *Creativity: Flow and the Psychology of Discovery and Invention.* New York: HarperCollins.

Davis, J. R., & Arend, B. D. (2013). *Facilitating Seven Ways of Learning: A Resource for More Purposeful, Effective, and Enjoyable College Teaching.* Sterling, VA: Stylus.

Fleith, D., Bruno-Faria, M., & Alancar, E. (2014). *Theory and Practice of Creativity Measurement.* Waco, TX: Prufrock Press.

Heist, P. (1967). *Education for Creativity: A Modern Myth?* Center for Research and Development in Higher Education, University of California, Berkeley.

Jackson, N. (2008). *Tackling the Wicked Problem of Creativity in Higher Education.* Background Paper for a Presentation at the ARC Centre for the Creative Industries and Innovation, International Conference Brisbane. http://imaginativecurriculumnetwork. pbworks.com/f/WICKED+PROBLEM+OF+CREATIVITY+IN+HIGHER+EDUC ATION.pdf

Jackson, N., Oliver, M., Shaw, M., & Wisdom, J. (2006). *Developing Creativity in Higher Education.* London: Routledge.

Kaufman, J. C., Plucker, J., & Baer, J. (2008). *Essentials of Creativity Assessment.* Hoboken, NJ: Wiley.

Kaufman, J. C., & Sternberg, Robert J. (Eds.). (2010). *The Cambridge Handbook of Creativity.* New York: Cambridge University Press.

Kovbasyuk, O., & Blessinger, P. (2013). The future of meaning-centered education (pp. 186–207). In O. Kovbasyuk & P. Blessinger (Eds.), *Meaning-Centered Education: International Perspectives and Explorations in Higher Education.* New York: Routledge.

Kuh, George. (2008). *High-Impact Practices: What They Are, Who Has Access to Them, and Why They Matter.* Washington, DC: AAC&U.

McIntosh, P., & Warren, D. (2013). *Creativity in the Classroom: Case Studies in Using the Arts in Teaching and Learning in Higher Education.* Bristol, UK: Intellect.

Nygaard, C., Courtney, N., & Holtham, C. (2012). *Teaching Creativity—Creativity in Teaching* (Learning in Higher Education Series). Oxfordshire: Libri.

Piirto, J. (2004). *Understanding Creativity.* Scottsdale, AZ: Great Potential Press.

Robinson, K. (2011). *Out of Our Minds: Learning to Be Creative.* Oxford: Capstone.

Sawyer, R. K. (2012). *Explaining Creativity: The Science of Human Innovation.* Oxford: Oxford University Press.

Sweet, C., & Carpenter, R. (2013). *Teaching Applied Creative Thinking: A New Pedagogy for the 21st Century.* Stillwater, OK: New Forums Press.

Treffinger, D. J., Young, G. C., Selby, E. C., & Shepardson, C. (2002). *Assessing Creativity: A Guide for Educators.* Storrs, CT: National Research Center on the Gifted and Talented.

Vartanian, O., Bristol, A., & Kaufman, J. (2013). *Neuroscience of Creativity.* Cambridge, MA: MIT Press.

PART I
Principles and Concepts

1

HISTORY AND NATURE OF CREATIVE LEARNING

Patrick Blessinger and Linda S. Watts

Defining Creativity

As discussed in the preface and as discussed by Csikszentmihalyi, Sawyer et al., creativity includes three key characteristics: (1) it is process and outcome oriented, (2) it is domain and field specific—the knowledge/symbols/rules and the experts/gatekeepers, respectively, and (3) it is connected to and embedded within the culture (i.e., the specific disciplinary culture as well as the broader socio-culture and environment) (Armstrong, 2006; Beghetto & Kaufman, 2010; Blessinger & Carfora, 2014, 2015a, 2015b; Blessinger & Wankel, 2013; Cropley, 2001; Csikszentmihalyi, 1996; Davis & Arend, 2013; Fleith, Bruno-Faria & Alancar, 2014; Heist, 1967; Jackson, 2008; Jackson, Oliver, Shaw & Wisdom, 2006; Kaufman, Plucker & Baer, 2008; Kaufman & Sternberg, 2010; Kovbasyuk & Blessinger, 2013; Kuh, 2008; McIntosh & Warren, 2013; Nygaard, Courtney & Holtham, 2012; Piirto, 2004; Robinson, 2011; Sawyer, 2012; Sweet & Carpenter, 2013; Treffinger, Young, Selby & Shepardson, 2002; Vartanian, Bristol & Kaufman, 2013).

For the purposes of this book, we are not talking about everyday personal creativity—those simple acts that make us feel creative like creating a new dish for dinner—but rather those major creative achievements that *change a domain* and are recognized as such by the domain's experts (the field). Creativity is a key aspect of what makes us human and it, say in the form of innovation, has become vital to economic development and competitiveness in the modern economy. Creative industries now represent an increasingly large part of economic output. According to Gantchev (2011), the creative industries account for over 11% of the gross domestic output in the United States. Increasingly, jobs that don't require some form of creativity are being outsourced or automated (Sawyer, 2006). As such, it is safe to presume that creativity will continue to grow in importance and that creative learning will start to emerge as a major focus area in all disciplines and at all levels of education.

Brief History of Creativity

The word "create" appeared in English in the 16th century as artists used it to differentiate themselves from craftsmen to denote how their works were different from a craft. This is perhaps why the creative process, even today, is often associated primarily with the artistic fields and with the qualities of inspiration, vision, spontaneity, and imagination. The rationalist view emphasizes that creativity comes from the rational mind by conscious, intentional effort. However, this view was challenged during the Romantic period of the 18th century, where the focus shifted to the imagination and the irrational unconscious as the main source of creativity. During this period, the idea of the creative genius became a popular notion in Europe (Engell, 1981, Taylor, 1989). The word "creative" began to be used in the 18th century. The word "creativity" was invented in the late 19th century when it appeared in 1875 in *History of Dramatic Literature*, but didn't appear in English dictionaries until after WWII. The word "creativity" is derived from the English word "create," which is derived from the Latin word *creatio*, meaning *to make* (Weiner, 2000).

Although imagination and creativity are linked, they are fundamentally different. Whereas the mind can imagine virtually anything, no matter how fantastical or implausible in real life, creativity is concerned with how to apply imagination in real life, with all its limitations, constraints, boundaries, and other practical considerations. Thus, another way to view creativity is the meaningful application of imagination (Robinson, 2011).

Creativity not only happens at the individual and micro level but also at the group and macro level. The process of evolution, for example, is a self-perpetuating creative act, and global systems such as the Internet and social networks evolve by the collective creation by many people rather than by a single individual, as well as teams of people collectively working together to come up with a solution to a specific problem. But this book is mainly concerned with creativity that starts with the individual and then flows through, emerges from, and is sanctioned by the respective domain and field. Thus, creativity changes the domain in some meaningful way and may also result in an innovation in the broader society and economy. The great economic, social, and technological revolutions that have occurred over the past several hundred years (e.g., the Printing Revolution, the Industrial Revolution, the Digital Revolution) have been sparked by highly creative discoveries or inventions. Without creativity, progress cannot be made.

Because of the growing importance of creativity in society and education, creativity research continues to grow. Modern research into creativity began in the 1950s. Sawyer (2006) describes four waves of creativity research over the past sixty-five years:

1. In the 1950s and '60s, the first wave of research focused on the study of personalities of highly creative people.
2. In the 1970s and '80s, the second wave focused on cognition and individual mental processes.
3. In the 1980s and '90s, the third wave focused on socio-cultural factors—a social systems approach.
4. In the fourth and current wave, creativity research is focused on an interdisciplinary approach to better understanding creativity, examining creativity from multiple points of view and multiple disciplinary domains (e.g., medicine, psychology, biology, social sciences, humanities, arts, philosophy, law, economics).

In addition, creativity can be defined from an individual perspective or from a socio-cultural perspective. The first and second waves of creativity research focused mainly on creativity from an individual perspective. From this perspective, creativity can be defined as a novel cognitive creation that is new to the world. This type of creativity is known as the "little c" of creativity. The individualist notion of creativity is associated with the individual mind and with the psychological study of the mind, with a focus more on the individual mind than on the creation itself (Kasof, 1995). Individualist approaches are reductionist in nature, in that they analyze creativity by breaking it down into its constituent parts of mental processes and behaviors that arise from these processes. The individualist approach tends to study creativity from the bottom up.

The third and fourth waves of creativity research focus mainly on creativity from a socio-cultural perspective. This perspective not only emphasizes individual processes and factors but also socio-cultural processes and factors. From this perspective, creativity can be defined as a creation of a novel and valuable outcome that is new to the world *and* judged as such by the appropriate experts in the domain. This type of creativity is known as the "Big C" of creativity. Since creativity starts with an individual or team, the "Big C" creativity also includes the "little c" creativity. For the purpose of this book, we focus on those types of creations that change the domain (e.g., creations that solve big problems, so-called wicked problems, creating new knowledge to the domain's knowledge base, innovations) (Sawyer, 2006). Unlike individualist approaches, socio-cultural approaches focus on real-world creativity and it takes a systems approach, studying the whole creative phenomenon as a system of interrelated and interdependent parts. The socio-cultural approach tends to study creativity from the top down.

Amabile (1988) describes an innovation as an organization's successful implementation of a new idea. Thus, innovations occur at the industry or macroeconomic level. Creativity may be the result of social creativity or natural creativity if the system is a social (group or community) or a natural (environmental or biological) system. For instance, a major creative solution to a big problem may be the result of the relatively smaller creative works (e.g., discoveries or inventions) of many people who have worked on a problem over centuries. The scientific method, for example, works this way by relying on the community of experts to continually generate new knowledge to expand the domain's knowledge base. New knowledge is built upon previous discoveries and inventions. The advent of collective learning (e.g., the preservation and dissemination of knowledge from one generation to the next) in human history is perhaps the chief reason for the development of human civilization.

Thus, new knowledge is created directly from the existing knowledge base of the domain (e.g., in the form of books, journals, libraries, and other forms of knowledge preservation and dissemination). The formal learning process, by way of educational institutions at all levels, is the primary way (and the most effective and most efficient way) by which people learn to acquire this knowledge and how knowledge is passed from one generation to another (Blessinger & Carfora, 2014; Blessinger & Stockley, 2016; Kovbasyuk & Blessinger, 2013).

Over the past hundred years, formal learning systems have served as the primary means of social reproduction and continuity. It is no surprise therefore that these systems are now highly developed into a virtuous cycle of knowledge reproduction and that they will continue to grow in importance for human progress and survival. The result of these modern developments, together with the Digital Revolution and other information and communication technologies, has been a rapid increase in how fast new knowledge is created and disseminated around the world. The rate at which the total amount of human knowledge doubles is now measured in months; one day soon it will be measured in weeks, then days, and probably in hours (Blessinger, 2015a, 2015b).

Much has been written about creativity in general and about creativity in primary/secondary education (e.g., gifted programs) but relatively less so about creative learning in higher education. Although much has been written about creativity in terms of innovation and much has been written about critical and analytical thinking, there is a relative dearth (but growing) of literature on creative thinking and creative learning, especially in the context of formal learning environments in higher education. The fact that relatively little has been written about creative learning is especially interesting given the fact that *creating* as a form of cognitive learning development is at the top of Bloom's taxonomy of learning objectives. This may suggest that the practical application of creating authentic creative learning environments is more challenging than it may appear.

Some approaches like undergraduate research are inherently focused on producing a learning environment where students must create new knowledge, but undergraduate research is just one means to foster creative learning. Given the relative paucity of academic literature specifically focused on creative learning in higher education, this book attempts to present an analysis supported by empirical data (via case studies and scholarly writing) to explain what creative learning is, how and why it works, and the practical implications of implementing it across disciplines and national cultures.

Assumptions About Creativity

As mentioned in the preface, new creations may be physical in nature such as a book, painting, invention, or other type of tangible product, or they may be mental in nature such as an idea, theory, method, or other type of intangible product. Creativity involves both cognitive (mental) processes (e.g., knowledge of the respective domain, divergent/convergent thinking, imaginative and critical problem-solving thinking, generation of new knowledge) and non-cognitive (affective and behavioral) processes (e.g., interest, motivation, self-efficacy, skill/ability) at the personal level, as well as disciplinary, socio-cultural, and other environmental factors (e.g., value of the creation to the domain, accepted as a new creation by the field). The defining characteristic of creativity is not the type of output but rather that the output is novel and valuable and accepted for inclusion in the domain by the domain's experts.

Given the right motivation and the right environment to foster creativity, it follows that creativity can be learned, to varying degrees like anything else, by anyone. Therefore, this book starts with the major premise that creative learning is an intentional act. This book serves as a practical resource for educators on how to cultivate and foster creative learning in their classrooms, their disciplines, and the broader educational environment. Because creativity is domain specific and domain dependent, an underlying assumption in this book is that if one learns to be creative in, say art, it will not automatically make her/him more creative in domains outside of art, say science.

Thus, being creative in one domain does not automatically guarantee that one will be creative in other domains, any more than having a high IQ in one domain, say math, will automatically guarantee that one will have a high IQ in another domain, say languages. The major domains involve different modes of inquiry, different rules/symbols, different ways to generate new knowledge, and different disciplinary cultures and historical developments. This suggests that before one can be creative, one must first master the respective discipline. Research strongly suggests that it takes, typically, about 10,000 hours over 10 years of hard work and deliberate practice to master a domain and have the requisite knowledge, skills, and competence to be in a position to make the "Big C" creative contributions (Ericsson, Krampe & Tesch-Romer, 1993; Gardner, 1993; Sawyer, 2012).

However, notwithstanding the fact that each domain must be learned on its own terms, we believe there is value in learning to be creative in multiple domains and learning to make connections across domains which is the essence of multidisciplinary, interdisciplinary and transdisciplinary learning. In fact, some of the greatest new creations are coming from these interdisciplinary intersections as we strive to solve problems that are seemingly intractable in nature.

Creativity is needed as much in the STEM domains as it is in any other domain. Thus, it all starts with schooling (K–12) that is comprehensive and rigorous in order to build a broad and in-depth knowledge in each child. Individuals and society at large would greatly benefit if education at all levels of teaching and learning processes were more creative.

Given the fact that each domain must be learned on its own terms and that a given domain must first be mastered before creative output can emerge, one could surmise that this is one of the reasons why perhaps there have been so relatively few people (e.g., polymaths) in human history who have been highly creative (with a large output of major creations/discoveries) in multiple domains. What this postulate means at a practical level is that approaches that try to teach one simplified set of overly generalized or generic creativity skills or exercises (on the assumption that they can be applied to any domain) may find limited success if those generic approaches are not tailored and contextualized around the unique characteristics of the specific domain. This book tries to shed light on these underlying assumptions.

In addition, Sawyer (2006) identified ten assumptions about creativity that are widely held in Western culture, but they are, relative to current research findings, either wrong or misleading (only partially true). They are:

1. Creative ideas come from a single moment of great insight or flash of brilliance.
2. Creative ideas come mysteriously from the unconscious.
3. Creative ideas happen when one rejects convention or rejects the rules of the domain.
4. Creative ideas are more likely to come from an outsider rather than an expert.
5. Creative ideas are more likely to emerge when a person works in isolation.
6. Creative ideas are always far ahead of their time.
7. Creativity is a personality trait (i.e., creativity is genetic and innate).
8. Creativity emerges from the right side of the brain.
9. Creativity and mental illness are linked.
10. Creative activities are always a form of self-actualization.

This book will not go into each one of these mistaken assumptions but may touch upon them tangentially as needed. Based on current research in the field of creativity, this book defines creativity as the process of creating (or discovering) something novel *and* valuable that changes the nature of the domain in some meaningful way. That is, the new creation or discovery is viewed as novel and valuable by the experts (field) in the domain (discipline) and is accepted for inclusion in the domain by the experts. Thus, before major creative output can emerge, it follows that one must first master the knowledge/symbols/rules of the respective domain in order to understand the domain's requirements and rules and in order to be seen as a legitimate member of the domain's community.

In contrast to these ten erroneous beliefs identified by Sawyer, truly novel and valuable creative ideas are much more likely to emerge and be successful in these situations:

- when they come from those who have first mastered the existing knowledge/ symbols/ rules of the domain (this principle therefore reinforces the importance of students establishing an in-depth and broad knowledge base);
- when they come from those who have worked long and hard in developing a uniquely valuable creative idea or solution to solve a very difficult problem;
- when the idea has been recognized to be novel and valuable to the domain;
- when the idea has been approved by the recognized experts in the respective domain.

According the "Big C" type of creativity, the domain's experts must first accept the idea for inclusion in the domain, otherwise anyone could self-proclaim to have created a great idea. So, the role of the experts is extremely important.

Creativity Across Cultures

Western cultures tend to associate creativity with novelty and originality. But it should be noted that this emphasis on novelty and originality is not shared by all cultures, especially non-Western cultures. In some cultures, rituals, traditions and similar cultural norms are valued over novelty and originality. In past centuries, imitating and reproducing the acknowledged masters of a given domain was highly valued, but the focus today seems to be on novelty, originality, and even improvisation. But as Sawyer (2012) notes, in today's world there is no such thing as a completely novel and original work, since all works are to varying degrees built upon the works created before them, and all creativity includes some aspects of tradition and established rituals, and all creativity is also a balance between tradition and invention. Each domain has its own established rituals, rules, cultural norms, symbols, and the like.

The Creative Process

Creativity research supports the view that creative people tend not to be creative in a general, universal way but rather in a domain-specific way (Csikszentmihalyi, 1996; Feldman, 1980; Kaufmann & Baer, 2005; Sawyer, 2012). The creative output typically emerges over a long period of time while engaged in the creative process. Sawyer (2012) describes the key stages involved in the creative process. These eight stages form an integrated framework. They are:

1. Understand and formulate the nature of the problem.
2. Acquire in-depth knowledge directly related to the problem (i.e., master the domain).

3. Acquire a broad range of potentially related knowledge about the problem.
4. Allow enough time for the idea to incubate.
5. Generate a large variety of potential ideas (i.e., potential solutions to the problem; divergent thinking, as well as inductive and deductive thinking).
6. Combine ideas in novel ways (i.e., cross-fertilization of related disciplines; analogic thinking).
7. Select the best ideas applying meaningful criteria (i.e., best solution to the problem; convergent thinking, as well as inductive and deductive thinking).
8. Externalize the idea, presenting it to the appropriate experts for review.

Sawyer (1998) provides some examples of well-known creators whose achievements exemplify the creative process as an intentional and rational process as opposed to a spontaneous flash of insight. For example, the paintings of Jackson Pollock "emerged from a long process of careful deliberation, and not from a sudden insight in the middle of the night" (p. 125), and the theory of natural selection by Charles Darwin emerged slowly over many years from many small incremental insights. Sawyer notes that creative ideas are more likely to emerge when one has acquired a great amount of direct and related knowledge on the topic, and major creative achievements typically come from those who can look at the problem from different conceptual frameworks and viewpoints (i.e., cross-fertilization).

Thus, this suggests that there is great creative value in being both a specialist and a generalist in order to more readily see the cross-disciplinary linkages and being able to draw on an immense knowledge base from which to come up with the best potential solution to a problem. This suggests that creativity starts with first developing a robust and fertile knowledge foundation (e.g., Level 1 as depicted in Bloom's taxonomy) from which creativity can take root. But knowledge alone won't yield creativity, so focus on knowledge building is necessary but not sufficient; one must also be able to effectively apply that raw knowledge in novel and valuable ways with the proper cognitive processes (e.g., divergent, analogic, convergent, inductive, deductive thinking), the proper affective and behavioral processes (e.g., interest, motivation, self-efficacy), and the proper socio-cultural processes and resources (i.e., externalizing the idea to effectively implement, test, and refine the solution in order to have it accepted as a new creation by the field).

Conclusion

This chapter highlights that creativity includes three key characteristics: (1) it is process and outcome oriented, (2) it is domain and field specific, and (3) it is connected to and embedded within the culture. Creativity involves both cognitive and non-cognitive processes at the personal level as well as disciplinary, socio-cultural, and other environmental factors. Creative learning is an intentional act.

The defining characteristic of creativity is that the output is novel and valuable and accepted for inclusion in the domain by the domain's experts. This type of creativity is known as "Big C" creativity.

The implication of the findings of creativity research is that creativity is the result of rigorous, consistently hard work over a long period of time. Given this, it seems reasonable to suggest that creative learning should start at the earliest grade levels, and it should be embedded in all domains and courses in such ways that continually cultivate creative thinking and problem solving. This may require a change or even a transformation in how curricula are structured and how courses are taught and learned. This, in turn, suggests that deep learning and learning-centered practices that require students not only to master the foundational content but also how to effectively apply, integrate, and evaluate (i.e., all levels of Bloom's taxonomy) that knowledge in meaningful, experiential, collaborative, and inquiry-based ways to create new knowledge and solve complex problems.

Bibliography

Amabile, T. (1988). A model of creativity and innovation in organizations. *Research in Organizational Behavior*, 10, 123–167.

Armstrong, L. (2006). "The creative university in a flat world." 11/6/2006, USC Templeton Lectures.

Beghetto, R., & Kaufman, J. (2010). *Nurturing creativity in the classroom*. Cambridge: Cambridge University Press.

Blessinger, P. (2015a). The world needs more international higher education. *University World News*. Retrieved from http://www.universityworldnews.com/article.php?story=20150422110029960

Blessinger, P. (2015b). Lifelong education as an equaliser. *University World News*. Retrieved from http://www.universityworldnews.com/article.php?story=20150803125916265

Blessinger, P., & Carfora, J. M. (2014). *Inquiry-based learning for the arts, humanities, and social sciences: A conceptual and practical resource for educators*. Bingley, UK: Emerald Group.

Blessinger, P., & Carfora, J. M. (2015a). *Inquiry-based learning for multidisciplinary programs: A conceptual and practical resource for educators*. Bingley, UK: Emerald Group.

Blessinger, P., & Carfora, J. M. (2015b). *Inquiry-based learning for science, technology, engineering, and math (STEM) programs: A conceptual and practical resource for educators*. Bingley, UK: Emerald Group.

Blessinger, P., & Stockley, D. (2016). *Emerging directions in doctoral education*. Bingley, UK: Emerald Group.

Blessinger, P., & Wankel, C. (2013). Creative approaches in higher education: An introduction to using classroom-mediated discourse technologies (pp. 3–16). In C. Wankel & P. Blessinger (Eds.), *Increasing student engagement and retention using classroom technologies: Classroom response systems and mediated discourse technologies*. Bingley, UK: Emerald Group.

Cropley, A. J. (2001). *Creativity in education and learning: A guide for teachers and educators*. London: Kegan Paul.

Csikszentmihalyi, M. (1996). *Creativity: Flow and the psychology of discovery and invention.* New York: HarperCollins.

Davis, J. R., & Arend, B. D. (2013). *Facilitating seven ways of learning: A resource for more purposeful, effective, and enjoyable college teaching.* Sterling, VA: Stylus.

Engell, J. (1981). *The creative imagination: Enlightenment to romanticism.* Cambridge, MA: Harvard.

Ericsson, K. A., Krampe, R. T., & Tesch-Romer, C. (1993). The role of deliberate practice in the acquisition of expert performance. *Psychological Review,* 100(3), 273–305.

Feldman, D. H. (1980). *Beyond universals in cognitive development.* Norwood, NJ: Ablex.

Fleith, D., Bruno-Faria, M., & Alancar, E. (2014). *Theory and practice of creativity measurement.* Waco, TX: Prufrock Press.

Gantchev, D. (2011). *The role of copyright for the development of creative industries.* Presentation at World Intellectual Property Organization, Nantong, China, 13–14 January 2011. Retrieved from http://www.ipkey.org/en/ip-law-document/download/1479/1741/23

Gardner, H. (1993). *Creating minds.* New York: Basic Books.

Heist, P. (1967). *Education for creativity: A modern myth?* Berkeley: University of California Center for Research and Development in Higher Education.

Jackson, N. (2008). *Tackling the wicked problem of creativity in higher education.* Background paper for a presentation at the ARC Centre for the Creative Industries and Innovation, International Conference Brisbane. Retrieved from http://imaginativecurriculum-network.pbworks.com/f/WICKED+PROBLEM+OF+CREATIVITY+IN+HIGHER+EDUCATION.pdf

Jackson, N., Oliver, M., Shaw, M., & Wisdom, J. (2006). *Developing creativity in higher education.* London: Routledge.

Kasof, J. (1995). Explaining creativity: The attributional perspective. *Creativity Research Journal,* 8(4), 311–366.

Kaufman, J. C., & Baer, J. (2005). *Creativity across domains: Faces of the muse.* Mahwah, NJ: Lawrence Erlbaum Associates.

Kaufman, J. C., Plucker, J., & Baer, J. (2008). *Essentials of creativity assessment.* Hoboken, NJ: Wiley.

Kaufman, J. C., & Sternberg, R. J. (Eds.). (2010). *The Cambridge handbook of creativity.* New York: Cambridge University Press.

Kovbasyuk, O., & Blessinger, P. (2013). The future of meaning-centered education (pp. 186–207). In O. Kovbasyuk & P. Blessinger (Eds.), *Meaning-centered education: International perspectives and explorations in higher education.* New York: Routledge.

Kuh, G. (2008). *High-impact practices: What they are, who has access to them, and why they matter.* Washington, DC: AAC&U.

McIntosh, P., & Warren, D. (2013). *Creativity in the classroom: Case studies in using the arts in teaching and learning in higher education.* Bristol, UK: Intellect.

Nygaard, C., Courtney, N., & Holtham, C. (2012). *Teaching creativity—Creativity in teaching.* (Learning in Higher Education series). Oxfordshire: Libri.

Piirto, J. (2004). *Understanding creativity.* Scottsdale, AZ: Great Potential Press.

Robinson, K. (2011). *Out of our minds: Learning to be creative.* Oxford: Capstone.

Sawyer, R. K. (2006). The schools of the future. In *Cambridge handbook of the learning sciences* (pp. 1–16). New York: Cambridge.

Sawyer, R. K. (2012). *Explaining creativity: The science of human innovation.* Oxford: Oxford University Press.

Sweet, C., & Carpenter, R. (2013). *Teaching applied creative thinking: A new pedagogy for the 21st century.* Stillwater, OK: New Forums Press.

Taylor, C. (1989). *Sources of the self: The making of the modern identity.* Cambridge: Cambridge University Press.

Treffinger, D. J., Young, G. C., Selby, E. C., & Shepardson, C. (2002). *Assessing creativity: A guide for educators.* Storrs, CT: National Research Center on the Gifted and Talented.

Vartanian, O., Bristol, A., & Kaufman, J. (2013). *Neuroscience of creativity.* Cambridge, MA: MIT Press.

Weiner, R. P. (2000). *Creativity & beyond: Cultures, values, and change.* Albany: State University of New York Press.

PART II

Successful Practices in Creative Learning

Cases

2

PROMOTING CREATIVE LEARNERS THROUGH INNOVATIVE PEDAGOGY

Fredricka Reisman

This chapter addresses creative learning in higher education, specifically at the graduate level. A selection of cases consisting of student discussion board posts includes tools and techniques students employed for enhancing and applying their creativity. These voices of students in Drexel University's online master's and EdD concentrations in Creativity and Innovation provide a view of how higher education instruction, focused on creativity, results both in awareness of the learner's own creativity in addition to applying creative strategies in real-world situations. Discussion board entries illustrate how students who mainly are middle level managers in large corporate worksites (many global) as well as in-service teachers and school district supervisors become a community of learners as they critique each other's posts, develop awareness of their creative strengths, and apply course content to identifying and solving personal and professional problems.

An online assessment, the Reisman Diagnostic Creativity Assessment (RDCA) (Reisman, Keiser & Otti, 2014), a free iPhone and iPad app that currently may be downloaded via iTunes, is incorporated as an initial tool for university students to become aware of their own creativity. The RDCA taps 11 creativity characteristics that have emerged from over 50 years of research—especially by Guilford (1967) and Torrance (1974). Table 2.1 shows definitions of the RDCA factors.

Participants can complete the RDCA in 10 minutes and get immediate online feedback. This chapter highlights strategies that relate to the RDCA factors with attention to original and fluent idea generation; resistance to premature closure; tolerance of ambiguity; intrinsic and extrinsic motivation; divergent-convergent thinking; smart risk taking; verbal, textual and picture elaboration; and flexibility in terms of using many categories of ideas. Students' voices make up mini-cases that illustrate their use of course content.

TABLE 2.1 RDCA Factor Definitions

Factor	Definition
Originality	Presents unique, unusual, and novel ideas
Fluency	Generates many ideas
Flexibility	Generates many categories of ideas
Elaboration	Adds detail (verbal or figural)
Tolerance of ambiguity	Is comfortable with the unknown
Resistance to premature closure	Keeps an open mind
Convergent thinking	Analyzes, evaluates, comes to closure
Divergent thinking	Generates many solutions (related to fluency)
Risk-taking	Is venturesome, daring, exploratory
Intrinsic motivation	Is satisfied by inner joy, ability to enjoy
Extrinsic motivation	Needs reward or reinforcement

Adapted with permission from Reisman, *Creativity in Business*, 2014 KIE Conference Book Series, Research Papers on Knowledge, Innovation and Enterprise, Volume II, Chapter 1, Page 21.

Creativity and Innovative Pedagogy Defined

What do we mean by creativity? There are several definitions of creativity from different perspectives—cognitive, intellectual, social, economic, spiritual (Mumford, Hunter & Bedell-Avers, 2008); from the viewpoint of different disciplines—business, science, music, art, dance, theatre, and so forth (Wilson, 2015), and from different countries (Kaufman & Sternberg, 2006). Here are summaries of a few common views of what creativity means:

- Carl Rodgers (psychologist)—the essence of creativity is novelty, and hence we have no standard by which to judge it (Rogers, 1961).
- John Haefele (CEO and entrepreneur)—the ability to make new combinations of social worth (Haefele, 1962).
- Mihaly Csikszentmihalyi (psychologist, academic, and writer)—any act, idea, or product that changes or transforms an existing domain into a new one (Csikszentmihalyi, 2013).
- Robert Sternberg (psychologist)—the ability to produce work that is novel (original) and adaptive with respect to task or situational constraints (Sternberg & Lubart, 1995).

This chapter, resulting from my working with Dr. E. Paul Torrance at the University of Georgia for 12 years, uses Torrance's expanded definition of creativity (which I acknowledge is a personal choice) that is threaded throughout the following reference:

a process of becoming sensitive to problems, deficiencies, gaps in knowledge, missing elements, disharmonies, and so on; identifying the difficult, searching for solutions, making guesses, or formulating hypotheses and possibly modifying them and retesting them; and finally communicating the results.

(Torrance, 1989, pp. 73–91)

Creative thinking is made up of two types of thinking; namely, divergent (exemplified by brainstorming or generating many ideas) and convergent (exemplified by critical thinking, which involves analysis and evaluation, and coming to closure when selecting a problem or a solution). Thus, creative thinking is the sequence of divergent-convergent thinking, as shown in Figure 2.1.

Further, creative thinking is the generating of original ideas and innovation is the implementation of these ideas.

What do we mean by innovative pedagogy? Innovative pedagogy has as a goal to prepare individuals to be creative, face changes, manage and analyze information, and work with knowledge. The role of the teacher has shifted from being a subject matter expert who transmits information. Now they act as facilitators of student learning, becoming catalysts to assist learners in successful problem solving; teamwork; becoming aware of their intellectual, creative, and social strengths; self-initiated learning; and other 21st-century skills. This does not imply that teachers need not have in-depth knowledge in their disciplines, but that they also are adept at the same skills they are helping their students to develop; namely, deal with changes, manage and analyze information, work with knowledge, engage in networking, and apply creativity and innovative thinking—now key outcomes for students.

A concept related to innovative pedagogy is *innovation pedagogy*. Traditionally, university instruction focuses on presenting knowledge that is new to the learner that they will apply later either in their professional career or personal life. On the other hand, innovation pedagogy integrates acquisition of new knowledge simultaneously with its application and, therefore, bridges university and post-university life. The traditionally separated contexts of education and

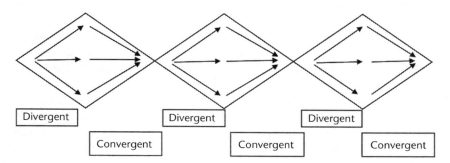

FIGURE 2.1 Creative Thinking Process

Source: With permission from Tanner and Reisman (2014), p. 98.

work become an interactive experience. Thus, innovation pedagogy does not start with knowledge and proceed to its application; rather, the new information is applied to practical situations immediately, even before the information is completely assimilated. It is assumed that the learning processes are deepened and strengthened when the previously gained knowledge is continuously applied in practical contexts.

This approach is evident in Drexel's Cooperative Education program (co-op), which balances classroom theory with periods of practical, hands-on experience prior to graduation.

Through the co-op program, students are able to alternate academic study with full-time employment, gaining practical experience in their field of study. Drexel University has been a pioneer in cooperative education since 1919, operating one of the largest cooperative education programs in the nation. Over 1,650 business, industrial, governmental, and other institutions "cooperate" with Drexel in offering students the opportunity to acquire practical experience in employment related to college studies. The co-op program has been extended into its graduate degree programs.

Creativity and innovation allow one to see new possibilities and alternatives and to embrace change rather than to become deep-rooted in customary ways of thinking. Today's information is ubiquitous and readily available, and students can access it when and where they want. With a future of uncertainty, creative thinking skills prepare university students as well as younger schoolchildren for the unknown, even if that means instructors must re-evaluate and change their own approaches to teaching.

Diagnostic Teaching and Learning

Diagnostic teaching is a creative problem solving instructional/learning model that is framed upon generic or core influences on learning, in-depth content knowledge, and pedagogy knowledge. Figure 2.2 shows the comparison between diagnostic teaching and creative problem solving.

Diagnostic learning suggests ways in which the learner is taught to identify possible gaps in his or her knowledge foundation that inhibits acquisition of new learning; become aware of generic influences on learning and their relationship to creative thinking factors (Table 2.2) and how these impact their learning; and how to use technologies and creative pedagogies to circumvent learning weaknesses and to enhance their learning and creative strengths.

How do we promote creative practices in higher education through instruction? How can we answer this question without asking: instruction for whom and for what content? Today's university student is a very different learner from the ones that most professors are used to. And most relevant to this chapter, often students and professors are not aware of their creative thinking strengths.

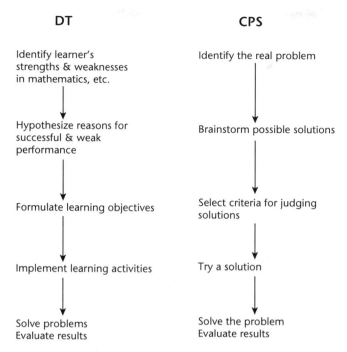

DT	CPS
Identify learner's strengths & weaknesses in mathematics, etc.	Identify the real problem
Hypothesize reasons for successful & weak performance	Brainstorm possible solutions
Formulate learning objectives	Select criteria for judging solutions
Implement learning activities	Try a solution
Solve problems Evaluate results	Solve the problem Evaluate results

FIGURE 2.2 Comparison of Diagnostic Teaching and Creative Problem Solving

Source: Adapted from Reisman (1982), with permission.

Furthermore, lecture does not always indicate poor instruction. Instruction needs to consider the content as well as the learner, and if we are dealing with factual or procedural information, lecture may be an adequate approach. But creative strategies such as Prezis (see https://www.prezi.com/support for a tutorial) can enhance lectures. Introduce videos; include interesting or little-known facts to spark curiosity from the very beginning; include strategies such as "think, pair, share," whereby students are to think about a problem initially on their own, pair with a partner, and finally share with the class; and provide opportunities for greater student interactions during lectures. The case studies in this chapter include scenarios that share creative pedagogies in consideration both of the learner and of the content to be learned.

The New Learner and the New Professor

Studies point to a growing disparity between what college graduates know and what they should know in order to be ready for work in the new global economy (Baer & Blais, 2010; Casner-Lotto & L. Barrington, 2006; Casner-Lotto & Wright, 2009; Gardner, 2010; Laurillard, 2008; McNamara, 2009). New technologies

TABLE 2.2 Selected Generic Influences Cross-Listed With Creativity Factors

Category	Generic Influence	Definition	Related RDCA Creativity Factor
Cognitive	Rate and Amount of Learning	Compared to Age Peers refers to the length of time taken to learn a given amount of material as well as the rapidity of making connections across concepts.	Fluency—generates many ideas
	Size of Vocabulary	Compared to Peers refers to the number of words a student understands and uses as well as the number of different meanings and nuances for a given word.	Elaboration—adds detail
	Ability to Form Relationships, Concepts, and Generalizations	Refers to the psychological nature of the content that is being learned. For example, constructing one-to-one correspondence is forming a relationship; abstracting the number property (three from a set of three objects) forms a concept; and putting two or more concepts together into some kind of relationship forms a generalization (e.g., combine concepts two and three into an addition relationship).	Divergent Thinking—generates many solutions (related to fluency)
	Ability to Make Decisions and Judgments	Involves recognizing salient aspects of a situation, using important information given, being aware of missing information, abstracting essential from nonessential details, evaluating relationships embedded in a situation, and making choices among alternatives.	Convergent Thinking—comes to closure
	Ability to Draw Inferences and Conclusions and to Hypothesize	Involves generating a set of possible alternatives, dealing with future ideas, and making judgments according to a set of criteria.	Flexibility—generates many categories of ideas
	Ability in General to Abstract and to Cope With Complexity	Includes classifying objects or ideas, finding new relationships or analogies, performing simple operations of logical deductions, and using similes and metaphors.	Originality—involves generating unique and novel ideas
Emotional	Feeling Afraid, Anxious, Frustrated, Joyous, Angry, Surprised	Involves conscious experience that can be communicated to another person.	Tolerance of Ambiguity—comfortable with the unknown

Social	Modeling Others' Behavior	Can be positive if acceptable behavior is modeled.	Intrinsic Motivation— inner drive
	Being Aware of Cues in the Environment	Involves knowing when to quiet down, when to speak up, responding appropriately to others' behavior.	Risk-Taking— adventuresome
	Relating To and Interacting With Other People	Includes cooperation and consideration.	Extrinsic Motivation— needs reward or reinforcement
	Understanding Another's Point of View and Empathizing	Includes having an emotional as well as a cognitive view of another's needs.	Resistance to Premature Closure—keeps an open mind

and ways of accessing information have provoked the need for higher education institutions to question whether the core pedagogical knowledge base of their professors is still in tune with recent advancements in learning research and with new skills that society expects and demands from today's students. The developmental stages of educational technology begin with the filmstrip projector (1920s) and move to radio and television (1950s), the computer (1960s), multimedia (1980s), the Internet and e-learning (from 2004 on), and now mobile computing (m-learning), which is a subset of e-learning but focuses on mobility and ubiquitousness.

On the other hand, many graduate students are used to years of structured and prescriptive instruction and are uncomfortable when given the opportunity to engage in self-directed learning. Some ask, "Is this what you want?" or "How long should my paper be?" or "Is this OK for my final project?"

One of my master's degree students who is on faculty at a community college outside of New York City, after a few courses in her Creativity and Innovation program (and who was visibly frustrated as she became aware of her rigidity), said that her husband noticed that she was relaxing more. She observed, "I guess I need to loosen my girdle." The change in her worldview was amazing once she became aware of her creative strengths and started to apply course content to her worksite leadership role. This student is profiled in Case 4 in this chapter.

Hart (2008) presented some features of today's learner that emphasize a constructivist paradigm whereby today's learners prefer to construct their own knowledge—assembling information and tools from different sources, enjoying collaborative learning, looking for ways to apply new knowledge to real-world problems, and preferring active participation in their learning rather than being passive recipients of lectures as so often is the main university pedagogy.

Creative Problem Solving (CPS) Grid: A Heuristic for Creating an Innovative Pedagogy

The CPS Grid is presented in Table 2.3 as a tool for developing creative pedagogies. Along the left margin are characteristics of possible innovative pedagogies, and along the top are criteria for evaluating the possible innovative pedagogies. The sample grid lists 22 characteristics of possible innovative pedagogies; selecting five to eight is probably sufficient.

TABLE 2.3 Creative Problem Solving Grid (CPS)

Characteristics of Possible Innovative Pedagogy	Evaluation Criteria							
	Desirable	Possible	Viable	Beneficial	Sustainable	Creative	Learner centered	Totals
Instructor facilitator								
Student problem solving								
Cooperative learning								
Reflective thinking								
Metacognition								
Persistence/grit								
Deal with change								
Manage/analyze information								
Trigger original/ novel ideas								
Generate many ideas								
Elaborate verbally/ in writing/ graphically								
Resist premature closure								
Tolerate ambiguity								
Divergent thinking								

Convergent thinking								
Intrinsic motivation								
Extrinsic motivation								
Generate many categories of ideas								
Take smart risks								
Self-initiated learning								
Self-efficacy								
Diagnostic teaching/ learning								

Directions

i. Rank each **Possible Future Initiative vertically within each Evaluation Criteria (assign most important/desirable/effective as follows: 1 – least to 5 – most). Note: five to eight options are usually a manageable list; thus the exhaustive 22 are presented so the reader may choose those most appropriate for his/her issue.**

ii. Add across **Evaluation Criteria by row and enter sum in Totals column.**

iii. Consider the **Characteristics of Possible Innovative Pedagogy with the highest total score as your first option for designing a creative pedagogy.**

iv. If you are not comfortable with the **Possible Future Initiative** with the highest score, then consider the next highest. Remember, this grid is merely a heuristic (tool) for making a decision.

The characteristics serve as a structure both for selecting a known creative activity and for designing your own. Implementation of the CPS Grid is illustrated through the case studies.

Case Studies

The discussion board entries disclose that the new techniques and tools students learned in their university studies are applied in the workplace to deal with difficult supervisors, introduce new ideas and ways to address worksite problems, deal with personal challenges, and further their professional and personal goals. Students review each other's weekly posts and final projects, provide feedback and comments, and even suggest a few resources. The instructor can also provide feedback and recommendations online. Students in Drexel's master's and EdD

Creativity and Innovation programs all are working in either industry or educational worksites and are part-time students.

Case 1

Student 1 has over 10 years of experience in the design, development and evaluation of air traffic control surface surveillance systems for the Federal Aviation Administration. Student 1 shares the following:

> This quarter we are working towards preparing a dissertation proposal ready for defense. Ensuring that our chapters one through three flow, our methodologies are defined, we've identified our measures, have composed invitations to participate and developed consent and other forms to satisfy the Institutional Review Board (IRB) requirements. A comparison to this process can be seen in the Michanek and Breiler (2014) statement, "Generating results through applied creativity that leads to innovation requires a structured process from the need phase to the delivery of a finished concept" (p. 34). Creativity is a necessary component in not only the formation of a dissertation topic, but also in the successful completion of the dissertation pathway. As a student in the creativity concentration I readily recognize that pursuing a doctorate involves creative problem solving, and the teachings and techniques I am studying about in the creativity courses are helping me to refine and focus my approach and processes. My dissertation topic delves into the widespread and persistent problem of doctoral student attrition in higher education. My study investigates the effect of including creativity instruments as a complementary admission assessment looking to broaden the profile of the doctoral student pool to acknowledge creative strengths as well as performance on traditional assessments such as the GRE, offer strategies to help alleviate creative thinking weaknesses, and thus increase the number who attain degree completion.

Student 1's literature review revealed that between 40% and 60% of students enrolled in a doctoral program fail to achieve their goal of obtaining their intended degree (Council of Graduate Schools, 2008; Gardner, 2009; Golde, 2015; Lovitts, 2001; Nettles & Millett, 2006; Perkins & Lowenthal, 2014) and that "paradoxically, the most academically capable, most academically successful, most stringently evaluated, and most carefully selected students in the entire higher education system—doctoral students—are the least likely to complete their chosen academic goals" (Golde, 2000, p. 199). Robert Sternberg has pointed out that standardized tests are measures of memory and analytical skills, and he has demonstrated at Tufts and Oklahoma State that creativity measures were a better predictor of college academic and nonacademic success than conventional standardized tests (Sternberg, 2009).

Student 1 proposes that the need exists to expand the selection criteria that has been in use for decades to include creativity assessments, particularly those that are easily scorable, which could provide admission boards with an easy to use measure that can be added to their already existing admissions requirements. Her assessments include the RDCA, a measure of persistence or grit (Duckworth, Peterson, Matthews & Kelly, 2007), and researcher-developed risk-taking and tolerance of ambiguity self-reports. The RDCA factors received the highest weighting, and she focused particularly on tolerance of ambiguity and risk-taking as well as on persistence in completing a task. The CPS Grid results shown in Table 2.4 supported her decisions regarding the creativity assessments that she will create and administer in addition to the RDCA.

Case 2

Student 2, in the Creativity and Innovation master's degree program, has worked for the past 15 years at a Fortune 500 industrial gas company. His company has been in the news lately after inducting a new CEO and board president about a year ago and undertaking a new vision and complete restructuring of the company. Student 2 is currently the export services team lead. His case study shows his creative problem-solving strengths, especially in dealing with squelchers from higher level management (We've already tried that before. It can't be done. It won't work. We're too small for that. We're too big for that. We have too many projects now.) as well as his grit in persevering. Student 2 shares:

> Over a year ago, my area manager who began working on some continuous improvement projects that were lying dormant for quite some time approached me. These were rather large and costly upgrades that were dropped due to a major system focus that took a long time to complete, took away many resources (people), and were of the highest priority for management at the time. After the implementation, and when things settled down a bit, management was more focused on getting back to those projects that were left lingering. I had begun taking on the projects, conducting brainstorming sessions and implementing new solutions. After many meetings and positive outcomes and recognition I did something bold. I prepared an email to the area manager proposing that a new communication system be put in place to regularly communicate ongoing project status, new system learning, and additionally a "red alert" process when new system issues arose and we needed to act on them quickly and provide the information to the response teams and then the affected teams at large. This was desperately needed since, especially during major system problems, there was always a fire drill of people walking around, barking instructions or rapid fire emails coming from many directions and no one leader taking control. I was worried about my manager's response because I knew this was something our group and company culturally did not do. My suspicions were not without merit. My manager responded that a systematic communication method would be too much work and was not a priority.

TABLE 2.4 Student 1's CPS Grid

Characteristics of Possible Innovative Pedagogy	Evaluation Criteria							
	Desirable	Possible	Viable	Beneficial	Sustainable	Creative	Learner Centered	Totals
1. Student problem solving	6	3	5	4	3	5	5	31
2. Persistence/grit	5	6	6	6	2	4	3	32
3. Manage/analyze information	1	1	1	3	1	1	1	9
4. Trigger original/novel ideas	4	5	4	5	6	6	6	36
Generate many ideas								
Elaborate verbally/in writing/graphically								
Resist premature closure								
Tolerate ambiguity								
Divergent thinking								
Convergent thinking								
Intrinsic motivation								
Extrinsic motivation								
Generate many categories of ideas								
Take smart risks								
5. Self-initiated learning	2	2	2	2	4	2	2	16
6. Self-efficacy	3	4	3	1	5	3	4	23

Direction

i. Rank each **Possible Future Initiative** vertically within each Evaluation Criteria (assign most important/desirable/effective as follows: 1 – least to 5 – most). **Note: five to eight options are usually a manageable list; thus the exhaustive 22 are presented so the reader may choose those most appropriate for his/her issue. Student 1 combined the RDCA factors as one characteristic yielding six Characteristics of Possible Innovative Pedagogy.**

ii. Add across **Evaluation Criteria** by row and enter sum in Totals column.

iii. Consider the **Characteristics of Possible Innovative Pedagogy** with the highest total score as your first option for designing a creative pedagogy.

iv. If you are not comfortable with the **Possible Future Initiative** with the highest score, then consider the next highest. Remember, this grid is merely a heuristic (tool) for making a decision.

I believe that creativity in the workplace is kind of like a dance. There's a point where the creative individual will need to lead the dance and a time when management needs to take the lead. However, both need to work together in a push and pull and back again relationship. To my delight, I saw in the Tanner and Reisman book (2014, p. 124) a quote that described my idea. "It's insufficient for an organization to have creative individuals. The environment must be structured for creative tension . . . and the space and freedom for people to 'dance with their idea' without fear of mistakes."

With the restructuring of the entire company and my move to another work area, I will be looking to create a communication method that will open up new avenues of learning and creative thinking. (As a note: Student 2's new CEO recognized his creative strengths and promoted him to Director of Creative Initiatives.)

Student 2's totals on the CPS Grid weighted highest on the following Characteristics of Possible Innovative Pedagogy: Persistence/grit, Deal with change, Tolerate ambiguity, and Take smart risks. I suggested that he employ the *Good Bad Interesting (GBI)* creative thinking activity, which involves considering your challenge and thinking about what's good about it, what's bad about it, and what's interesting about it. The GBI activity originates from de Bono's concept of lateral thinking (1967) that involves employing unorthodox methods to arrive at your end ideas. GBI involves generating as many examples of each idea as you can think of; try to be fairly equal in each category. Too much of one or another demonstrates bias in your thinking. This is not about finding the "right" answer. It's about looking at all the possible interpretations of an idea. Most people react to a new idea by either liking or disliking it. The GBI exercise forces creative thinking to generate multiple perspectives on an idea. It shows that ideas can be seen as good, bad, or interesting, depending on your particular frame of mind. Participants can learn that any idea can be looked at in a different way by reframing it. The idea changes in the mind of a person depending on how they are looking at it. This is important to remember in all negotiations between people with opposing viewpoints. The GBI creative thinking exercise enables the participant to understand other people much better, resulting in a more flexible thinker and therefore, an effective problem solver. This exercise helps to see a problem from many perspectives and to reframe ideas so that different aspects of an idea emerge.

Case 3

Student 3, also in the online Creativity and Innovation master's degree program, is Administrator for Curriculum and Teacher Development in a southern district where she began her teaching career 20 years ago. Student 3 uses the Stepladder technique, which is a specific way to get her participants involved so that all voices can be heard and not just the usual voices that always take over every meeting. Student 3 explains:

> Stepladder (Rogelberg, Barnes-Farrell & Lowe, 1992) is a process that allows each member of a group to generate their own ideas first. It is comprised of five steps.
>
> **Step 1:** Each group member receives the task or problem and is given time to think about ways to address the situation.
>
> **Step 2:** Establish pairs of two participants and have them brainstorm solutions.
>
> **Step 3:** Add a third group member who presents ideas to the first two members *before* hearing the ideas that have already been generated; then the three discuss the options.
>
> **Step 4:** Repeat the same process by adding a fourth member, a fifth, a sixth, and so on.
>
> **Step 5:** Reach a consensus after all members have presented their ideas.

Another strategy that Student 3 might employ is the Brutethink creative thinking technique (Michalko, 2006, pp. 159–172), which involves forcing a random idea into a challenge or problem situation (e.g., you produce out of the ordinary choices to solve a problem). Steps in the Brutethink process are as follows:

1. Bring a random word into the problem (from a dictionary, newspaper, book, etc.).
2. Think of things associated with the random word.
3. Force connections between the random word and the challenge, and also between the associated things and the challenge.
4. List all your ideas.

As curriculum and teacher development administrator, Student 3 encounters issues that combine both of her areas, as curriculum design often involves teacher development. Introducing new creativity enhancing techniques excites her teachers who welcome a new activity—especially one that they in turn can use with their students. She also might use de Bono's Six Thinking Hats exercise, which allows for taking different views of a situation (de Bono, 1985). The six colored hats represent six modes of thinking and elicit fuller input from more people, which is just what Student 3 is working toward. This activity allows people to metaphorically switch thinking by actually wearing one of the hats that they can take off and replace with another role (e.g., go from fact finder to devil's advocate to creative thinker). Table 2.5 describes the metaphorical meaning of the different hats.

TABLE 2.5 de Bono's Six Thinking Hats Exercise

The *Blue* Hat is the facilitator or manager of the thinking process. This role represents thinking about the thinking function—reflection.

The *White* Hat calls for information and is the fact finder.

The *Yellow* Hat symbolizes optimism and tells why something will work.

The *Red* Hat signifies emotion—gut feelings, intuition.

The *Black* Hat represents judgment—the devil's advocate, or why something may not work.

The *Green* Hat represents creative thinking.

Case 4

Student 4, a community college administrator, who is in the online Creativity and Innovation EdD concentration, uses the Cherry Split technique (Michalko, 2006) with students who are struggling academically. The activity involves iterations of dividing a problem into two or more components and then recombining these new concepts to form new ideas. Student 4 shares:

> I ask the student to write down exactly what they think the issue is for academic success. I brainstorm with a student to help them list things that are preventing them from being successful during the semester (e.g., don't always go to class, miss the bus, can't handle early classes, poor study habits, lack of confidence, like to study with a friend). By writing down these ideas, it makes it more real for the students. Then we proceed to use the Cherry Split technique to break down the issues further.

The Cherry Split is a technique that involves helping students to break down a problem into manageable components. The technique includes the following six steps:

1. State the challenge—in two words.
2. Split the challenge into two attributes.
3. Split each attribute into two further attributes.
4. Continue splitting each attribute into two more attributes, until you have enough to work with.
5. Look at each attribute and think of ways to change or improve it.
6. Reassemble the attributes.

As the college learning specialist, Student 4 works with students in two major ways; namely, academic support for those with learning issues and next steps in their education or career.

Case 5

Student 5, an oral surgeon who is pursuing his EdD, shares the following:

> The concept put forth in this week's readings was within-company communication. The gist of this chapter in Robinson and Stern (1998) is that organizations need to foster creativity by increasing communication from outside normal channels of reporting. According to the authors, "The majority of creative acts in companies are unplanned and bring together components from unexpected places" (p. 214). They go on to state, "sometimes, different employees in scattered departments each have a piece of the puzzle, and until they find each other, nothing at all will happen" (p. 215). Organizations can find creative ways to make these interactions possible. With an expectation of improved communication and subsequent better patient service, I am applying these ideas to my dental office, which has a partnership of several dentists, an onsite lab for manufacturing dentures, caps, other articles, and a staff of hygienists, dental assistants, receptionists, an office manager, and the lab employees.

Student 5 assessed the present situation using a SWOT analysis of the dental office, identifying the following components: Strengths, Weaknesses, Opportunities, and Threats faced by colleagues, staff, and lab employees while considering internal and external factors. The results led to weekly memos that communicated a variety of news, including employee suggestions for streamlining patient scheduling to cut down on wait time, enhanced patient interactions with the front office staff, and more collaboration and collegiality among all members of the practice.

Case 6

Student 6 in the EdD Creativity concentration program, recently appointed Dean of Academic Services & College Transitions at a local college, shares another story regarding with in-company communication:

> One year ago, we formed an enrollment management group in order to assist in moving away from the silo mentality that is often pervasive at higher education institutions. This was also done purposefully to ensure alignment between offices. What we initially (quickly!) discovered was that many individuals had incorrect perceptions of what other offices were doing and the extent of responsibility. To combat this, we began a monthly meeting called "SOS—Serving Our Students" where all members of this group were required to attend while extending a general invitation to all academic schools and other offices. These sessions have served in creating a rotation of timely and informative system sharing. We have also recognized

the culture of the area shifting to be inclusive and supportive of each other. We used the Slice & Dice activity to accomplish our goal. To slice and dice is to break a body of information down into smaller parts or to examine it from different viewpoints so that you can understand it better.

Student 6's CPS Grid results were highest in Instructor facilitator, Cooperative learning, and Manage/analyze information. His highest ranked RDCA factors were Tolerate ambiguity and Resist premature closure. One of his major challenges relates to recruitment and increasing student numbers. Student 6's recruitment goal was hindered by the old guard wanting to maintain what they were doing even though student numbers were declining. Sometimes "experts" in a field become so committed to a standard way of doing something that they do not even consider alternative approaches. This is an example of coming to premature closure due to blindly accepting the status quo. Torrance (1979) stated that when

> faced with any incompleteness or unsolved problem, almost everyone tends to jump to some conclusion immediately. Frequently, this jump is made prematurely—before the person has taken the time to understand the problem, considered important factors involved in the problem, and thought of alternative solutions.
>
> *(p. 74)*

It is necessary for Student 6 to counsel some of his colleagues to defer judgment, in order to resist premature closure and remain open to new recruitment strategies. One approach might be to question their assumptions. Many institutions, including higher education, hold on to a set of deeply held, often tacit beliefs that resemble the squelcher persona (i.e., this is how we do things around here). This is akin to a set of blinders on a horse; the animal plods straight ahead, unable to see what lies to the right or left. By questioning assumptions at key points in a discussion, new ideas and possibilities can emerge. To use this technique, Student 6 might first decide how to frame his creative challenge to the way recruitment has always been done. Next, he requests from his colleagues 20–30 assumptions, true or false, and selects a few of these assumptions as idea stimulants to generate new ideas. By involving the old guard in this activity, he allows them to begin questioning their recruitment assumptions.

Case 7

Student 7, in the EdD program, utilized the SCAMPER creativity technique in her application of course content to a personal issue (she is A's fiancée). She shares:

> This observational case study outlines the background behind a conflict between two brothers (A and B) that involves use of basement space by B

who has operated his business out of A's basement. A has been asking B to move his things out of the house since he moved out, but has consistently replied that he will get around to it when he has time and space.

I (Student 7) am instituting the SCAMPER technique as an approach to problem solving, where the participants review suggestions generated and discuss how the ideas can be reconfigured into a working solution. The words in the initial ideas are Substituted for synonyms to generate further ideas. The ideas, words and phrases can be Combined in unique ways. If the ideas are not practicable, they can be Adapted, Modified, Maximized, or Minimized with other ideas. When the ideas have been reconfigured, the brothers can determine ways that less doable ideas could be Eliminated. One final way that the brothers can consider solutions is to Reverse the order of the ideas. If A and B utilize the SCAMPER technique for problem solving they will have an extensive list of solutions, and from these options be able to discuss one clear plan of action that best suits the needs of everyone involved.

In order to get to this point, Student 7 realized that the brothers must first establish an effective line of communication between one another. Student 7 suggested that a third party mediator intervene to help the brothers see that this issue of space is negatively impacting their relationship with one another and also with their family, because their parents are worried about the unresolved issue. A neutral, outside mediator (the family pastor) was consulted, and he agreed to help establish an environment in which the brothers could comfortably discuss their needs and wants regarding the basement space in order to come to a workable solution through utilizing the steps of the SCAMPER technique (Eberle, 1984).

Promoting Creative Practices in Higher Education Through Instruction

Coming back to our original goal of promoting creativity in higher education learning, we return to the creativity factors tapped by the RDCA. In addition to these factors (especially originality that entails pursuing unique and novel ideas, resistance to premature closure that involves keeping an open mind, and risk-taking) is college student *curiosity*. Curiosity can be nourished by instructors who allow students to explore and expand their thought processes by engaging in student dialogue and by encouraging students to question and require evidence for information being presented. Incorporating ways to transform learning from passive listening to active engagement can be accomplished by teaming students to discuss a probing question offered by the instructor. Strategies such as "think, pair, share" are great at encouraging active learning and participation. Some of the creativity activities shared within the cases serve to integrate creativity into college instruction (e.g., Cherry Split, Stepladder, Star bursting, Brainstorming, and recognizing and dealing with squelchers). In addition to curiosity are determination or *grit* and imagination. *Grit* involves perseverance and relates to the RDCA factors of avoiding premature closure and tolerating ambiguity—both by the instructor and the student. *Imagination* as defined by the Merriam-Webster dictionary (2015) is "the ability to imagine things that are not real, the ability to form a picture in your mind of something that you have not seen or experienced, the ability to think of new things, something that only exists or happens in your mind."

Duckworth, Peterson, Matthews and Kelly (2007) have explored individual differences that predict success. Their focus on grit is defined as "perseverance and passion for long-term goals. Grit entails working strenuously toward challenges, maintaining effort and interest over years despite failure, adversity, and plateaus in progress" (p. 1087). They further state that "grit is essential to high achievement evolved during interviews with professionals in investment banking, painting, journalism, academia, medicine, and law" (p. 1088). Grit in terms of this chapter could be described as a quality that allows some university students to persist and succeed when others may abandon a task, course of study, or project altogether. An instructor who resists providing help too quickly to a student who is struggling with a particular idea enables that student to work things out for himself or herself. Furthermore, when higher education instructors share their own learning challenges, they encourage students to see that finding something difficult often results in a creative pathway to solving a problem or understanding a heretofore difficult concept. *Imagination* is an essential part of creativity, but needs time for reflection, visualization and meditation, which instructors need to build in to the learning experience for university students. In addition, giving students time and space to leave work in progress nurtures student resourcefulness, because they will have time to figure out how to make it the best that it can be. Time to think is a valuable higher education commodity, and giving a *think* assignment can yield creative outcomes. Effective creative pedagogies include asking students to think about the tools and resources at their disposal in order to reach a particular solution. Giving an assignment that involves using others as sounding boards for ideas encourages team work and collaboration. Another creative pedagogy involves providing a think assignment that requires mental rehearsal to visualize problems and work toward their resolution.

Exciting Technologies Happening

Open Studio (https://www.youtube.com/user/NRELOpenStudio) is a cross-platform (Windows, Mac, and Linux) software tool to support whole building energy modeling using Energy Plus and advanced daylight. It is a heuristic for STEM, and engineering courses in particular.

The educational mission of the NeuroTechnology Center at Columbia University in New York (NTC) is to educate undergraduates, graduate students, postdoctoral researchers, and faculty in the newest neurotechnologies, training a new generation of interdisciplinary neurotechnology researchers for the 21st century. The center includes faculty from the School of Arts and Sciences (A&S), the School of Engineering and Applied Science (SEAS), the Zuckerman Mind, Brain, and Behavior Institute (ZMBBI), and the Kavli Institute for Brain Science. The NTC will support only synergistic interdisciplinary graduate student and postdoctoral research projects; single-PI (Primary Investigator) projects will not be supported. Additional information is available at http://www.ntc.columbia.edu/.

The University of Southern California Institute for Creative Technologies (ICT) focuses on artificial intelligence, graphics, virtual reality (VR), and low-cost immersive techniques and technologies to solve problems facing service members, students, and society. ICT brings film and game industry artists together with computer and social scientists to study and develop immersive media for military training, health therapies, education, and more. Research projects explore and expand how people engage with computers through virtual characters, video games, and simulated scenarios in the development of virtual humans who look, think, and behave like real people. ICT prototypes deal with decision-making, cultural awareness, leadership, and coping. An in-depth look at ICT's activities is available on YouTube at https://www.youtube.com/user/USCICT.

Summary

This chapter addressed creative learning in higher education. Cases representing voices of students in Drexel's online Creativity and Innovation master's and EdD degree programs provided applications of coursework to their personal and professional lives. The cases provided a backdrop for addressing how higher education instruction can be creative, including applying Characteristics of Possible Innovative Pedagogy to designing your own creative pedagogies and utilizing discussion board interaction. An online assessment, the Reisman Diagnostic Creativity Assessment (RDCA), was incorporated as a diagnostic tool to help students and instructors become aware of their creative strengths and weaknesses. Most creativity assessments focus on predicting creativity, whereas the RDCA was designed for users to identify their strengths and weaknesses related to the 11 factors tapped by the RDCA. This places the user in control so that they can decide if they wish to enhance or live with the results. For example, one may accept a low score in fluency if generating many ideas is not a personal priority. On the other hand, if one comes to premature closure to the detriment of arriving at a solution to a problem, then a low score on this factor may suggest that attention is needed to resist converging too quickly. Creativity-infused activities were presented, which address creative learning pedagogy and introduce university learners and their instructors to a culture that promotes creative learning practices.

This chapter acknowledges that the current student population in higher education, including at the graduate level, is diverse from previous student populations in many ways—they are technologically savvy, often attend part time due to concurrent employment, enjoy collaborating with their fellow classmates, and are serious about their studies. Many have stated that becoming aware of their creative strengths has changed their lives.

Bibliography

Baer, L., & Blais. M. A. (2010). *Handbook of clinical rating scales and assessment in psychiatry and mental health.* New York: Humana Press.

Casner, J., & Wright, M. (2009). The ill prepared U.S. workforce: Exploring the challenges of employer-provided workforce readiness training. http://www.conference board.org/Publications/describe.cfm?id=1676.

Casner-Lotto, J., & Barrington, L. (2006). *Are they really ready to work? Employers' perspectives on the basic knowledge and applied skills of new entrants to the 21st century workforce.* New York: The Conference Board.

Council of Graduate Schools. (2008). *PhD completion and attrition: Analysis of baseline program data from the PhD completion project.* Washington, DC: Author.

Csikszentmihalyi, M. (2013). *Creativity: The psychology of discovery and invention.* New York: HarperCollins.

de Bono, E. (1967). *Lateral thinking: Creativity step by step.* New York: Harper and Row.

de Bono, E. (1985). *Six thinking hats.* Boston: Little, Brown & Company.

Duckworth, A., Peterson, B., Matthews, M., & Kelly, D. (2007). Grit: Perseverance and passion for long-term goals. *Journal of Personality and Social Psychology, 92*(6), 1087–1101.

Eberle, R. F. (1984). *SCAMPER.* East Aurora, NY: Games for Imagination Development.

Gardner, H. (2009). *Five minds for the future.* Boston: Harvard Business Review Press.

Gardner, H. (2010). Multiple intelligences. http://www.howardgardner.com/MI/mi.html.

Golde, C. (2000). Should I stay or should I go? Student descriptions of the doctoral attrition process. *Review of Higher Education, 23*(2), 119–122.

Golde, C. M. (2015). Should I stay or should I go? Student descriptions of the doctoral attrition process. *Review of Higher Education, 23*, 199–227.

Guilford, J. P. (1967). *The nature of human intelligence.* New York: McGraw-Hill.

Haefele, J. W. (1962). *Creativity and innovation.* New York: Reinhold Publishing Corporation.

Hart, J. (2008). Understanding today's learner. *Learning Solutions Magazine* (22 September).

Kaufman, J. C., & Sternberg, R. J. (eds.) (2006). *The international handbook of creativity.* New York: Cambridge University Press, pp. 1–9.

Laurillard, D. (2008). Technology enhanced learning as a tool for pedagogical innovation. *Journal of Philosophy of Education, Special Edition on the New Philosophies of Learning,* R. Cigman & Andrew Davis, eds., 1–11.

Lovitts, B. E. (2001). *Leaving the ivory tower: The causes and consequences of departure from doctoral study.* Lanham, MD: Rowman & Littlefield.

McNamara, C. (2009). General guidelines for conducting interviews. http://management help.org/evaluatn/intrview.htm.

Merriam-Webster's Collegiate Dictionary. (2015). Springfield, MA: Merriam-Webster.

Michalko, M. (2006). *Thinkertoys: A handbook of creative-thinking techniques* (2nd ed.). New York: Ten Speed Press.

Michanek, J., & Breiler, A. (2014). *The idea agent: The handbook on creative processes* (2nd ed.). New York: Routledge.

Mumford, M., Hunter, S. T., & Bedell-Avers, K. E. (2008). Multi-level issues in creativity and innovation. In F. J. Yammarino & F. Dansereau, *Research in multi-level issues, Volume 7.* Maryland Heights, MO: Elsevier.

Nettles, M., & Millett, C. (2006). *Three magic letters: Getting to Ph.D.* Baltimore: Johns Hopkins University Press.

Perkins, R., & Lowenthal, P. R. (2014). Establishing an equitable and fair admissions system for an online doctoral program. *TechTrends,* 58(4), 27–35.

Reisman, F. K. (1982). *A guide to the diagnostic teaching of arithmetic.* Columbus, OH: Charles E. Merrill, p. 20.

Reisman, F., Keiser, L., & Otti, O. (2014). *Development, use and implications of diagnostic creativity assessment app: Reisman Diagnostic Creativity Assessment (RDCA)-Update.* Paper presented at the 2014 University of Georgia Torrance Center conference, Athens, Georgia.

Robinson, A.G., & Stern, S. (1998). *Corporate creativity: How innovation and improvement actually happen.* San Francisco: Berrett-Koehler.

Rogelberg, S., Barnes-Farrell, J., & Lowe, C. (1992). The stepladder technique: An alternative group structure facilitating effective group decision making. *Journal of Applied Psychology,* 77(5), 730–737.

Rogers, C. R. (1961). *On becoming a person: A psychotherapist's view of psychotherapy.* Boston: Houghton Mifflin.

Sternberg, R. J. (2009). *Cognitive Psychology* (5th ed.). Belmont, CA: Wadsworth/Cengage Learning.

Sternberg, R. J., & Lubart, T. I. (1995). *Defying the crowd: Cultivating creativity in a culture of conformity.* New York: Free Press.

Tanner, D., & Reisman, F. (2014). *Creativity as a bridge between education and industry: Fostering new innovations.* North Charleston, SC: CreateSpace.

Torrance, E. P. (1974). *Torrance tests of creative thinking.* Bensenville, IL: Scholastic Testing Service.

Torrance, E. P. (1979, March). An instructional model for enhancing incubation. *Journal of Creative Behavior,* 13(1), 23–35.

Torrance, E. P. (1989). Scientific views of creativity and factors affecting its growth. In J. Kagan, ed., *Creativity and learning.* Boston: Houghton Mifflin, pp. 73–91.

Wilson, L. O. (2015). http://thesecondprinciple.com/creativity/creativity-essentials/on-definitions-of-creativity/)/.

3

PARTICIPATORY CHOREOGRAPHIES, OUR FUTURE CITIES, AND THE PLACE OF CREATIVE LEARNING IN INTERNATIONAL ARTS EXCHANGES

Kanta Kochhar-Lindgren

> Artistic practices are "ways of doing and making" that intervene in the general distribution of ways of doing and making as well as in the relationship they maintain to modes of being and forms of visibility.
>
> The Politics of Aesthetics, *Jacques Rancière (2014: 8)*

> Educators ought to recognize. . . . the necessity of their participation in the project of materializing democracy on a dramatically new scale and in a fundamentally new form.
>
> *"Decolonial pedagogy and the ethics of the global,"*
> *Noah De Lissovoy (2010: 279)*

Participatory Choreographies, Future Cities, a series of international arts exchange projects, investigates how creative learning models that link the arts, cities, and the environment can lead to new curricular paradigms for international higher education. Numerous campus-community frameworks that link the local with the global through workshops, performances, and site-based projects can provide a dynamic context for building cross-cultural understanding, learning about the significance of diverse cultural heritages, and stimulating new thinking about how we can work together toward our shared futures.

As we engage with issues that cut across national boundaries such as water, natural disasters, terror, migration, and the interconnectivity of global cities, creative learning modes that draw on the techniques of the arts can lead to the development of more fluid, and truly international, pedagogies. These undertakings generate high levels of participation for broad-based audiences and lead to dialogue that will subsequently strengthen capacities for community change, arts diplomacy, and global citizenship.

In the summer of 2015, *Water in Kerala: Art, Performance, Science* (WK), an international arts exchange project, provided a series of workshops, performances, roundtables, and community outreach activities for students at the Amritapuri Campus-Amrita University (Kollam) and Sacred Heart College of Thevara (Kochi). The project considered how sharing our water stories through dance, theatre, music, and mixed media formats can help us generate new ideas on how to move toward a more sustainable water future across our global landscape. International exchange occurred at three levels: among the arts team, the arts team and the students, and the arts team and the broader community. The primary arts team—three US artists, three Indian artists, and a project director from the United States currently based in Hong Kong—developed performance work on water stories on both the Periyar River in Kerala and the Mississippi River in the United States.

This comparative approach informed the structure of the student workshops. As students learned about water in Kerala and in the United States through both workshop and the performances, they built an understanding of water scarcity and pollution as a shared issue. This approach invited the university and college students to consider ways to engage differently with our water future through the various dance explorations. Such a "translocal" approach, as a lens and a practice, "deliberately confuses the boundaries of the local in order to capture the increasingly complicated nature of spatial processes and identities, yet it insists on viewing such processes and identities as place-based rather than mobile, uprooted or 'travelling'" (Oakes and Schein, 2006: 20). WK was an initial effort to activate forms of translocal partnerships between international teams of artists and campuses within the context of the immediate project that has implications for innovative formats for creative learning in international higher education.

Such structures and styles of working together can help us practice ways to co-create part of what Noah De Lissovoy has invoked in regard to higher education as whole: "a vision of a *globality* that we live in, that offers life and meaning to people everywhere" (2010: 279). The leveraging of the term "globality" here is crucial in two significant ways. First, globality is typically defined as the condition that occurs post-globalization that signals a major shift in the flow of commerce in multiple directions. This shift leads to the parallel development of governance structures that supports these changes. In order to respond to these rapidly transforming conditions, new approaches to stimulating capacity regarding how to think and act across borders, or what I would term a type of global consciousness, are required. Second, participation in an emerging globality necessitates the development of a global citizenry in ways that simultaneously honor the local and connect to the global.

WK, as a type of participatory choreographies, or set of artistically based interactive and immersive pedagogical methods, focused on how to generate shared cultural spaces that foster the emergence of new visions for our collective future, particularly in relation to participants who are from diverse cultural locations. This approach requires methods that account for and make new types of collectively devised physical and social spaces in order to honor different histories and perspectives. In this context, participants learn to develop a high level of trust and collaboration quickly in order to successfully create and produce collectively devised theatre and other forms of participatory cultural heritage experiences. These methods generate exchanges that fold together pedagogy and arts-making, and as a result, they provide very powerful tools for deepening positive relationships between and across diverse communities.

Background

WK focused on blending artistic and scientific approaches to the study of water in a translocal context. Two interlocking components framed this undertaking. The artist team itself collaborated on the development of a signature traveling performance work, *River to River*. The student participants engaged in series of workshop sessions on basic performance training and methods of collaboration in order to create *In Praise of Water*, a dance work that showcased original student work. The WK project team centered their investigation on the cultural legacies of diverse groups of people along and across specific places, routes, rivers, and seafronts—in Kerala, for example, along the Periyar River, and in the United States, along the Mississippi River. Performance activities examined stories about the histories of the people, cultural performance forms, and the landscapes of these two places in relation to water, and then sought to create new stories—through the performance workshops—that offer new possibilities for our future water stories.

The artistic team consisted of project lead Kanta Kochhar-Lindgren, Founding Artistic Director, *Folded Paper Dance and Theatre* (Seattle/Hong Kong); Sen Jansen TF (Sacred Heart College of Thevara, Kochi); and Rag Saseendrababu (Sruthi School of Dance and Music, Kollam). In addition, there were three other US artists (Beth Gracyzk and Morgen Chang, both dancers; Aaron Gabriel, musician, composer, and lyricist) and one other Indian artist (Jebin Jesmes, director, playwright, and filmmaker). An initial preparatory residency took place in Fort Kochi, where the team—while collecting film materials, developing the project website, and outlining the workshops—focused on devising its signature performance piece, *River to River*. Rehearsals continued on an almost daily basis over the following three and a half weeks so that we continued to refine *River to River*, develop other performance work, refine and deepen the workshop structures, and expand the project website.

The first residency at Amritapuri Campus-Amrita University in Kollam, India, provided thirty-five students with an intensive five-day workshop on dance, theatre, music creation, collaboration, team building, and water stories. It culminated in a one-day performance series that included *In Praise of Water*, and the premiere of *River to River*. A one-day residency at Siddhartha Central School, Kollam, involved *River to River* and a Q&A session. Another five-day workshop series and two-day series of public events with four performances and roundtable took place at Sacred Heart College of Thevara in Kochi.

The larger context for the events is the planetary crisis around water and its just distribution. Climate change, pollution, and the increasing lack of access to clean water are inextricably intertwined with global economics and the widening gap between wealth and poverty. As world economic power shifts from Europe and the United States toward India and China, how does this scenario play out at local levels in India? Much work remains to be done bridging conversations about water in relation to cultures as the placeholder for the symbolism of water, anthropology as the site of daily living, and the natural and built systems as purveyors of urban systems. The focus on creating a new appreciation of water is both practical and symbolic, since care for rivers is vital for sustaining life and culture.

Methods that create cross-sector opportunities for target audiences in both US and Indian communities to engage in the conversation concerning water are more important than ever, since water crises (which are intensifying) are not simply political or environmental problems, but are also of cultural and social concern. The arts provide a needed active and shared space for telling our cultural stories and investigating ordinary, day-to-day practices about access to water, in order to build understanding about the impact of the lack of access to water resources. From the art processes including theatre, dance, and media, possibilities for new relationships with water and our communities unfold through performance onstage, through education, and other community settings.

Theoretical Frame for Participatory Choreographies

Participatory choreographies aim to generate a series of international arts research projects, as forms of cross-cultural exchanges, that are focused on a range of pressing transnational issues. Diverse formats can include site-based projects, dance workshops, and performance-based laboratories focused on generating new research methodologies, attuned to cultural diversity. Specialized workshops, training sessions, and symposia can help build bridges to and across dance, theatre, the vernacular humanities, and transnational studies. As our understanding of the emerging globality increases, a series of transnational research collectives that I am calling "Expressive Urbanisms" can bridge diverse campuses and communities. Such efforts are well positioned to respond rapidly and, crucially, on the ground through people-to-people exchanges. Such an intensive approach enables the participants, artists, students, and community alike to explore a range of related, and pressing, issues in an immediate, and felt, manner. As a result, arts-based approaches act upon the participants, and vice versa, and taking action in the world can gain vibrancy, urgency, and tangibility.

This method involves what Jacques Rancière calls "the distribution of the sensible [that] reveals who can have a share in what is common to the community on what they do and on the time and space in which the activity is performed" (2014: 8). The *sensible*, in this context, refers to all the facets of the sensorium—a complex organization of what is available to the senses (that is able to be seen, heard, or touched) based on the historical construction of what Rancière has termed a "regime of art." The arts, as the primary approach for thinking through the senses, are the most viable way for creating and considering alternative formulations of the sensible.

Participatory choreographies consider what is "common to the community" and then, through a range of interpretative processes, articulate where and what the community-at-large needs. It begins as an alternative pedagogical configuration in order to redistribute the power of and access to the arts. It acts as a viable field of exchange both in and outside the typical campus-community configuration; it is tacked on to standard curricular programming, including that of most "art education." Participatory choreographies therefore operate as an alternative pedagogical approach outside of (or at least alongside) the university.

This approach focuses on what Rancière terms the "potentiality inherent in the innovative sensible modes of experience that anticipate a community to come" (2014: 25). A particular project focuses, first, on the specifics of the international arts exchange as its own entity with a specific raison d'être; then it asks how and under what terms it can also interface with a college or university.

Participatory choreographies activate Rancière's "aesthetic regime," or forms of making and doing imbued with a "heterogeneous power":

> In the aesthetic regime, artistic phenomena are identified by their adherence to a specific regime of the sensible, which is extricated from its ordinary connections and is inhabited by a heterogeneous power, the power of a form of thought that has become foreign to itself . . . This idea of a regime of the sensible that has become foreign to itself, the locus for a form of thought that has become foreign to itself, is the invariable core in the identifications of art that have configured the aesthetic mode of thought from the outset.
>
> *(2014: 16–18)*

This is a complicated series of conceptual moves, but it essentially means that arts-making takes difference into itself; it unsettles and transforms the sensible; it opens up the possible. Rancière leverages the word "foreign" as the name for this difference. The foreign, typically seen as that which is "of or related to another country" or "strange and unfamiliar," can by virtue of its power challenge location, relationship, and ideation. It sets in motion processes of what Deleuze and Guattari have termed "de-territorialization" (2004: 161).

In the case of participatory choreographies, it (at least temporarily) unmoors or decouples institutional structures, social structures (for the artist teams, staff, and students), and cultural structures (through the interplay of aesthetic practices). The "foreign" does trigger anxieties and disorientations—forms of institutional, social, and cultural vertigo—when the sensible is "extricated from its ordinary connections." This "power of form" activates a self that is unfamiliar to itself or the community that does not yet know what it is.

It is revelatory that "foreign" has an etymology that includes its origin (Latin *foris*, "outside," literally "out of doors"; related to *foris*, "a door"). In order to define that which is "out of doors," there must, of course, be a door—a threshold between two spaces. Following architectural theorist Bernard Cache's work on the structural thresholds of the built environment, the inside and outside spaces exist by virtue of the specific thresholds.

The threshold identifies and dis-identifies at the same time. This complexity of spatial and relational location means that, in terms of the aesthetic regime, hopes for any simple forms of "passing through" is no easy task. Here, participatory choreographies structurally interface with the university as an independent project that offers a certain type of creative disruption and reconstitution to the university. It acts as a door and the out of doors as well as the "not a door"—or, in other words, that which signals and can make something beyond its own foreignness.

The term "foreign," then, already gestures toward the complexities of dislocation and re-location that will take place in truly creative learning. It simultaneously marks the passage of having left one place and arrived at another while at the same time connecting places with one another. Through these projects, we are already at the door. We are locally placed *and* we are in constant movement. The image of a threshold—before the door, at the door, and beyond the door—between where one has been and where one is going helps mark the ways in which translocal arts practices can both travel *across* and *link* geographies and temporalities. Theatre and dance provide a shared space for knowledge generation, exploring identities—both individual and collective—and for multiplying the doorways as we generate new modes of analysis, cultural practices, and forms of theatrical mapping as forms of trans-location.

The doorway, literally and metaphorically, is a key signature of WK. All of the performance and workshop modules raise questions about how we see each other, how we can change our perspectives, why we would change those perspectives, and how that will impact what kinds of stories we do and could tell about ourselves as well as each other. The performances include segments where shifting the performance angles and scale act as framing devices for heightening the experience of viewing the story as well as each other from different angles. As the performers and/or workshop participants bring previously hidden stories to light or tell seemingly familiar stories in new ways, the target audiences are invited to see new possibilities for how we can understand our past and move toward future stories.

In "The Revelation of a World That Was Always Already There," Rick Dolphijn notes that it is "art that occupies, that releases the suppressed and that takes over and thus has the power to stage another world. Art realizes occupation as it thinks through involvement" (2014: 192). This potentiality of art—as occupation, release, and taking over—leaps simultaneously into and beyond its own history. Therefore, participatory choreographies, as they tune into the diverse histories, bodies, and learning styles, can help to recalibrate spatial practices in higher education and invite us "to explore what the body's movements and sensations mean for thought, *challenge educators to shift how we make bodies matter in pedagogy*" (Ellsworth, 2004: 17), in relation to the ongoing processes of pedagogical exchange.

In *Places of Learning: Media, Architecture, Pedagogy*, Elizabeth Ellsworth writes:

> Architects, artists, performers, media producers of content-based experiences, museum exhibitions, and public spaces are inventing "processual paths," "communicative instruments," urban "critical vehicles," theatrical performances, provocative interactive encounters, architectural spaces, and mediated cityscapes—with pedagogical intent, and they are doing so in ways that emphasize noncognitive, nonrepresentational processes and events such as movement, sensation, intensity, rhythm, passage, and self-augmenting change.
>
> *(2004: 6)*

Here the body is a co-constituent of the sensible, a type of sense body. Through this type of interactivity, the body makes itself and its architectural surround as it goes. It is transient and contingent; it appears as it disappears, leaving ripples in the social space. This phenomenon frames how we may encounter each other—differentially—in a folded and folding play of bodies, through the skin. It makes manifest spaces of material encounter as it activates an ontology of hybrid bodies rife with new registers for experience and learning, with the self and/or others.

If we are to change our ways of responding to the challenges of globality, we have to change our actual practices. When we move, we touch the world. But touch is already the layering of history, cultural coding, and physical practices. Touch activates the folding and unfolding of ourselves into the world and requires us as active participants engaging with our environments to orient ourselves to the world relationally and spatially. Through the recalibration of touch or turning attention to the felt sense of experience, we can become aware of how deeply the built environment and movement hold each other in place and we can begin to change it.

Students need to learn not only how to talk about and critique institutions of power, but also how to *act differently* and set new cultural models in motion. More simply put, we need to attend to both the thinking life as well as the feeling and behavioral life of the students in order to generate change as we gather in a provisional third space, that of the multidimensional city-stage that both holds us and propels us toward our shared futures.

Case Study: WK as Creative Learning Through Collaboration, Imagination, and Trans-location

Cross-cultural collaboration—as an innovative forming of and intervention in the sensible—requires a coming together of diverse groups of people and related institutions on a topic that hits the community "nerve," a point of felt importance. Dialogue building, collaborative artistic exploration across a range of scales, and the necessary related research—which is embedded in arts-making and community stories—sets in motion the collective synapses of creativity—the unpredictable ways in which new ideas and practices emerge and take shape. This type of "firing up" happens through practices of reciprocity: the exchange of things, ideas, and activities for mutual benefit in ways that honor the past and point to the future.

At Sacred Heart College of Thevara, the five-day workshop series was held for approximately six hours per day for selected college students. The series provided a range of arts-based activities that included specific training as well as opportunities to devise performance pieces on water. The workshop invited both trained and untrained student performers—many had a primary frame of reference in Indian performance and limited exposure to American modern dance and musical traditions—to explore ways that folded together what they already knew with a range of explorations, based in American modern dance, that could broaden and deepen their performance range.

In order to facilitate a sense of shared space needed for collaborative work on performance compositions, the workshop participants explored diverse methods for building a common movement-based vocabulary (so that we could share ideas across diverse positions), observing oneself and others while in action (so that we can learn as we are engaging in forms of doing and making), and generating multiple frames or perspectives (so that we can investigate topics from different directions and angles). These methods helped open up a collective, though still differentiated, space for the workshop participants.

My performance-based approach, while eclectic,[1] draws in specific ways from Laban Movement Analysis—a basic movement vocabulary developed by Rudolf Laban and his protégés[2] designed to make movement and dance accessible to a wide community of participants, including participants with disabilities. The use of the Laban Movement vocabulary, in particular, breaks movement activity into some combination of four elements: space, shape, effort, and body.[3] Space regards how the mover uses the environment; shape, the form the body takes in space; effort, the qualities of movement; and the body, its biomechanics. This vocabulary generates an understanding of everyday movement as well as specific performance idioms. Laban Movement can be used as a basic vocabulary for dance improvisation and a range of creative approaches to performance composition. It also can be used as a way of making new choices in relation to an already familiar dance idiom for the workshops participants, such as Bharatanatyam, a classical

Indian dance form. The Laban Movement vocabulary informs varied movement choices, and therefore can act as a translational device for understanding and engaging with moving bodies as they pass through space in numerous contexts, including cross-cultural ones.

The establishment of this baseline tends to foster a spirit of common enterprise. It enables creative work to happen quickly across diverse performance traditions in ways that can honor the performance idioms as they are, and/or it can act to transform them into blended genres. This approach results in performance structures that grow out of the movement choices of the participants and their specific reference points as they respond to, explore, and embody the collective and ongoing spirit and research of the performance project.

On the first day of the workshop, most of the students stated they joined the workshop because they wanted to dance. They also indicated that they did not know much, if anything, about the water situation in Kerala. As a result, we needed to build a common starting point. Our initial method for exploring water stories was to track, through a performance-based dialogue, what the participants knew or already carried with them. As a result, for instance, after an initial introduction to ways to improvise moving through the workshop as a group and begin to become sensitive to the group flow and rhythm, we launched into our first session on "shape." After a broad-based exploration of shape as actual forms of the body in space as well as methods for how body shapes itself in space, we engaged in a series of structured improvisations using the specific Laban vocabulary:

- Shape flow, the form of the body in relationship to itself;
- Directional movement, the form of the body as it reaches out into space;
- Carving, the form the body takes as it acts on the environment.

It is beyond the scope of this chapter to delineate available research on how the modes of shape change relate to the early stage of physical developmental processes for engaging with one's environment. Nevertheless, it is important to note that ongoing exploration of these structures enhances clarity and range of movement as well as attention to the environment.

In order to further explore and apply the vocabulary, the students worked in small groups to create movement phrases—using the modes of shape change—in ways that depicted the qualities of water as it travels down the riverbed. The phrases became ways for the students to discover what they already knew about water and its qualities. Some students indicated later that it was the first time they had thought about what water "feels" like. This exercise explores the participants' relationships to the river. Many students remarked on the power they felt in embodying these images and qualities. Other students articulated that this exercise began to heighten their sense of spatial awareness as well as their relationships to their fellow performers. These workshop sessions are one example of what Ellsworth means when she argues for the valorization of pedagogy that prioritizes methods that "explore what the body's movements and sensations mean for thought" (2004: 17).

Over the next three days, some of the workshops modules involved continuing to work with the Laban vocabulary. The sessions led to group work on performance compositions that focused on the elements of space to generate a new section that showed "building on the river," and the elements of effort to generate a phrase that explored "turbulence" and water. These performance phrases begin to articulate how the "lines of the river are not universal, but rather products of a particular literacy through which water is read, written, and drawn on the earth's surface, on paper, and in the imagination" (Mathur and Da Cunha, 2014: 5). Together, the three phrases displayed imaginative and suggestive engagements with the performance of a river that often honored the histories of rivers in the region, but almost always depicted the river as a site of power.

The practice of generating multiple frames fosters reciprocity in the collaboration process. Such reciprocity flourishes through the creation of a space that emphasizes a dynamic approach to this work as (1) inclusive, (2) process oriented, and (3) iterative. Inclusiveness requires that we continue to generate new and effective working methods that effectively incorporate multiple forms of cultural difference. A process focus prioritizes an emphasis on *discovery* and *making* that emerges from the activities at hand. Iterative processes, such as Anna and Lawrence Halprin's RSVP cycles,[4] underscore loops of trial, test, feedback, and revision required for collaborative work.

These community collaborations open and transform public space. As forms of "progressive dialogues and actions," collaboration simultaneously occurs within the circle of a specific project and expands beyond the edges of the project proper. The collaboration that "spills over" into the surrounding spaces is a form of listening and responding to the diverse pathways of connections that accumulate across numerous stakeholders: artists, organizations, local populations, and online constituencies. This work generates reciprocating formulations of the arts that—striking a nerve and firing collective synapses—enlarge community dialogue and actively expand our visions for the future. One example of this type of spilling over can be seen in the principal's invitation to the students to apply what they were learning in the workshop by creating their own blended performance projects, which they then take out into the surrounding communities.

The spilling-over effect can also be seen in how the progressive engagement in the workshop processes took on a type of cumulative impact. Subsequent workshops involved dialogue and artistic exploration around the participants' own research into cultural stories and oral histories as well as scientific information about the status of water in Kerala. These findings ranged from cultural stories about how the Ganges River came into being when the goddess Ganga was unleashed to the earth from Shiva's coiled hair to a number of daily stories.

Daily observations included those poor neighbors who live in the same building for whom the water pipes did not work and who must walk daily to the nearest water station. Relatives who live in Kanamally, a neighborhood outside Kochi, who did not have any access to clean water. As a result, they had to wait for the irregularly scheduled lorry to bring water. Other findings spanned scientific data about the pollution in the Periyar River caused by a range of activities including, but not limited to, industrial waste dumping, overly rapid land development, and religious rites involving releasing the dead into the river. Other findings included studies of the all too unmitigated ecological and human destruction caused by building dams on rivers across India, as well as the way in which climate change has resulted in much lower levels of rainfall—thus available clean freshwater—during the monsoon season.

As the students shared their own findings with each other in small groups, they were asked to decide what aspects resonated the most for them and then to pick a core story or image. In other words, what did they want to explore further and begin to craft into performance pieces? The students were invited to use skills that they were learning in the workshop and other performance training to craft short performances or songs that captured what they wanted to say. This approach—giving them choices about how they craft their expressions without telling them which structure to pursue—tended to open up a more complex and dynamic space for the workshop.

As we moved into this particular workshop section, two intertwining sets of feelings began to surface: sorrow and anger. As the students moved into creating more content specific performance sections, they began to view the activities in the workshop—that is, the creation of these expressive pieces—as a form of taking action, and they also began asserting that more needed to be done. One student, for example, wrote the following song:

> Through the creations and the destructions the land of God has seen it all,
> You fill our land with culture,
> And you fill our hearts too
> Lord Brahma has a river,
> Lord Shiva has one too
> You make our land holy,
> And you make us a whole too
> O river, holy water of our land
> You flow through us with so your grace,
> Just to finally die by our hand.
>
> *(SH of Thevara, August 2015)*

Once these smaller performance compositions take shape and begin to have identifiable rhythmic structures, they can be combined into one larger work. New elements such as text, image, materials, music, sound, or film can be added that either amplify and underscore the emerging work, or disrupt, delay, or trans-figure the collective work. And, variously, other cross-media entry points can be used to generate performance structures, such as moving from text to move-ment, movement to sound, sound to materials, or materials to movement. As the project develops, questions of size, scale, types of participation from audience and performers, and location(s) for the work become answerable.

Within the collaborative processes of these workshops, students from diverse backgrounds share their perspectives on the topic at hand through their respec-tive art forms as they intersect with new artistic forms and ways to express their ideas. In the epigraph at the beginning of the this chapter, Rancière asserts that "artistic practices are 'ways of doing and making' that intervene in the general distribution of ways of doing and making as well as in the relationship they maintain to modes of being and forms of visibility" (2014: 8). The SH of Thevara workshop led to public performances, while each focused on a specific theme, showcased the distinct performance heritages, and also blended them together at the same time around the theme of *Water in Kerala*. Audiences saw their local stories reflected to them, and they also learned about other stories regarding our cities at the water's edge. This form of educational diplomacy through the arts and the related dialogical processes revolved around telling our water stories and imagining new ones.

In *The Future as Cultural Fact: Essays on the Global Condition*, Arjun Appadurai considering the vast numbers of people who face different forms of brutality and oppression and the ways in which the trauma of ordinary living can supplant a sense of hope, writes that

> this affective crisis, which also inhabits a geography that is not uniform, planetary, or universal, needs to be engaged fully by those who seek to design the future . . . a space for democratic design that must begin with the recognition that the future is cultural fact.
>
> *(2013: 299)*

In delineating the extreme living conditions of much of the world, Appadu-rai, like many others, finds the lack of attention toward understanding of the "future" seriously remiss.

Given our understanding of the arts as a cultural laboratory, the ways all of them can operate a repository for diverse histories, as a site for dialogue and the creation of new stories, and as a doorway toward hope, participatory choreog-raphies will continue to explore the relevance of this research through interna-tional arts exchanges—as new forms of translocal theatre education and creative learning in higher education. Dolphijn writes:

> To occupy nature thus means that we cannot, like the dualist, conservative and anthropocentric environmentalist, start with asking ourselves "how

we might *save* the world." We cannot and we should not save the world. We ought to dismantle the world and ourselves . . . through a world proposed to us by art. Only thus new forms of subjectivity more worthy of the crisis we are in can come into being.

(2014: 203)

As a whole, WK resulted in performance work that incorporated the telling of water stories through dance, theatre, and the use of mixed media; research on water in the context of the collection of oral histories, video footage, and field observations of how people experience water on a daily basis; and environmental science that tracks changes in the physical landscape of rivers through narratives, images, and maps. The use of theatre and related media forms, with the emphasis on telling stories through dance, acting, singing, and film, was an effective way to communicate research on water to multiple audiences.

These participatory cultural heritage experiences, creative learning in action, lead to high-impact shifts in awareness and practice as the participants share what they know and expand their understanding through embodied arts practices. The workshops and the performances trigger empathy and new, even if provisional, shared social spaces. These exchanges, which from the beginning include multiple voices, added momentum to the processes of artistic diplomacy that can create more imaginative, effective local and global citizens.

Notes

1. This movement-based approach to entering into the development of a shared project is informed by diverse methods such as Augusto Boal's Theatre of the Oppressed and Image Theatre, modern dance improvisation, my study of butoh, Kalaripayattu (and other Indian performance forms), my work on disability/deaf theatres, as well as studies in the histories and theories of collaboration and creativity. For more on my work on the interplay of movement explorations, cross-cultural communication, and arts-based research, see Kochhar-Lindgren (2008, 2013a, 2013b, 2014).
2. For more on Laban Movement Analysis, see, for example, Ciane Fernandes's *The Moving Researcher: Laban/Bartenieff Movement Analysis in the Performing Arts and Creative Arts Therapies* (2014).
3. Laban Movement Analysis is also a system used to notate movement, and in recent years it has been used in a number of computer-driven programs that involve motion capture, forms of movement rendering, and analysis. See, for example, Lian Loke et al.'s "Understanding Movement for Interaction Design: Frameworks and Approaches" (2007). While it can be leveraged as a "scientific" or "universal" vocabulary, it is nevertheless a product of its cultural history. Further work on the use of this vocabulary in such types of cross-cultural workshops would benefit from a comparative analysis of the vocabulary and a deepening of how the terms are effectively deployed in the respective workshops. For more on this discussion, see, for example, Brenda Farnell's "Moving Bodies, Acting Selves" (1999).
4. For more on the RSVP cycles, see Lawrence Halprin's *The RSVP Cycles: Creative Processes in the Human Environment* (1970).

Bibliography

Appadurai, Arjun. (2013). *The Future as Cultural Fact: Essays on the Global Condition.* London: Verso.

Deleuze, Gilles and Felix Guattari. (2004). *A Thousand Plateaus Anti-Oedipus: Capitalism and Schizophrenia.* London: Continuum.

De Lissovoy, Noah. (2010). "Decolonial Pedagogy and the Ethics of the Global." *Discourse: Studies in the Cultural Politics of Education.* Vol. 31, No. 3, 279–293.

Dolphijn, Rick. (2014). "The Revelation of the World That Was Already There: The Creative Act as an Occupation." In *This Deleuzian Century: Art, Activism, Life* (pp. 185–206). Eds. Rosi Braidotti and Rick Dolphijn. Leiden: Rodopoi Press.

Ellsworth, Elizabeth. (2004). *Places of Learning: Media, Architecture, Pedagogy.* New York: Routledge.

Farnell, Brenda. (1999). "Moving Bodies, Acting Selves." *Annual Review of Anthropology.* Vol. 28, 341–373.

Fernandes, Ciane. (2014). *The Moving Researcher: Laban/Bartenieff Movement Analysis in the Performing Arts and Creative Arts Therapies.* London: Jessica Kingsley.

Halprin, Lawrence. (1970). *The RSVP Cycles: Creative Processes in the Human Environment.* New York: George Braziller.

Kochhar-Lindgren, Kanta. (2008). "Uneasy Alliances: Art as Observation, Site, and Social Innovation." *Working Papers in Art and Design.* Vol. 5. University of Hertfordshire. http://www.herts.ac.uk/__data/assets/pdf_file/0013/12424/WPIAAD_vol5_lindgren.pdf

———. (2013a). "Dramatizing Translation: Performance, Cultural Tourism, and the Transnational." *Journal of Contemporary Thought.* Vol. 38, 73–84.

———. (2013b). "Dramatizing Water: Performance, Anthropology, and the Transnational." *Rupkatha Journal on Interdisciplinary Studies in Humanities.* Vol. 5, No. 2, 22–33. http://rupkatha.com/v5n2.php

———. (2014). "The Turbulence Project: Touching Cities, Visual Tactility, and Windows." *Performance Research International.* Ed. Paul Carter. Vol. 19, No. 5, 13–22.

Loke, Lian, Astrid T. Larssen, Toni Roberts and Jenny Edwards. (2007). "Understanding Movement for Interaction Design: Frameworks and Approaches." *Personal and Ubiquitous Computing.* Vol. 11, No. 8, 691–701.

Mathur, Anurradha and Dilip Da Cunha. (2014). "Waters Everywhere." *Design in the Terrain of Water* (pp. 1–23). Eds. Anuradha Mathur and Dilip Da Cunha. Philadelphia: Applied Research+Design with the University of Pennsylvania.

Oakes, Tim and Louisa Schein. (2006). "Translocal China: An Introduction." *Translocal China: Linkages, Identities and the Re-imagining of Space* (pp. 1–35). Eds. Tim Oakes and Louisa Schein. New York: Routledge.

Rancière, Jacques. (2014). *The Politics of Aesthetics: The Distribution of the Sensible.* Ed. and Trans. Gabriel Rockhill. London: Bloomsbury.

4

CONFIGURING INTERDISCIPLINARITY

The Common Core at the University of Hong Kong

Gray Kochhar-Lindgren

We all sense that we urgently need a decisive change in teaching, a change that will eventually have repercussions on the entire space of our global society and its obsolete institutions.

Michel Serres, Thumbelina *(2014, p. 13)*

We learn nothing from those who say "Do as I do." Our only teachers are those who tell us to "do with me," and are able to emit signs to be developed in heterogeneity rather than propose gestures for us to reproduce.

Gilles Deleuze, Difference and Repetition *(1994, p. 23)*

Interdisciplinarity: The Space Between

By activating the dynamic space of the *inter-*, the University of Hong Kong's (HKU) Common Core (http://commoncore.hku.hk/) provides a generative reflective platform for the *practice of interdisciplinary creativity* for all of its undergraduate students. Given the forces of globalization, technology, migration, and digitization that are so powerfully shaping the contemporary university, such a reconfiguring of interdisciplinarity enables students to prepare more fully for the knowledge and experience economy, to make connections between their majors and other areas of learning, and to begin to think about the meaning of ethics in the context of extremely complex dilemmas.

How might we understand the *inter-*: the space of the between? How might we most creatively activate it? For any learning to occur, the strange topology of the between must be constantly traversed as we develop assignments, courses, curricula, and university-wide initiatives. The term "*inter*disciplinary" will gesture toward curricula that explicitly moves between "established" disciplines, while also being cognizant of the fact that all of these are themselves always in flux; that the disciplines have been historically cobbled together for a great many reasons which do not have to do primarily with the space of a "pure" intellectual inquiry; and that "traditional" departments, schools, and faculties remain the most powerful internal forces in the organizational chart of a university. The university, as an idea and as a set of interlinked practices, is now in tremendous flux, and reconfiguring interdisciplinarity as a form of student learning adds an essential dimension to the possibilities of making creative interventions in the flows of the local and the global.

At HKU interdisciplinarity occurs across many domains—both at the undergraduate and graduate level—but I will focus on the Common Core. This was launched in 2012 when all eight publicly funded universities in the city transitioned from a three-year to a four-year undergraduate degree structure. Each university designed its own curricular structure to address the additional year, although all were mandated to organize some form of a general education program rather than simply extending the credits required for majors. HKU underwent an extremely intensive process of comparative review with international peer institutions, consultations with local and distant experts, and complex and iterative internal process of decision-making before establishing the Core.

The Common Core requires that students be given opportunities as soon as they enter the university, rather than waiting until they become sufficiently "expert" in a discipline, so that the two complementary practices of (inter)disciplining can develop hand in hand. An interdisciplinary set of approximately 160 courses designed by faculty members from across the entire university (including the professional schools), the Core requirement consists of six courses that for the most part must be completed within the students' first three years of study. The courses are placed in one of four Areas of Inquiry (AoIs)—Scientific and Technological Literacy, Global Issues, Humanities and Arts, and China—and students must complete at least one course in every AoI, plus two additional courses of their choice.

The criteria for a successful course proposal—which must be approved both at the AoI and Curriculum Committee level—are that the course be inflected toward interdisciplinary concerns, organized around a topic of "profound significance," and that engages students with the active learning methods of practices such as projects, fieldwork, media production, experiments, debates, and role-plays as the means of assessment. The courses are reviewed after two years in order to recommend continuation or discontinuation, and each year the teachers revise the courses after considering student feedback. In addition, external examiners, mainly from North American universities, review the courses in each AoI and across the program as a whole.

Like all curricula, the Common Core creates both knowledge and dispositions. As C. W. Mills (1959) so eloquently observed more than sixty years ago (and we could of course go back to philosophical and religious examples from many millennia ago):

> There is a playfulness of mind back of such combining [of ideas that were not expected to be combinable] as well as a truly fierce drive to make sense of the world, which the technician as such usually lacks. Perhaps he is too well trained, too precisely trained. Since one can be *trained* only in what is already known, training sometimes incapacitates one from learning new ways; it makes one rebel against what is bound to be at first loose and even sloppy.
>
> *(p. 212)*

In the Core, there is certainly a type of training occurring—especially around the skills of collaboration, communication, and project-based exhibits—but there is also the "fierce drive to make sense of the world" and to change for the better, in a very modest manner, the quality of life for Hong Kong and beyond.

Reflective and Pragmatic Inventiveness

The Core seeks to be an inviting space of reflective inventiveness where the unexpectedness of new knowledge and new practices can emerge, where the "loose and sloppy"—also known as creative chaos—can be an aspect of intellectual rigor, and where the "playful" and the "serious" are able to move back and forth in a distinctive rhythm. It is grounded less in the development of abstract domain-specific knowledge and more in what Sullivan and Rosin (2008) have called a "pedagogy of practical reason," which "requires moving back and forth between specific events and the general ideas and common traditions that might illuminate them, in order to interpret and engage the particular situation more fruitfully" (p. xvii). "Practical reason" combines a "know how to" with a "know what for" that is enacted around particular questions, and often around particular locales. This is the usefulness of students taking field trips throughout Hong Kong, from the Wan Chai Cut to film studios to geological sites, and even across the border to the nuclear power plant at Daya Bay.

Student and staff engagement, then, is not purely on a discursive or theoretical plane, but also on a plane of self-reflexive practice that requires movement between differences of locale, cultures, disciplinary formations, types of assessment, and learning goals for the courses and the program as a whole. The Common Core is a primary site within the overall HKU curriculum to foreground this activity for incoming and continuing undergraduates (including exchange students from abroad, who are able to sign up for a number of the courses). How, though, does this work more specifically in practice?

Many courses work on a number of different types of student projects, but one of the recent presentations that I visited comes out of "Journey into Madness: Conceptions of Mental Health and Mental Illness" (CCHU9022).[1] The students read material—targeted at an appropriate level of difficulty—from psychology, anthropology, Chinese medicine, biochemistry, and social media as they explored the social and medical construction of mental illness across categories and cultures, with an emphasis on Hong Kong. Then, with the "use of experiential exercises, case student and film viewing" (Common Core Student Handbook, p. 76), they further reflected on their encounter with mental illness in their daily lives. Finally, in partnership with a local nongovernmental organization (NGO) centered around forms of social interaction with the mentally ill, the students were divided into groups. They were asked to do a field visit; create different interactions with the members of the community; do a reflection on the experience; make a short video; and present their work the class as a whole and to visiting NGO members.

This is a systematic reconfiguration of required undergraduate learning as it moves through the classroom and back; as it creates a new relationship between the ongoing dynamics of theory and practice; and as it uses student learning to conjoin with a social intervention. None of these curricular experiences is, of course, unique to HKU, and all of them have many instantiations around the world. But the systemic nature of such a change that emphasizes, along different axes, a participatory rather than a primarily receptive model for learning does serve as an index of the forces at work that are serving as the conditions of change for higher education.

Perhaps we could simply give them, for the moment, the abbreviated names of "globalization" and "technosociality." The curricular networks that form a university are historical indices of a *zeitgeist* (one translation: "haunted time"). The contemporary university, a loosely organized ensemble of disciplines that tend to centrifugally move away from one another, is a dense node of a network of geo-, techno-, and social relationships that are rapidly changing shape. Since the founding of the University of Berlin in 1802, the comprehensive research university has always been (and always will be) beset by the tensions between teaching and research, between disciplines and the *inter-*, and between the production of knowledge and the formation of capacities for undergraduate students. The question, then, is how we might best activate these tensions toward creativity instead of allowing the tensions to freeze an institution, or even parts of the institution, into the stasis of the status quo.

The Crossings of Interdisciplinarity and Specialization

What will we make of the new institutional puzzles in which learning now occurs, which must find mechanisms to carry along selected traditions, cast off other traditions, and create the space for the "new" without the new simply being a space to be filled by capitalist production and consumption? Locally, how will these demands shape the *inter-* of the Common Core, and how, in turn, might the *inter-* reconfigure the long-term structure and pedagogy of a university? "Fundamentally, there are two logics," Jacques Rancière (2011) has reminded us:

> The one that divides thought into specific competences and domains for specialists, who fragment it into differences that are the small change of a

principled inquiry; or the logic that thinks it as an undivided power, similar in all of its exercises, shareable among anyone or whoever. My vision of philosophy is first of all a vison of thought as a power of declassification of the redistribution of territorial divisions among disciplines and competences. Philosophy says that thought belongs to all.

(p. 23)

Hedgehogs and foxes—to borrow Isaiah Berlin's famous classification—all the way down and all the way across. Those with different priorities and angles of vision will always coexist and, however collegially, battle for resources, visibility, and prestige. As simply one discipline among others, philosophy *also* offers for Rancière a name that indicates a hope, a sign, and occasionally even another mode of thinking than the technoempiricism that currently dominates the research landscape. Philosophy, in Rancière's sense, works at the redistribution of value, works across disciplines, and springs forth from an ontological equality of thought for all. But this is only if philosophy—or any other departmentalized discipline—addresses the constitutive nature of the *inter-* within its own structure. Where are the doors, windows, fire escapes, and trapdoors of the disciplines? In a program such as the Common Core, how might they not only communicate with one another but also, in a reflexive act of creativity, be changed by that encounter?

*Inter*disciplinarity operates, by definition, in the middle of the action. The middle, however,

> [is] by no means the average; on the contrary, it is where things pick up speed. *Between* things does not designate a localizable relation going from one thing to another and back again, but a perpendicular direction, a transversal movement that sweeps one and the other away, a stream without beginning or end that undermines its banks and picks up speed in the middle.
>
> *(Deleuze and Guattari, 1987, p. 25)*

The solution of the tension between Rancière's "two logics"—and those of C. P. Snow that are even more familiar—is conceptually simple, but institutionally complicated: invite the foxes and hedgehogs to work on mutually interesting projects and create a proliferating bestiary on campus. See what foxes and hedgehogs might become as hybrids. Let them work together to co-create the Common Core and its analogues. Give it a shot; see what happens.

One of the most common rationales for the enactment of advanced interdisciplinary expertise is that all of our contemporary conundrums are "wicked problems," not amenable to solution within a discipline (although I in no way want to dismiss the wickedness of these difficulties as well, since in a certain manner "wickedness"—an insoluble complexity—belongs inherently to all the fundamental questioning of thought and experience). The world is not simple—bounded and with determinate solutions after which we can make a checkmark—but a composite of (quasi)intractabilities. Speaking of the natural sciences, a 1986 UNESCO forum noted that:

> In the last century, science was geared to the solution of relatively simple problems lying within a field of homogenous relationships which could be embraced by a single discipline. Today, one of the essential features of the problems arising is their great complexity. The contemporary world poses problems involving a considerable number of factors in which social and technical aspects overlap, multiple and essential interactions abound, precision is mingled with a great of uncertainty, and the field of relationship is heterogeneous.
>
> *(D'Hainaut, 1986, p. 5)*

Heterogeneity is the essential condition for creativity—difference gives rise to the difference marked as "the new"—and the pathways created *between* disciplines, zigzagging across the terrain of learning, enable students to more intensely practice their own learning. Recently, for example, Common Core student groups were out on campus making measurements in the streets, using portable blue solar spectrometers, and following a *"129erive* app" to test the boundaries of their freedom of motion on campus in places such as chemistry labs, administrative offices, and the faculty dining area. For undergraduates, who are early apprentices in the arts of the *inter-*, these activities serve as catalysts for questions, collaborations, and observations, a glimpse of a way of being that they are often noticing for the first time.

As the interdisciplinary team at the Future and Emerging Technologies reminds us, however, it is not simply a conceptual map that we are creating, but new means of *working together* across significant and often viscous differences of language, assumptions, methods, and values (not to mention time zones). While complexity does in fact drive interdisciplinarity,

> what are often missing in such a construction are the pathways between the disciplines to really learn from one another . . . [such a process] at least initially, deconstructs more than it constructs, because everyone involved is forced to put into question the fundamental assumptions of its own view of the world. This is hard work and risky business.
>
> *(FET, n.d., p. 2)*

This, too, is why programs such as the Common Core are invaluable even for beginning undergraduates, for they set students to work with one another across intellectual and dispositional differences on projects that matter to them.

The extraordinary precision of the most specialized expertise across all the domains of knowledge remains absolutely necessary—this is one of the central powers of the sciences of whatever stripe—but there is an urgently correlative question that shadows this development of expertise: how do we establish creative and ethical *connectors* in and beyond the university?

As David Harvey (2011) has insisted, it is now essential for those with a

> deep knowledge of how the relation to nature works need to ally with those deeply familiar with how institutional and administrative arrangements function, how science and technology can be mobilized, how daily life and social relations can most easily be re-organized, how mental conceptions can be changed, and how production and labor process can be reconfigured.
>
> *(p. 138)*

Although undergraduates need to continue to develop a more densely layered knowledge in the majors, none of them will be truly "expert" after four years of study, and they are well served by the learning that assists them in becoming far more adept practitioners of the skills of navigating the *inter-*. We need to cultivate, as I say in my orientations with students at HKU, an *inspired pragmatism* for all of us so that we can not only learn how to *do* things more adeptly, but also how to *care* more deeply about what, how, and why we are doing what we are doing.

Globalization, Holistic Learning, and Creativity

"The space of the lecture hall," as Serres (2014) has observed,

> was designed as a field of forces whose orchestral center of gravity was the stage, with its focal point at the lectern, which was literally a *power point*. What was situated there was the heavy density of knowledge, which scarcely existed on the periphery. Now, knowledge is distributed everywhere, moving freely in a homogenous and decentered space.
>
> *(p. 34)*

When the center can no longer hold, it is not necessarily the "blood-dimmed tide" of Yeats that ensues, but perhaps a fluidity of networks-in-motion. The disciplinary major—the figure for specialization, and thus, presumably from most students' perspectives, simple linear success in the job hunt—has in North America long been supplemented by one form of general education or another, which has served, in its turn, as the figure for the connectivity of the whole.

This is "whole-person education" for the "well-rounded" student, a model that has been going global for some time now. Both multinational and local employers realize the need for a different type of learning experience, preparing students for the knowledge economy rather than for the standardization of the factory, the suburb, and the classroom where a kind of homogenized memory, repetition, and standardization reign. This has certainly been the case in Hong Kong, where employers' advocacy for different skills and ways of approaching issues was a major part of why the city decided to move to a four-year degree (which also aligns better with the degrees structures in North America and mainland China).

In our historical moment of globalization, financialization, violence, and mobilities of all sorts—which has radically reshaped the university since the Reagan-Thatcher years—different experiences of "heaviness" are also close at hand. Zygmunt Bauman (2000) has noted, "We live in a world of universal flexibility, under conditions of acute and prospectless *Unsicherheit*, penetrating all aspects of individual life" (p. 135).

> Work has drifted from the universe of order-building and future-control to the realm of a game; acts of work become more like the strategy of a player who sets himself modestly short-term objectives reaching no further than one or two moves ahead.
>
> *(p. 138)*

Innovation, creativity, problem solving, communication skills, flexibility, and collaboration are the qualities in the highest demand by the workforce of global capital, which is very visible on the streets and across the skyline of Hong Kong. None of these offers "guarantees," however, since there is no such thing as a guarantee in the high-risk game and casino world of global capital. Spin the wheel; bet on red.

It is, however, this same force, strangely aligned with the traditional discourse of "whole-person education," that is driving much of the move, at least in Hong Kong and Asia, toward cross-disciplinary and actively taught curricula. In this age of globalization, then, "interdisciplinarity" is a mark of a reconfiguring of the disciplines, forms of assessment, and the understanding of the purpose of a university education. The Common Core at HKU, as it addresses this reconfiguration, provides an exposure to interdisciplinary experience—which impacts forms of learning as much as bodies of knowledge—that is built into undergraduate experience from its very outset. Some argue that this is pedagogically inappropriate and technically undoable, since students are asked to perform the *inter-* before they have really entered into, much less mastered, a discipline. How can there be a "between" before there are structures in place between which to construct the bridge of a between?

There are several responses to this argument. The students are entering into their disciplinary lives—whether in the professional schools or in the liberal arts at HKU—as they also begin the Core, so these experiences are constantly interweaving with one another. The *inter-* is complementary to the disciplines and vice versa. Second, the students will certainly *not* be masters of their disciplines at graduation, after they have "finished" their undergraduate training. No one is master of any discipline, since the disciplines are always expanding and are always already too expansive for us to reach around in a comprehensive manner. This structural excess though, is the very essence of thinking, of coming toward knowledge, and so is both irresolvable and inevitable. That's a good thing. We do not master disciplines, but the disciplines—though in a sense broader than the departmental institutionality of the university—keep calling us back to do their own work in a labor of love that consumes us.

Finally, the interdisciplinarity of the Common Core is more about the development of *performative learning capacities* than about repeating already established bodies of knowledge. Learning always has an intellectual content, so the students are learning a great deal of content in all of their courses, which, emphatically, are *not* designed as "Introductions to X" but are organized around thematizable questions and problems that cross disciplines. Most are taught, however, by colleagues that are trained in a single discipline—that is, after all, what a PhD implies—and this training shows in the ways the courses are organized, although all courses, as I have mentioned, must inflect toward the *inter-*.

Let me give another example of a Common Core course that works to remodel undergraduate general education: "Shaping the Landscape: A Quest for Harmony between Nature and the City" (CCHU9023). The project for this year's course was entitled "Voices of the Water," in which the students, with the facilitation of the instructor and the tutors, were to

> create a series of land art works that can speak from the perspective of the natural resource of water and its associated landscapes. . . . Seldom do we listen to the voice of the land. Therefore, this project aims to treat elements of the landscape as the "first person" telling us their stories, and from their perspectives also tell their experiences and opinions of the water supply story. Through these "narrations" of landscape elements, we hope to collect and present information about the waterworks system to the audience, at the same time to allow participants and audience, through the medium of art, to imagine/interpret/dive in to the first-person experience of how the environment feels about all these ever-changing situations of fresh water supply issues.
>
> *(Course Assignment, format revised)*

The project landscape elements were "Water as Commodity (Commodification of Nature); Employed Materials at Waterworks (Operations); Forgotten Changes to the Natural Landscapes, *past and present* (Memory); Sound of Waterworks, *past and present* (Sound)" (Course Assignment, format revised). This kind of project—which involved a great deal of reading, writing and on-site research—resulted in a temporary art installation on the sites of the Pokfulam Reservoir, the Tai Tam Reservoir, and the Bowen Aqueduct. These sites are essential aspects, either historically or in the present, of Hong Kong's water-management system. Students roam about the world—intellectually, emotionally, and physically—and make a project together which they then share in multiple ways. This is the power of integrated learning that occurs in the *inter-* of both disciplinarity and of the campus-city network.

Since the encyclopedia of attained knowledge is available today at a swipe across our electronic devices, what does tertiary learning contribute to individual, cultural, and economic development? What distinguishes us from the increasingly capable robots and the emergence of ubiquitous computing that more and more closely mimics artificial intelligence (AI)? It is the capacity, still, to symbolize differently than in the past that is being negotiated, often brutally but sometimes only with the necessary violence, which is the least violent option, of discourse.

The Common Core, with its interdisciplinary topics and projects, works out of a practical reason—a *phronesis* rather than a *theoria*—that

> aims at a kind of synthetic knowing that links self-conscious awareness to responsive engagement in projects in the world . . . The agenda of practical reason could be said to be about re-grounding the ideals of the Enlightenment. This agenda grounds the meaning of critical rationality in human purposes that are wider and deeper than criticism, in part inherited and in part constructed in social relationships.
>
> *(Sullivan and Rosin, 2008, p. 104)*

Practical reason—a tradition that draws upon (among others) Aristotle, Kant, and Dewey—includes multiple opportunities for "critique," but these extend beyond the areas of theoretical discourse and a traditional "hermeneutics of suspicion." Critique is creative. In addition, for Kant—where this distinction is most thoroughly articulated—practical reason provides the opening for freedom, which is required if there is to be knowledge, ethics, inquiry-based learning, debates that lead to conclusions, or discovery through experimentation.

We are all now responsible, as modest designers but not as masters, for inventing the future. "Find something new to hook up with and you'll have a desire, make something different," Deleuze and Guattari (1987) have reminded us. "It's recombinations; it's random acts of assembling. It's LEGOs and tinker-toys. Metaphors; academic trainings and disciplines; different floorings in the chemistry and the philosophy building; the architecture of computers, buildings, or of reason. The logic of the dream" (p. 14). Try new things; combine and recombine; hook up the everyday to the everyday and the unexpected will emerge. Ask physics to talk to anthropology or mathematics to talk with painting and see what happens. That which manifests will teach and delight us, as well as prove useful for finding solutions to perplexing problems.

The Common Core at HKU is one of many examples across Asia of experimenting to establish a different, more creative learning experience for students.

The responses by students and staff to the creation, implementation, and refinement of the Core has ranged from enthusiastic participation to deep resistance, but the central thrust of the administrative and pedagogical work has become to enhance the experience for everyone involved. This will be accomplished through a continual assessment of courses; the formation of an advisory board with student ambassadors; and a number of structural changes within student enrollment, the types and timing of the courses, and ongoing development workshops for tutors and teachers.

Through an array of different methods, there is an ongoing system of assessment of the tutors, teachers, courses, and program as a whole. We ask international external examiners to review collections of courses across the four Areas of Inquiry as well as the whole enterprise; we have a number of surveys for students and staff around their specific and general experience of the Core; and the Curriculum Committee has a schedule for reviewing courses in detail and recommending continuation, improvements, or discontinuation. Finally, the Hong Kong University Student Union recently sponsored a formal debate on the motion, "The University should abolish the Common Core," which the popularly elected councilors roundly defeated. In their defense of this still new curricular experiment, the students were quite eloquent about the purpose of a university education and about how the Core supported such a purpose by broadening their perspectives, providing a site for them to come to know friends across the faculties, and complementing their majors as they looked beyond their graduation to what might come next.

Constellations of Rivers: Re-stitching Transversal Creativity

Serres (2014) has asked how disciplines might be "re-stitched" to create an experience that gestures toward the whole:

> A river, for example . . . but how can we unite these classifications, dissolve these borders, gather together the already cut and formatted pages, superimpose the designs of the university, unify the lecture halls, pack up the departments in one suitcase, and make all the high-level experts—each of whom thinks they process the exclusive definition of intelligence—listen to each other?
>
> *(p. 38)*

Interdisciplinary undergraduate education aims at a dynamic vision of the whole person and of the whole world, as well as toward a variety of articulations of the interconnections between the parts. The whole, however, is not an accumulation of knowledge from across all the disciplines that will then *add up* to a totality. The whole is not an attainable empirical accomplishment based on a quantitatively achieved sum, but instead serves as both an a priori assumption of the possible experience of the good—the world is an essentially differentiated one—and a regulative ideal to strive toward: from the fragmented *toward* the fully lived.

Creative learning, in this context, is an interactive multiscalar practice that actively constructs connections between sites, questions, capacities, materials, methods, and experiences that, incrementally shaping collective and individual dispositions, creates a tendency *toward*. It is an experiment in motion that moves between the classrooms on campus and toward the huge new engineering dig creating the train link between Hong Kong and Guangzhou, toward an eco-village in the New Territories, or the Museum of the Monetary Authority in the IFC Tower. Creative learning crisscrosses the streets in Kennedy Town that are constantly changing under the pressure of the new MTR station and the arrival of greater capital investment, the traditional Pokfulam Village, and the CAVE where students can enter a 3D virtual world. Learning of this sort is always contextually oriented and transportable across multiple boundaries, and, as a force for (re)configuration of relationships, it transforms the world in ever so modest but nonetheless important ways. It requires professors to be facilitative translators rather than the focalized point for the transmission of knowledge.

Whether active in the Common Core or in other sites, the *inter-* activates, infinitely. It cannot be contained since it creates unexpected relations between always emerging domains of knowledge. The question is how we, always provisionally, organize the *inter-* into programs, classes, experiences, and on occasion, degrees. The suitcase—full of equations, masks, ocean ridges, galaxies, paintings, pathogens, tribes, buildings, laws, robots, plankton, and poems—clicks open and out spring the most marvelous surprises, the most unexpected constellations of contact. For all of us in the contemporary globalizing university, this is an experiment in motion, creativity in the mode of its most serious play.

Note

1. I am extremely grateful to Paul Wong and Vincci Mak, the instructors of the two courses that I use as extended examples, for permission to use their class material. The courses were also very adeptly supported by the tutors in the respective courses: Martina Rehnu Ambrose and Gizem Arat in the first, and Maxime Decaudin, Andrea Palmioli, Bryan Woo, and Viola Yucong Zhang in the second.

Bibliography

Bauman, Zygmunt. (2000). *Liquid Modernity.* Cambridge: Polity Press. *Common Core Student Handbook 2015–16*, University of Hong Kong. <http://commoncore.hku.hk/files/CC2015-low-p.pdf?150720> Accessed 7 December 2015.

Deleuze, Gilles. (1994). *Difference & Repetition.* Trans. Paul Patton. New York: Columbia University Press.

Deleuze, Gilles and Felix Guattari. (1987). *A Thousand Plateaus: Capitalism and Schizophrenia.* Trans. Brian Massumi. Minneapolis: University of Minnesota Press.

D'Hainaut, Louis. (1986). *Interdisciplinarity in General Education*. Paris: UNESCO, Division of Educational Sciences, Contents and Methods of Education.

FET [Future and Emerging Technologies]. "Living Interdisciplinarity," *Digital Agenda for Europe*: 1–3. <http://ec.europa.ed/digital-agenda/en/news/fet-living-interdisciplinarity>

Harvey, David. (2011). *The Enigma of Capital and the Crisis of Capitalism*. Oxford: Oxford University Press.

Mak, Vincci. "CCHU9023 Shaping the Landscape: A Quest for Harmony Between Nature and the City," University of Hong Kong, Autumn 2015.

Mills, C. W. (1959). *The Sociological Imagination*. New York: Oxford University Press.

Rancière, Jacques. (2011). A Politics of Aesthetic Indetermination: An Interview With Frank Ruda & Jan Voelker, *Everything Is in Everything: Jacques Rancière Between Intellectual Emancipation and Aesthetic Education*, Eds. Jason E. Smith and Annette Weisser. Pasadena, CA: Art Center Graduate Press, 10–33.

Serres, Michel. (2014). *Thumbelina: The Culture and Technology of Millennials*. Trans. Daniel W. Smith. Lanham, MD: Rowman & Littlefield.

Sullivan, William M. and Matthew S. Rosin. (2008). *A New Agenda for Higher Education: Shaping a Life of the Mind for Practice*. San Francisco: Jossey-Bass.

Wong, Paul. "CCHU9022 Journey Into Madness: Conceptions of Mental Health and Mental Illness," University of Hong Kong, Autumn 2015.

5

CREATING MEANINGFUL LEARNING SPACES THROUGH PHENOMENOLOGICAL STRATEGIES

David Giles and Clare McCarty

Introduction

As teachers with more than thirty years of experience, we have found ourselves returning to our understandings of the nature of the teacher–student relationship and indeed the priority of this relationship for teaching and learning in Higher Education. As academic colleagues in the same School of Education, we have found ourselves asking questions that we consider important about our pedagogical practices, questions that call us into an ongoing dialogue:

- What might we have taken for granted about the teacher–student relationship?
- Have we unintentionally slipped into privileging transactional models of teaching and learning?
- Have we lost sight of the holistic and experiential nature of teaching and learning, whether intentional or otherwise?
- What is the nature of the student's first year experiences within a university?
- As teaching staff in a university, how well do we hear students' voices in relation to our learning intentions?
- Have our learning expectations, assessment requirements and the fixation for the 'evidence' of learning constrained the creativity and innovation for those who teach in Higher Education?
- Are there examples of pedagogical practices that appear to release a deepening creative experience?

If those questions are not difficult enough, we have also opened up some ontological and phenomenological questions, such as:

- Where does the teacher–student relationship exist ontologically?
- How is the phenomenon of relationships experienced subconsciously?

- When is teaching, pedagogy, and indeed leadership, not relational?
- What do authentic relationships and dialogue have in common?

The purpose for stating these questions is to give you, the reader, a 'feel' for our position and stance on the priority that ought to be given to students' educational experiences in Higher Education, and the centrality of the teacher-student relationship within these experiences. We will argue in this chapter that the teacher-student relationship is always mattering within our teaching-learning experiences, whether we attend to this or not. Moreover, we argue that pedagogy, being the 'art' and 'science' of teaching and learning, is always relational in nature, and as such is central to our everyday teaching strategies. The challenge for those who teach is their need to deeply appreciate under-standing from phenomenological research that relationships exist between us (Giles, 2008). Moreover, the teacher-student relationship is experienced as an improvised play that has uncertainties for both the teacher and the student (Giles, 2010).

We have structured this chapter as follows:

- Initially, we describe a relational foundation to educational endeavour in Higher Education by scoping the phenomenological nature of the teacher-student relationship as 'existing' in a creative space 'between' those relating.
- We then turn to two cases of creative and meaningful learning which utilise hermeneutic processes for interpretive writing that focuses on meanings and understandings of the phenomenon we call 'teaching.'
- In the third section we recount our experience of constructing meaning-ful and engaged learning spaces for first year university students through a university-wide initiative across different cohorts.
- The final case describes innovative pedagogical approaches in action which calls students to experience their learning through performing arts within an educational core topic.

The Phenomenological Nature of the Teacher-Student Relationship in Higher Education

A key finding from a research project on the teacher-student relationship in Higher Education was that, from a phenomenological lens, relationships exist in the space between those relating (Giles, 2008). While at first glance this find-ing might appear simplistic, the finding has particular significance to those who teach in Higher Education.

When we objectify the teacher-student relationship to the 'people' involved, we can take for granted that the relationship is not just one person or another relating, rather the relationship exists as a creative, open and living space between those relating which is charged with possibility. Moreover, those relating influ-ence the dynamic relational space and are morally responsible for the nature and care of the space and the 'other' (Joldersma, 2001). For instance, sometimes it is a teacher's way of being that influences the nature of the space, while on other occasions teachers experience students who are very apt and adept at influencing their peers and the teacher's lived experience of a particular moment (Giles, 2011b; van Manen, 1990; van Manen & Li, 2002).

Another finding from the same phenomenological research is that an individual's way of being—that is, 'who they are' and 'how they are'—is integral to how the relational space is experienced (Giles, 2011a, 2011b). Teachers and students are continually feeling and reading the verbal and non-verbal movements within the moments shared with another in their relational space (Joldersma, 2001). When a creative pedagogical space emerges, then the 'who' and the 'how we are' of relating is critical to an individual's experience of the space. In this way, relating and teaching is always experienced holistically. In this engagement, authenticity, genuineness and care are felt experientially. The nature of the engagement is integral to the creation of meaningful learning spaces.

The movement of the relationship has both a familiarity and an uncertainty, given that there is no script for how the relating actually unfolds. Inauthentic relating by game-playing teachers, using their position of authority as power over students, can douse the life of the relating (Giles, 2010). The point here is that the teacher-student relationship is always mattering in the unfolding uncertainties of learning experiences. Gadamer (1994) likened the relational experience to that of being caught up in a festival, where the lack of script was a taken-for-granted characteristic of the festival. The seriousness of being 'in' the relational space behoves teachers to regularly reflect on the relational nature of their teaching and learning, and *contemplate* what specific experiences show about the life of their teaching and the nature of the students' lived experiences. A particular case will be reported later in the chapter.

Our research shows that highly relational teachers live out a very deep moral imperative with an articulated rationale for their everyday pedagogical practice. Similarly, teachers who privilege relationships in their everyday practice embody and enact their concern for relationship as pivotal to authentically 'walking the talk.' Further, teachers and students show particular sensibilities in the way they engender and hold open spaces for each other's creativity and innovation (Giles, 2010, 2014; van Manen & Li, 2002). These are not traits that can be isolated from experience, nor are they a checklist for success. These relational sensibilities show how teachers' or students' tacit knowing can amplify the life-centric nature of the relating and how the absence of tacit knowing impacts on the relational context for learning. While the sensibilities are not the primary message of this chapter, we signal the role of the sensibilities as integral to opening and sustaining the 'life' within the everyday relationship between teachers and students (Giles, 2010, 2014; Giles, Smythe & Spence, 2012). We list some sensibilities for further consideration: nous, tact, improvisation, resoluteness, moral judgement, pedagogical thoughtfulness, phronesis, episteme and techne (Giles, 2014; van

Manen, 2002). Our position is that the shared humanity of the teacher-student relationship with Higher Education needs to be reflected in creative and innovative learning spaces.

Four Cases of Creative and Meaningful Learning Which Utilise Hermeneutic Processes for Interpretive Writing That Focus on Meanings and Understandings of the Phenomenon We Call 'Teaching'

In this section, we outline four cases where phenomenological endeavour and understandings are embedded in the teaching and learning strategies.

Case 1: Hermeneutically Exploring Our Experiences of Teaching and Learning

In Case 1, we describe a particular pedagogical strategy that we have used with undergraduate pre-service teachers in Higher Education and with educational leaders studying in postgraduate courses. Underpinning our teaching strategy was the work of Emmanuel Levinas (1998; Joldersma, 2001), who suggests that others see us more fully than we see ourselves. In addition we draw upon Heidegger's (1992) notion of contemplative thinking which involves a process of allowing as-yet-unthought thoughts to find us. Such a contemplative stance stands in stark contrast to everyday thinking that tends to be more akin to a calculative thinking approach that is deductive and rational.

Our approach engages students in interpretive and hermeneutic writing processes that relate to their everyday lived experiences. This scaffolded learning experience involves contemplative thinking and hermeneutic writing which seeks to open significant meanings about teaching from within students' own experiential accounts (Giles & Morrison, 2010). Students start by descriptively writing about everyday experiences of being 'in' a teacher's role and being 'with' other experienced teachers. Critical to the success of the teaching strategy is the need to ensure that students write about experiences and not about their theories about an experience. Short, thick, grounded descriptions, akin to phenomenological data-gathering approaches, are sought (van Manen, 1990).

Having written a minimum of two stories, information is given about the pedagogical processes to follow, the role of hermeneutic processes in interpreting meanings and understandings from stories, as well as an introduction to calculative and contemplative thinking (Heidegger, 1992). We affectionately refer to this interpretive exercise as 'reading white font,' that is, reading for meaning in the spaces between the words in black font. After this, students are expected to be chewing on their written accounts and recording insights for sharing with the class. Most typically, students share ontological thoughts that relate to the relational nature of teaching.

Once the experiences have been described, the interpretation commences. The interpretive activity involves students in groups of four (Giles & Morrison, 2010). This activity involves students reading aloud their experiences from the past, and then listening as others interpret the stories by expressing potential interpretations and taken-for-granted understandings within the story. This interpretive process begins with the question, 'what does this story show us about teaching?'

The author of the story is asked to listen without speaking or recording any thoughts, as what is shared is both specific to the actual story and phenomeno- logical in nature. The silencing of the author occurs for several reasons (Jolder- sma, 2001). First, we wanted to close down a 'rightness and wrongness' dialogue. Second, we wanted to affirm the idea that as human beings we live in a way that takes for granted deeper meanings within our experiences (Pinar & Reynolds, 1992). Third, the interpretive process was not about the meanings within a per- son's experience but those meanings that were seen across all the students' stories within the group.

In their group of four, having read their stories aloud and listened to many interpretive comments, students must then collaboratively identify ontologi- cal understandings in the form of powerful and emergent themes, which show essential understandings about the nature of being a teacher and/or teaching. Invariably, students refer the primacy of relationships, the influence of context, and the degree of agency. As teachers, we are moved by the manner in which students reconstruct their experiences creatively, bringing to the fore their higher order thinking in a deep engagement with a phenomenon of interest.

Case 2: Appreciative Appraisals

A second case for creating a deeply meaningful and creative learning space involves the use of the appreciate inquiry in a process we call an appreciative appraisal (Chapman & Giles, 2009; Giles & Alderson, 2008; Giles & Kung, 2010). This strategy was developed initially for practicing and emergent educational leaders enrolled in a postgraduate course. We have used the strategy with under- graduate students setting personal goals for an upcoming professional teaching experience. In a structured six-week timeline, as teachers, we act as an appre- ciative coach, critical friend and facilitator of this process. The process involves significant dialogue and contemplative thinking for the student and teacher.

The process for an appreciative appraisal is in the title itself. First, the pro- cess has an appreciative lens, meaning we have adapted an appreciative inquiry process. Second, the process involves an appraisal or stocktake of the individu- al's current context, be it teaching or leadership. The process for an apprecia- tive appraisal begins with students describing six everyday experiences that had a sense of 'life' in their practice. These might be high points, or experiences where they were so immersed in the moment that they lost track of time. These experiences are written descriptively, with a copy of each of the stories going to the teacher as the critical friend.

Working separately, the student and critical friend embark on discovering emergent themes across the stories that show particular characteristics that appear to engender a sense of life in practice. The process seeks the positive core of a person's practice (Hammond, 1998; Whitney & Cooperrider, 1998; Whitney, Trosten-Bloom & Rader, 2010).

The challenge continues as the student is required to explain their understandings about the 'life' within the stories, and then identify four emergent themes across the stories for the critical friend (teacher). Then the critical friend repeats the process, tabling ideas as to the appearance of ontological understandings within the experiences. Our approach utilises our interpretive and hermeneutic abilities to engage with the stories. This important discussion may require a second meeting.

The third phase, after writing and analysing the stories together, involves the construction of several provocative propositions that resemble aspirational statements that describe the contextual conditions which best support the student's practices. This aspect of the process is difficult for students and usually requires our assistance. The final aspect of the process is to construct an action plan, which contextualises the students' propositions in the context of their future practice. The process is engaging, energising and taken seriously as students grapple with the life-giving characteristics within their former experiences. The importance continues over the interpretations. The experience of working closely with a critical friend is akin to a challenging professional dialogue that invariably 'emotionally moves' the student and critical friend. Students point to understandings they had not previously seen.

Students are required to construct a report on the experience of the process and the outcomes. Recently, one postgraduate student said, 'in over 30 years of being a school principal, I have never thought so deeply about . . . my practice. I've never been asked what gives life to my practice as a leader.' We remain fully committed to these time-consuming activities and interpretive responsibilities associated with an appreciative appraisal, given the significant influence these experiences have for the student and the teacher.

This process of shared understandings, interpretation and critical appraisal was integral to changes in pastoral care and pedagogy in a large first year bachelor of education cohort.

Case 3: Describes the Co-construction of Meaningful, Engaged and Caring Learning Spaces for First Year University Students

On arrival at university, students are frequently vulnerable, insecure, lacking confidence, alienated and without a 'voice' in many senses (Noddings, 2005).

In relation to these characteristics, across our university action has been taken in respect of student orientation, transition and retention. In our case, this was manifested in the pastoral care of new students by professionally developed tutors and the introduction of student-mentors in drop-in centres and embedded in classes. We called our approach 'Feeling at Home at Flinders' and described it as 'a secure foundation of pastoral care.' Students referred to it as providing 'comfortability' and the warmth of friendship.

Quality teaching sat on this secure foundation. We sought to enhance, through ongoing professional development, the role of first year tutors to encompass the academic, personal and social aspects of their educational relationship with students. Transformative pedagogy was at the heart of our approach (Mezirow, 1991, 1995; Mezirow & Associates, 2000). Student 'voice' had a further implication within this changed learning experience (Mezirow & Associates, 2000). The interdependence of language and thought had to be developed further to achieve empathetic, critical, higher order thinking—notable aims for Higher Education and humanity.

Language is the predominant, though not exclusive, means whereby we are able to think, learn and create. It predominates because of its relationship to thought. As such it allows us to evoke, manipulate and organise images and experiences and to reflect on these. There are transformative elements that actively integrate and generate the relations among ideas, building internal and external connections as well as making new ones (Mayer, 2008; Vygotsky, 1978; Wenger, 1999).

The very act of speech makes meanings and understanding available to others, which are critical to the relational influence of these understandings and to the creative learning groups which are formed (Vygotsky, 1978; Wenger, 1999). Bullock (1975) states that 'in group discussion the spoken contribution of each member may be worked upon by speaker and listeners alike and in the immediacy of face-to face speech they make corporate enquiry a powerful mode of learning' (p. 50). In a similar way, Berger and Luckmann (1967) observed that 'I hear myself as I speak; my own subjective meanings are . . . continuously available to me and "ipso facto" become more real to me' (p. 52). Buber (2002) reminds us of the centrality of dialogue to relationship.

The tutors in our 'Feeling at Home at Flinders' experience had to understand the nature of pastoral care and the role of language in learning. To this end, five professional workshops were held on these practices to augment what the tutors, having been teachers in schools, knew and could implement. The process we adopted turned out to be a very important one in relation to transition, engagement and learning. During each of the first four weeks, students sat with different students whom they did not know. This was to avoid the insularity of former school friends staying isolated and unapproachable. They went through introductions, shared experiences and stayed in a group for the duration of the tutorial. The introduction was crafted so that a student need only describe themselves within their comfort zone to one other, who then introduced them to the other members of the group. By the end of this process, after several weeks, they had sufficient knowledge of other students to choose a partner.

These pairs each joined another pair as a group of four that continued for the remainder of the semester. In this way they were socially comfortable through informed choice (Buber, 2002). Perhaps even more importantly, the groups spent every week together sharing and discussing their written reading responses followed by a variety of different learning activities. In this way they built up considerable knowledge of educational issues through a constructivist process (Vygotsky, 1978).

During this process tutors also learned and practised how to respect each other, to have an opinion which could be justified, and to connect their previous experience to new ideas from lectures, readings and class discussion. How to discuss and enable discussion was the responsibility of every group member.

Reflection was an early practice, where individual experiences were recreated through written contemplations of learning and teaching memories at school. These were shared in pairs and then with the whole class, and included the tutors and student-mentors. The activity culminated in a circle. The students faced outwards and the circle was silent. Then, one by one, each student turned inwards and completed the following sentence: 'When I'm a teacher I will. . . .' These comments have repeatedly been delivered with emotion and commitment. Their intention is palpable.

In the following weeks, again in their pairs, students discussed and shared their views on a newspaper article on education with the whole class, connecting now with the contemporary world and the possibility of acting upon it.

We know through three years of evaluative research that we had met our intentions of greater student retention and higher academic results. Nine out of ten students indicated that they looked forward to attending their tutorial with the considerable relational engagement. They also placed a very strong emphasis on the topic content being interesting, engaging, relevant and important. Numerical data shows fewer failures and higher academic results. The number of withdrawals is not only relatively very small but reduced further in 2014. The outstanding statistics were the reduction of withdrawals to 1.8% and the number of High Distinctions grades that were given were double those of 2012.

The 'voices' of the various participants in relation to our intentions are rich and varied. These are the words of two student-mentors after a drop-in session, demonstrating a mix of practical wisdom and empathy:

> The sweetest girl came to see us about the first assignment. We had a great chat—she seemed a little lonely and shy but was looking forward to seeing us again next week and attending the lecture. We helped her

with the assignment, [gave her] library information, filled her in on the 'Introduction to Uni Workshops' she'd missed and showed her how to use the Flinders map. We also went through the Topic Guide with her. **The following week:** A great 50 minutes spent with the same person from last week. This week we have helped her get a little more organised with her up-coming assignments. More importantly we emailed her Topic coordinator, on her behalf, in regards to a difficulty with a third year Topic that she and other first year students have been put in. . . . We also gave her a . . . voucher and informed her how to use the loop bus.

These excerpts demonstrate the mixture of concerns that first year students can experience from the apparently trivial to the serious. They are also a mixture of the essential components of our programme: orientation, physical, academic, transition and retention.

This next journal note comes from one of the earliest student-mentor's experiences:

I walked out of this session feeling overwhelmed with joy as I honestly felt as though a number of students had begun to understand that their learning experiences are a two way street and the effort they put in will be reflected in their results. I really enjoy helping people and I value the opportunity to be able to assist with the student's transition to university and their success in their first year. If I could I would attend every tutorial if it meant reaching a higher number of students.

The pride and delight in being able to help first year students is evident in these descriptions by the student-mentor. The intermingling of the personal and professional, the academic and the social are also clearly demonstrated. The following quotations came from four students' contemplative writing and shows the complexity of the tutor, student-mentor and student relationship interwoven with learning and cultural understandings:

I have found, in the tutorials, that my role has shifted slightly to what was originally intended. Although I am still mentoring students on 'normal' first year concerns, my role in the tutorial class room has become more of a 'community connection' or to better put a 'point of relevance.' To reinforce a learning outcome or understanding, the tutor will ask me to demonstrate how I have used or come across this issue in my own teaching or teacher education. I feel that this is giving the students a chance to see how a graduate uses these understandings in real practice rather than having it explained by a distinguished tutor. Paired with the tutorials becoming more engaging and interactive, I think my role in the tutorials has enriched the student's educational experiences.

I had a very long chat afterwards with a student who was having a hard time adapting to life while studying in University who had moved from the country and is living on his own for the first time. He sought my help through the experiences I had from moving out of home (from the country) to come and study here (at university) and I found similarities in his story that coincided with mine.

I had such a great time in this tutorial on cultural diversity. I was glad for my last tutorial visit, I was able to use some of my own personal experiences to bridge the gap between theory and practice with stories of my schooling in Japan, USA, and rural Australia. As someone who has experienced many different types and styles of schooling, the tutor's experience of being a teacher in different types and styles of schooling really gave the students insight on how the experience affects both teachers and students in a culturally diverse classroom.

I'm really sad to leave this group because not only was I building stronger relationships with the students and the way they were learning and understanding the course, but I had a really great time collaborating with the tutor as a student mentor and in class assistant.

The life and learning that occurs through the additional 'adult other than teacher' in the room is extraordinary in the way that it both supports and extends the students' learning on so many levels: academic, social, cultural, emotional and expressive. Finally, a reflection from a first year student that demonstrates the combined strength of the individual strands of pastoral care and meaningful learning:

When I started university I felt very overwhelmed, frightened and unsure and I cried every night, but after listening to my tutor I organised a Counsellor's appointment where I was able to talk through my issues and the Counsellor was able to give me ways to calm my anxiety and suggested I come back every two weeks to talk though my emotions. I have found it difficult adjusting to driving a long distance and being on another side of town that I am unfamiliar with, but I am finding that with each day it is becoming easier. . . . At first I found it unsettling being on such a big campus, with a huge number of students, but I have been spending my free period between practicals and lectures on Wednesday morning finding my bearings. All things considered, for the first time last week, I am starting to enjoy university life and its free choice options. I am beginning to talk to new people in my courses. I love my topic choice. . . . I can now see myself as a willing, compassionate teacher not only for the current generation but for many more to come. I cannot wait for placement this year and the years to come and I am extremely excited to start my many years of teaching ahead of me.

Meaningful learning spaces have evolved between students, tutors, and the student-mentors. Moving from just a pastoral role, the student-mentors were given a pedagogical presence alongside the tutor. The case which follows is about the same cohort of first year students but the pedagogical change here has creativity at its centre.

Case 4: Performing Arts Within an Educational Core
Topic: Creative Performance as Innovative Praxis

Creativity is defined most simply as a transformative act which produces something new or original for a purpose. This last word 'purpose' is particularly important and relevant in education.

> Purpose is essential to creative expression—nobody carves a statue without intending to do so . . . I suspect that few people will question the malleability of purposes and intentions. How best to get students to intend to be creative—to take creative behaviour as a goal—is a legitimate question.
>
> *(Nickerson, 1999, p. 408)*

Universities face difficulties in providing experiences for first year students which relate to academic orientation and transition and also to increasing retention and engagement. In addition, educational expectations, especially ideological, are not engaging to typical first year students, who typically baulk at discussing ideologies. The inclusion of creativity as a creative resource and a product as a central tenet of a compulsory unit of study for first year education students arose from a desire to deepen and enliven the students' experience through increased engagement.

The 'quality resource' chosen as the catalyst in the process was a play called *Educating Fronnie*, written by Dr Paul Jewell in 2006 when he was a Lecturer in Education at Flinders University. The play was performed live several times that year. It was also performed at the 2008 Adelaide Fringe Festival. The play takes place on a spaceship. The five characters, chaired by an additional character, Francis Fronesis, discuss education suitable for 'the sort of society we are going to set up in the new world.' They are to make recommendations to the 'assembly' (the audience) who at the end of the performance 'select the character whose views are closest to your own' by voting.

The play is a vehicle for looking at educational concepts through five different lenses in an attempt to find common ground. It presents educational perspectives through common discourse, making a bridge between what is already known and what is still to be learned in the students' transition: a constructivist process (Vygotsky, 1978). We build new understandings based on prior knowledge through the learning processes of active engagement, inquiry, problem solving and collaboration with others. Most importantly, it is an engaging and productive learning experience for students.

These words by former student and actor Emma Maguire (2008) crystallise the benefit of *Educating Fronnie* when it was used in the past. We intended to enhance this significantly in 2014:

> The format of this play has many differences from the more traditional ways of learning at University like readings and lectures. The most effective, I feel, is the embodiment of complex conceptual arguments by characters within the play. For example, the many ideas and theories that make up the conservative, economic rationalist argument come together in one body to form the character of Rex Right.
>
> In this way each of the characters are grouping mechanisms for the themes of the great education debate which rages in Australian society today and in many other parts of the world. They also represent ways of thinking throughout history. This technique makes the complexities of educational ideas accessible for first years who may be unaccustomed to, and intimidated by, academic language and argument. It also provides an introduction to the basic arguments within education and the ways in which they connect with and oppose one another, which will become part of their professional knowledge as teachers. My encounter with 'Educating Fronnie' in first year provided a base structure which I have built on to understand better the roles of different educational arguments and my place within such arguments.

This pedagogy was a creative one. Not only was it driven by an art work, the play also sought to engage students through dialogue, purpose and product in a 'creative' process. The purpose was to enter, understand and be active in an intellectual discourse of education (Buber, 2002; Kedian, Giles, Morrison & Fletcher, 2015).

The final product was a mini-play devised by groups of six students—the same number of characters as were in the original play—but on new, related, topical and contemporary educational issues.

> To understand is to discover, or reconstruct by rediscovery, and such conditions must be complied with if in the future individuals are to be formed who are capable of production and creativity and not simply repetition.
>
> *(Piaget, 1973, p. 20)*

The plays were all performed in the last week of the semester, 120 plays involving 680 students—an unusual event in in the life of the University. While students often fail to submit essays, no one has yet missed performing in their mini-play except in exceptional circumstances, where sickness was the cause, when they have either been incorporated in the play by video or performed solo later. This intense support for each other, or collegiality, is particularly relevant for a future professional lie.

This process entailed transferring understanding of the concepts being studied to an advanced level of being able to apply them to new, student-directed educational issues. The performances were seen by the other students in the class and again, as occurred throughout the topic, they were interpreted, discussed and evaluated. Some of the outstanding scripts and videoed plays formed additional content for future students. The embedding of this pedagogy was both broad and deep. The quality of the weekly discussions on each new educational issue, scaffolded through *Educating Fronnie*, had an effect on each of their ongoing assignments, which were assessed and evaluated progressively.

The effectiveness of the initiative was evaluated and compared to students in previous years. Tutors stated that the various pedagogical activities associated with the play *Educating Fronnie* had a very positive and productive effect on students' engagement. By analysing the different perspectives of each of the characters in the play and responding to particular quotations through a critical analysis, students were able to focus deeply on, and identify, a diverse range of opinions, giving serious thought to another point of view different from their own (Mezirow & Associates, 2000).

Quotations from the play were also useful and contextual in connecting words and meanings from the play to tutorial and lecture ideas in a holistic and consistent way. By taking on the perspective of the character, students were able to learn more for future reference when they had to act out their particular character's perspective in the mini-play assignment. Other tutorial activities enhanced these skills further including writing the mini-play script, general group work, role plays, oral presentations and readings that students felt related to the play.

Many of the tutors who worked in 2012, 2013 and 2014 commented that students had learned to think more deeply and more critically in 2014. Students also became more capable of making connections between ideas and demonstrated a deeper learning and appreciation of educational and teaching contexts. It was evident both in their written assignments and group activities. Tutors identified students' growing ability to reflect on their understandings and engage with the ideas as they began to understand them. The pedagogical activities provided the students with a context to engage in meaningful sessional and out-of-class conversations (Kedian et al., 2015).

Tutors wrote that as a direct result of the various pedagogical activities students made connections between the topic's content and educational contexts that were relevant and developed deeper understanding for themselves as educators. Students had fed back to tutors that the pedagogical activities that were used were engaging, fun, entertaining and supported students to further their learning in a meaningful way.

It is difficult to convey the enthusiasm, delight and energy that springs from the live acting of the play. The following remarks from three tutors get close to the flavour:

> On arrival at the School of Education on Monday, I saw several students walking along mumbling words. Many groups rehearsing in nooks and crannies—they were all rehearsing for their play performances: The school was alive with acting.

Hearing students talk about hidden curriculum, the requirement of having ethically and empathetically constructed systems and facilities for learning was wonderful. During the mini-plays the evidence of how much the students had learned was mind boggling. At times I would write a question on the back of the rubric—for example one group looked at sexual education—and for quite some time no mention was made of sexual differences (LGBTQ) so I wrote 'what about the LGBT community and student?' which I then had to cross off as being addressed. The plays were amazing.

I think the social nature of working and learning in tutorials was more vibrant this year. Student Comment: 'This 4pm Friday tutorial is like happy hour at the end of the week! We talk about important things, and when we head off at 6pm, it's the weekend!'

While performing arts activities need meticulous planning and careful people management, the opportunities for meaningful learning spaces abound. In the service of a holistic formation of the adult students within Higher Education, learning experiences must be just that: learning through experiences, as experiential learning.

Conclusion

Meaningful learning spaces can be created in Higher Education using learning strategies underpinned by phenomenology. In these learning strategies, students' own stories and everyday experiences becomes the narrative that serves an interpretive pedagogy. More specifically, the students' being is cared for in ways that enable, equip and evoke students' voices in meaning-centred activity. From the outset, the intentional curriculum is understood to be serving the experiential priorities of creative reconstructions of everyday experiences.

As teacher educators, our phenomenological research and lived experiences must continue to show the centrality of relationships whether exploring teaching and learning, being in an appreciative appraisal, organising cross cohort mentoring or embarking on performance within core topics. Relationships exist in the space between those relating, as does dialogue.

Meaningful learning spaces in Higher Education are always relational and dialogic. When we construct learning activities that draw upon phenomenological concerns, we find ourselves attending to, as Heidegger notes, our way of 'being-together-in-the-world.' Simply, student engagement is enhanced through experiential learning where meanings and understandings of students' stories are hermeneutical, worked for essential themes associated with our shared humanity. In this way, academics must improvise a pedagogy that attunes to the way students are in their learning, and how the movement of learning calls for deep listening and decision-making.

Invariably, where students' stories and everyday experiences are available to contemplation and dialogue, students deepen their awareness of self and others. Such learning spaces focus on 'being' as opposed to the more common shallow conversation around required assessments. Arguably, the academic demonstrates an educational concern that is lifelong, dynamic, and available for further reconstructions beyond the end of the course.

Bibliography

Berger, P. L., & Luckmann, T. (1967). *The social construction of reality*. Harmondsworth: Penguin.

Buber, M. (2002). *Between man and man* (R. Gregor-Smith, Trans.). London: Routledge.

Bullock Report. (1975). *A language for life*. London: HMSO.

Chapman, L., & Giles, D. L. (2009). Using appreciative inquiry to explore the professional practice of a midwife lecturer. *Studies in Continuing Education, 31*(3), 297–305.

Gadamer, H. G. (1994). *Truth and method*. New York: Continuum.

Giles, D. L. (2008). *Exploring the teacher-student relationship in teacher education: A hermeneutic phenomenological inquiry*. Unpublished doctoral thesis, Auckland University of Technology, Auckland. http://aut.researchgateway.ac.nz/handle/10292/537

Giles, D. L. (2010). Developing pathic sensibilities: A critical priority for teacher education programmes. *Teaching and Teacher Education, 26*(8), 1511–1519.

Giles, D. L. (2011a). Relationships always matter in education: Findings from a phenomenological inquiry. *Australian Journal of Teacher Education, 36*(6), 80–91.

Giles, D. L. (2011b). 'Who we are' and 'how we are' are integral to relational experiences: exploring comportment in teacher education. *Australian Journal of Teacher Education, 36*(1), 60–72.

Giles, D. L. (2014). Appreciatively building higher educator's relational sensibilities. *Journal of Meaning-Centered Education, 2*(1), Article 1, http://www.meaningcentered.org/appreciatively-building-higher-educators-relational-sensibilities

Giles, D. L., & Alderson, S. (2008). An appreciative inquiry into the transformative learning experiences of students in a family literacy project. *Australian Journal of Adult Learning, 48*(3), 465–478.

Giles, D. L., & Kung, S. (2010). Using appreciative inquiry to explore the professional practice of a lecturer in higher education: Moving towards life-centric practice. *Australian Journal of Adult Learning, 50*(2), 308–322.

Giles, D. L., & Morrison, M. (2010). Exploring leadership as a phenomenon in an educational leadership paper: An innovative pedagogical approach opens the unexpected. *International Journal on Teaching and Learning in Higher Education, 22*(1), 64–70.

Giles, D. L., Smythe, E. A., & Spence, D. G. (2012). Exploring relationships in education: A phenomenological inquiry. *Australian Journal of Adult Learning, 52*(2), 214–236.

Hammond, S. A. (1998). *The thin book of appreciative inquiry*. Plano, TX: Thin Book.

Heidegger, M. (1992). What calls for thinking? In D. F. Krell (Ed.), *Martin Heidegger: Basic writings* (pp. 341–367). San Francisco: HarperCollins.

Jewell, P. (2014). *Educating Fronnie*. Frenchs Forest, NSW: Pearson Australia.

Joldersma, C. W. (2001). Pedagogy of the other: A Levinasian approach to the teacher-student relationship. *Philosophy of Education* (2001), 181–188.

Kedian, J., Giles, D. L., Morrison, M., & Fletcher, M. (2015). Leadership development as a dialogic process: The rationale and concept of an international leadership institute.

International Journal of Leadership in Education: Theory and Practice, 19(2), 182–202. http://dx.doi.org/10.1080/13603124.2014.997800

Levinas, E. (1998). *Entre nous: Thinking-of-the-other* (M. B. Smith & B. Harshav, Trans.). London: Athlone Press.

Maguire, E. (2008). Faculty Teaching Excellence Award submission, School of Education, Flinders University, South Australia.

Mayer, R. E. (2008). *Learning and instruction.* Upper Saddle River, NJ: Pearson.

Mezirow, J. (1991). *Transformative dimensions of adult learning.* San Francisco: Jossey-Bass.

Mezirow, J. (1995). Transformation theory of adult learning. In M. Welton (Ed.), *In defense of the lifeworld* (pp. 39–70). Albany: State University of New York Press.

Mezirow, J., & Associates. (2000). *Learning as transformation: Critical perspectives on a theory in progress.* San Francisco: Jossey-Bass.

Nickerson, R. S. (1999). Enhancing creativity. In R. Sternberg (Ed.), *Handbook of creativity* (pp. 392–430). New York: Cambridge University Press.

Noddings, N. (2005). *The challenge to care in schools: An alternative approach to education* (Vol. 2). New York: Teachers College Press.

Piaget, J. (1973). *To understand is to invent: The future of education* (first English translation). New York: Viking Press.

Pinar, W. F., & Reynolds, W. M. (Eds.). (1992). *Understanding curriculum as phenomenological and deconstructed text.* London: Teachers College Press.

van Manen, M. (1990). *Researching lived experiences.* Albany: State University of New York Press.

van Manen, M. (2002). *The tone of teaching: The language of pedagogy.* London, ON: Althouse Press.

van Manen, M., & Li, S. (2002). The pathic principle of pedagogical language. *Teaching and Teacher Education, 18*(2), 215–224.

Vygotsky, L. (1978). *Mind and society: The development of higher mental processes.* Cambridge, MA: Harvard University Press.

Wenger, E. (1999). Learning as social participation. *Knowledge Management Review, 1*(6), 30–33.

Whitney, D., & Cooperrider, D. L. (1998). The appreciative inquiry summit: Overview and applications. *Employment Relations Today, 25*(2), 17–28.

Whitney, D., Trosten-Bloom, A., & Rader, K. (2010). *Appreciative leadership: Focus on what works to drive winning performance and build a thriving organization.* New York: McGraw-Hill.

6

CREATIVE LEARNING STRATEGIES

Learning How to Cooperate

Nives Dolšak and Cinnamon Hillyard[1]

Introduction

Social and behavioral science scholars identify social capital and trust as core factors fostering cooperation to solve social choice dilemmas. Past successes in solving social choice dilemmas equip individuals with strategies that enable them to build trust, thereby increasing their ability to successfully cooperate with others in another situation of interdependence. The question then is whether such strategies can be taught in a classroom.

Creativity pedagogies may be the key in teaching these cooperation skills. Jackson (2008) notes that creative education can help prepare students for the increasingly complex world, is "necessary to achieving difficult things for an individual and our collective well being," and is important "to the health and prosperity for our society and economy" (p. 4). This chapter provides an example of how social capital and trust can be conditions for and outcomes of creative learning.

We used a common pool experiment, developed by Elinor Ostrom and her colleagues (Ahn, Ostrom, and Walker, 2010) in the Ostrom Workshop at Indiana University, Bloomington, to develop students' understandings of and creative solutions to a social choice dilemma. This experiment simulated a situation of interdependence where students' costs and benefits depend not only on their own choices, but also on the decisions of others.

This chapter examines how this in-class experiment can create the opportunity for students to experience a real-life scenario, see the relationship between decisions and outcomes, explore strategies toward a solution, learn how to cooperate, and reflect on individual roles and group decisions in a process to create optimal solutions. We first review the literature on social capital and quantitative reasoning suggesting several core elements of teaching cooperation that are also common to developing creativity. Then, we briefly summarize two freshman courses in which these skills were taught at the University of Washington, Bothell. We then describe an experiment that allows students to learn about their own strategies, the strategies of others, and the impact they have on the collective outcome. We conclude with a discussion of strengths and weaknesses of such approach for classroom learning and provide recommendations for use of this experiment in the future.

Social Capital Concepts and Skills

The definition of social capital varies across scholars. Putnam (1995) broadly explains that "social capital refers to features of social organization such as networks, norms, and social trust that facilitate coordination and cooperation for mutual benefit" (p. 67). Cooperative behavior, an important aspect of social capital, is the result of multiple persons, animals, or organizations working toward a common goal. A study of cooperative behavior is a core theme in biological, social, and behavioral sciences. Biologists provide numerous examples of cooperative behavior among animals and evolutionary advantages of cooperative behavior (Dugatkin, 1997; Nowak, 2006). Social and behavioral scientists identify the role of cooperation in economic development (North, 1990; Putnam, Leonardi, and Nanetti, 1993), in fostering positive interpersonal relationships and psychological health (Johnson and Johnson, 2009), building better schools (Stone, Henig, Jones, and Pierannunzi, 2001), and protecting shared environmental resources (Dolšak and Ostrom, 2003; Ostrom, 1990). Thus cooperative behavior is key in creating positive outcomes for all.

Yet, scholars also remind us of various challenges in fostering cooperation. First, each individual is free to do what pleases her. Individual freedom enables individuals to pursue their happiness and engage in activities that maximize their individual benefits. The second reason is that when deciding their strategy, individuals consider only the benefits they will reap, rather than the benefits to the entire society. While the extent an individual considers broader societal benefits depends on her value system, most current cultures have strong individualistic elements. Finally, even if an activity of an individual imposes costs on the society, each individual pays only a fraction of the social marginal costs, making these costs less relevant for her decision.

Motivation for Teaching Cooperation

Calls for American educators to instill cooperative values and teach cooperative skills are not new. In 1916, Dewey asked American educators to teach young individuals about social goals and habits of groups in order to maintain a strong democracy. In the 1960s, scholars of political socialization highlighted the importance of building shared knowledge of political values. Easton and Hess (1962) stressed the need to help children develop such values because

> the range of alternative behaviors open to the adult is also intimately related to his experiences as a child . . . the kind of political reality the adult perceives and his attitudes about it are restricted by what he has learned during his early years.
>
> *(p. 229)*

These scholars suggest that teaching cooperation during school years is important for our individual and shared knowledge of political processes and values.

In the mid-1990s, Elinor Ostrom (1996, p. 756), in her presidential address to the American Political Science Association, warned about the "decline in civic engagement, political efficacy, and in the capacity of citizens to organize themselves. . . . American people (especially younger people) no longer have the customs of local self-organization and civic engagement, the core strengths of associational activity that democracy in America exhibited in the middle of the 19th century." She echoed the findings of Robert Putnam (1995), who pointed out that Americans are no longer building social capital through their face-to-face interactions in hobby groups, such as bowling leagues. Americans are now *bowling alone*. Norman Jackson (2008) also mentions this focus on the individual as a problem with higher education, citing that our current system paradoxically "values individual academic achievement while preparing people for a lifetime of cooperation and co-creation" (p. 7). These scholars all note that a focus on the individual instead of the collective results in a lack of shared understanding necessary for a democratic society.

Some American educators have sought to overcome these obstacles by teaching cooperation and building trust and social capital. They have developed a curriculum for training cooperative behavior (Fan, 2000; Gillies, 1999; Niemi and Junn, 1998; Torney-Purta, Lehmann, Oswald, and Schulz, 2001), required collaborative learning activities (Astin, 1987; Blumenfeld, Marx, Soloway, and Krajcik, 1996), and provided opportunities for service learning projects (Dudley and Gitelson, 2002). These approaches have had mixed success. While training can have positive impacts (Gillies, 1999), the impact is often short-lived (Fan, 2000). Niemi and Junn (1998) and Torney-Purta et al. (2001) report of the positive impact of civics-related courses on children's political knowledge, but not necessarily on civic engagement.

Core Concepts and Skills We Can Teach

We want students to be able to distill lessons from their past collaborative interactions and apply them to another situation of interdependence. Successful cooperation requires that individuals understand the logic of interdependence—that their success in achieving a certain outcome depends on the behaviors of other individuals. Further, they must appreciate the role of communication in helping them to collectively devise better strategies. Finally, if the devised strategies are not followed, they need to be able to resolve the conflict and implement an incentive system (persuasion, reward, or punishment) to secure better outcomes in the future (Ostrom, 1990). In this chapter we briefly address core concepts that can assist in these steps.

One tool to understand interdependence is using the economic measure of payoff (or return on an investment) from a decision. In particular, individuals must have and be able to *use information about payoffs associated with different strategies everyone in their group used*. Quantitative reasoning skills can assist in this step. Scholars find that the ability of and comfort with using numbers in real life is a key factor in structuring the decision-making process. Specifically, Nye and Hillyard (2013) illustrate that a person's quantitative reasoning ability influences their financial decision-making, and Lipkus and Peters (2009) illustrate the importance of quantitative reasoning in decisions about personal health.

Assessing how others will behave in the situation of interdependence is another key skill. Past interactions assist individuals to predict other individuals' strategies and provide some level of confidence (trust) that if another person commits to a specific behavior (s)he will indeed behave in that particular way. Past group projects can provide such information and assurance for students. However, when students have not interacted with one another in the past, a curriculum focused on cooperation can teach students about key types of individuals and their social value orientations to assist in this step. Four social value orientation types have been identified:

- Individuals with *cooperative* orientation will value maximization of joint outcomes.
- Individuals with *competitive* orientation will maximize relative difference between their and others' payoffs.
- Individuals with *altruistic* orientation will maximize the partner's outcome without regard for their own outcome.
- Individuals with *individualistic* orientation will maximize their own outcome without regard for the partners' outcome.

Experimental work has shown that individuals' orientations/types are stable over time (Casari and Plot, 2003; Kurzban and Houser, 2005). If the majority of individuals value reciprocity (Kurzban and Houser, 2005)—that is, respond to cooperation with cooperation, and to defection with defection—then we can equip students with two strategies for fostering cooperation. First, make sure that others are able to monitor your own cooperative behavior. Signal cooperative intent in a clear and credible way. Second, devise the group decision in several stages to allow individuals to observe reciprocity at different points in time.

Consequently, this will allow individuals to respond with cooperation (defection) in an earlier stage by others with their own cooperation (defection) in the subsequent stage (Axelrod, 1984).

Communication with group members and opportunities to negotiate superior individual and group strategies can assist groups in achieving an optimum group outcome. Students can be taught to clearly communicate their decisions and to get others to make explicit commitments. Students can be taught the importance of building reputations and using this argument in persuading others to follow the strategies that lead to group optimum. When negotiating future decisions of individuals in the group, students can be taught to build a shared identity for a group (Kramer and Brewer, 1984). *Resolving group conflict and implementing incentives* (persuasion, rewards, or punishment) can build on these skills.

The aforementioned concepts and skills can be taught in courses and practiced in a number of creative learning activities. In the next section we report our use of a common pool resource experiment in this regard. While such experiments have historically been used in microeconomics and negotiations courses in business, we show that they can be productively used in other courses, including a social science course and a scientific methods course. In the subsequent section, we review the core elements of the two courses in which we used the experiment. Then, we turn to the description of the experiment and its results in the two courses.

Practicing Cooperation With an Experiment

Experiments and Their Effectiveness in the Classroom

Instructors have used cooperation experiments to introduce core concepts of an interdependence and to discuss its real-world applications (Marks, Lehr, and Brastow, 2006). In terms of cognitive learning and retention, Holtzman (2005) reports that students participating in active learning perform better on quizzes, have higher appreciation for how in-class learning pertains to their own lives, and express less anxiety about the course. In a meta-analysis of 225 studies, Freeman et al. (2014) showed that the introduction of any active learning component in a course "increases examination performance by just under half a SD [standard deviation]" (p. 8412). Importantly, these gains hold across a variety of classroom settings. Kolb and Kolb (2005) reviewed studies on experiential learning from across 16 academic fields. They found that experiential learning, or learning from a practical experience, is an effective tool for developing students' ability to apply skills and knowledge in the real world and can bridge the gap between varied learning styles and abilities in the classroom. Further, Jackson (2008) also points out that experimentation pedagogies can foster creativity as they allow students to work in new and interesting ways while being challenged with new ideas within a real context.

In terms of impact on changing attitudes, the literature does not offer a uniform assessment of the impact of simulation games and experiments. While some authors report positive impacts on changing attitudes (less dogmatic opinions, reduced racial barriers to interaction, increased empathy, positive attitudes toward self and others), others report no impact or even negative impact (an increase in cynicism, pessimism, intolerance, and lack of appreciation for diversity) (Dorn, 1989, and sources cited therein). In terms of learning how to cooperate, authors report that simulation games improve students' interpersonal skills and increase self-confidence in decision-making (Dorn, 1989).

Courses in Which We Administered the Experiment

We administered a common pool resource experiment (Ahn et al., 2010) in two different freshman courses during the same quarter at the University of Washington, Bothell: a natural science course in which students were taught scientific and quantitative reasoning and a social science course in which students were provided with multidisciplinary strategies to foster cooperation. We sought to control for the external environment (campus level, state level, or the country level) in which students in different courses were situated.

The first course, titled "Cooperation, Competition, and Conflict" (henceforth referred to as the Cooperation course), adopted an interdisciplinary approach, drawing on readings from biology, economics, management, and political science. This approach examined factors promoting cooperation, including altruism, natural selection, reciprocity, retaliation, power relationships, norms, rules, culture, and social and psychological dynamics. While cooperation is often stereotyped as something good and competition and conflict are often seen as negative social phenomena, the course also highlighted the role of conflict for development of skills, clarification of preferences and prioritization of goals, strengthening of group identity, and development of compromise. Group work and assessment of collaborative efforts accounted for 55% of the students' grade.

The second course, titled "Coffee: Science, History, and Economics" (henceforth referred to as the Science course), was an interdisciplinary science course that explored several aspects of coffee, including the economic importance of coffee and the biological and chemical aspects of growing and processing coffee. A connecting theme of the course was the use of the scientific method to address a wide range of important and interesting questions. The course included readings on scientific methods, chemistry, health, the ecological benefits of organic coffee farming, and the economics of organic coffee farming. The core learning goals for the class were demonstrating communication, critical reading, quantitative and statistical reasoning, and analytical thinking skills necessary to understand the claims made in the context of an applied scientific question. Collaborative learning was central to the class and was formalized through study groups and research clusters. About 20% of the course grade was acquired in these collaborative settings.

The Experiment and Its Administration

This experiment simulates individuals' decisions to invest in fishing boats (incur costs) with which they will harvest fish from a shared fishery and sell the catch in a market (generate revenue). The fish context, taken directly from the Ostrom Workshop, was chosen as a topic that students could readily understand with little background knowledge. The payoff in this experiment is calculated as the difference between the revenue and the costs from fishing. Students know that each will receive a university bookstore gift card in the amount of their total individual payoffs across all rounds in the experiment. This monetary payment for a class activity was done purposefully to ensure students had motivation to participate as they would in similar real-world scenarios. The experiment simulates a situation of interdependence where students' costs and benefits of fishing depend on the levels at which other group members are harvesting the shared fishery. Students are randomly assigned to groups of seven. Before students begin the experiment, the instructors complete several exercises illustrating how each individual's decision will impact their own outcomes as well as the group's outcomes. These practice examples as well as the experiment instructions are reported the Ostrom Workshop description (Ahn et al., 2010).

The core decision each individual makes is how many tokens (units of investment) to invest in this fishery. Token investment translates to monetary costs depending on the number of tokens the student invests and the average cost of a token. Average cost of a token depends on the level of investments by everybody in the group. This experiment illustrates the upward-sloping marginal cost curve. Namely, the more others invest in fishing in the shared fishery, the more costly it becomes for an individual to fish. Increasing the number of fishing boats leads to increases in the duration of each fishing trip and/or makes it necessary to fish during the periods when it is more dangerous to fish, such as in bad weather. The relationship between the token investments and fishing revenue is outlined in a schedule of benefits (see Ahn et al., 2010). Students receive this table at the beginning of the exercises in which they practice for the experiment. The core challenge of this experiment, then, is for students in each group to cooperate and curtail their investments at the level where the difference between the cost of fishing and the revenue from fishing is at a maximum. Yet, students face incentives to invest more than the optimum from the perspective of the group.

When making their token investment decisions, students may or may not cooperate. If they cooperate, they maximize net revenues/payoffs for the entire group. If they are maximizing their own payoffs while everybody is behaving cooperatively, they can receive higher payoffs. Next we illustrate benefits of cheating, that is, investing in more tokens when everybody else in the group is cooperating to keep the costs of tokens low.

Given the schedule of benefits and the increasing costs of tokens, the group receives maximum revenue when each group member invests 9 tokens. When investing 9 tokens each, the net revenue for each student is $3.40. However, if six other group members invest 9 tokens, and one student invests more, this student will benefit from lower average token cost while obtaining benefits of investing more tokens. The optimum level of investment for a non-cooperative individual is 20 tokens if everybody else is investing 9 tokens. In this case, the student investing 20 tokens receives the net revenue, $4.90. With a six-round experiment, a cooperative student receives a gift card for $20.40, if everybody in her group also cooperates. On the other hand, if a student invests 20 tokens while everybody else in the group is investing 9 tokens, the 20-token investor receives the total of $29.40 across the six rounds. The $9.00 higher payoff could buy lunch for one additional day for a student. Therefore, students in this experiment have noticeable, non-trivial incentives to try to get everybody else to cooperate and invest 9 tokens when they invest 20 tokens. While these particular levels of investment are not discussed in the practices prior to the experiment, the practice examples (see Ahn et al., 2010) assist students in understanding the outcomes of their own investment decisions given the level of the total group investment.

The experiment consists of six rounds illustrating different strategies groups can use to increase cooperation. At the beginning, students are told the number of their group, but other members of the group are not identified. After each round, students are told what the average cost of fishing in each group was. The first two rounds do not allow for any communication across various groups. Rounds 3 and 4 allow students *to communicate* with the rest of the class to discuss how various groups are doing, but are not allowed to reveal what group they are in. In most cases, students realize that they have invested too many tokens, leading to higher competition for the shared fish and increased costs, resulting in lower payoffs. In order to improve their payoffs, they need *to find out at what level each individual should invest* so that the group can have maximum payoff. They have little information about their group. They do not know who is in the group, but they are told after each round how many tokens each group invested, enabling each student to analyze how effective their group was in comparison to other groups. Therefore, group members can begin to feel a group identity and this can stimulate them to cooperate in the group by investing at the group optimum level to "outperform" other groups. They can make general appeals to others in the group with the same number. However, they cannot yet negotiate with specific members in their group.

At the end of round 4, students are told who is in each group. Therefore, in rounds 5 and 6, students in each group are moved to a separate location where they can further discuss the strategy for their group. While they do not need to tell others how much each had invested before, they can discuss the specific challenges of their group and set the optimum level of investments. They can also develop strategies how the group will reach the optimum level of token investments. They can use persuasion, but are not allowed to threaten or bribe others in the group. Each group is monitored by an instructor, and if such behavior is detected, the experiment is stopped for the entire class.

In sum, this experiment encourages and enables students to use their creativity, quantitative analysis, cooperation, and communication skills to understand the impact their decisions have on their communities, to evaluate the importance of the communities on their own well-being, and to create strategies for fostering cooperation in situations of interdependence. This experiment requires students to develop cooperative strategies (e.g., agreeing on a fishing quota or limiting who and when certain members can fish) for using a resource they own jointly: a fishery. The experiment is played in several rounds, enabling students to study what happened in each round and to experiment with strategies to foster cooperation in subsequent rounds. Students calculate individual payoffs they received in each round. These payoffs depend on their own decisions and on decisions of the rest of the group. The payoffs of their individual decisions (a university bookstore gift card in the amount of their total payoff across all rounds of the experiment) are modest yet sufficient to provide incentives to invest more than the group optimum. If members of the group succumb to incentives to maximize their own outcome without concern for the group, their group members see their own payoffs decline and realize that someone is cheating. At that point, the challenge for the group is to devise a better agreement (one that leads to cooperative and socially optimum outcome) or to take "revenge" by overharvesting the resource and substantially reducing the payoffs for all others in the group. In the next section, we review the results of this experiment for students in the Cooperation and Science course.

Results

We administered the experiment in two phases. We ran the experiment with only four rounds at the beginning of the quarter (phase 1). We wanted to be able to measure whether repetition of this experiment led to learning and a higher level of cooperation the second time we administered the experiment (phase 2). To avoid the possibility for retaliation in phase 2, we ran the first phase with only four rounds, thereby not revealing the identity of group members. This standard pre/post design allowed us to evaluate whether learning of the experiment as well as student interactions in the class and the course curriculum impacted a group's ability to devise strategies for fostering cooperation. After the second phase, we returned to both classes and discussed the decisions groups had to make, strategies they applied, and how effective they were.

Participation in the experiment was voluntary. Individuals' token investments were kept confidential. While students knew in rounds 5 and 6 who was in their group, they were not told by the instructors what token investments each group member made. Similarly, the instructor recorded only students' random ID numbers, not their names. All individual decisions were submitted on token order forms. Each student used a random number that only (s)he knew. This random number was also used to calculate individual payoffs for each round and issue gift cards in the appropriate amount at the end of the experiment.

Figure 6.1 depicts token investments for individual group members, by groups, by course. The left panel depicts groups in the Cooperation course and the right panel groups in the Science course. We do not note significant differences

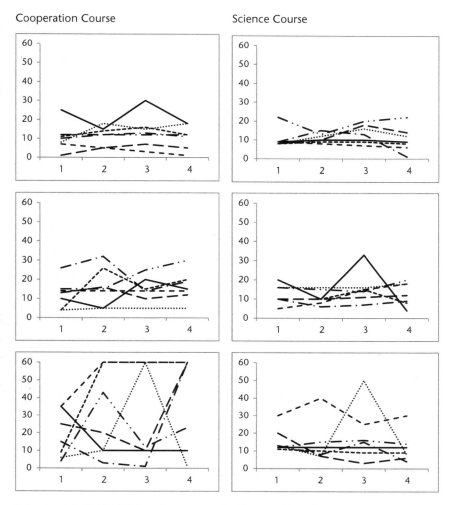

FIGURE 6.1 Individual Token Investments, by Groups, Phase 1

between the courses. We find that most groups have individual token investments between 5 and 25. However, and interestingly so, there is also one group in each course that has higher variability in token investments with some individuals investing as high as 60 tokens. The 60-token investment is not rational. The highest investment yielding positive benefits for an individual is 31 tokens, and even that only when all others in the group invest no tokens. Therefore, the 60-token investments can be explained in one of two ways. First, as a conscious strategy to make it impossible for anybody in the group to make any positive benefits. Casari and Plot (2003) identified individuals who have no regard for their own payoffs in order to make sure others are not benefitting. Second, as a lack of understanding of the basic characteristics of the situation. Given the self-assessment of the two individuals who chose 60 tokens as being "good at math" (see Table 6.1), we believe that this investment was not made in error, but rather as a decision to spoil the experiment for others. In sum, results of phase 1 seem to suggest that this creative learning approach can be successfully administered in a social science course, a quantitative reasoning course, or in a science course to provide students with opportunities to practice cooperation.

TABLE 6.1 Token Investments, by Student in a Group, by Round, by Phase

Student	Course	Phase 1 token investments per round				Phase 2 token investments per round						"Good at math"[1]
		R1	R2	R3	R4	R1	R2	R3	R4	R5	R6	
1	Science	20	10	33	4	14	22	22	15	7	8	3
2	Science	9	10	10	9	9	10	8	9	7	7	4
3	Science	8	10	18	14	10	8	7	10	7	7	2
4	Science	9	15	13	1	15	25	20	20	7	7	4
5	Science	12	12	12	12	12	12	12	12	7	7	4
6	Science	20	7	3	6	4	2	5	3	7	7	2
7	Science	10	10	11	12	10	10	9	9	8	8	4
1	Cooperation	10	5	20	15	10	20	15	25	10	10	3
2	Cooperation	35	10	10	10	6	5	5	5	10	5	5
3	Cooperation	25	15	30	18	30	15	15	15	10	10	3
4	Cooperation	25	20	10	60	12	14	17	10	10	10	4
5	Cooperation	15	3	1	60	5	5	4	10	10	20	4
6	Cooperation	13	16	10	12	6	10	9	8	10	10	2
7	Cooperation	1	5	7	5	6	7	9	15	10	10	2

Notes:

Optimum token investments: group optimum is 9; individual optimum is 20 if everybody else is at the group optimum.

[1] "Good at math"—Students' agreement with the statement "I am good at math": 1 = strongly disagree; 2 = disagree; 3 = neutral, 4 = agree; 5 = strongly agree.

Phase 2 was administered at the end of the quarter. Student attendance at this phase was substantially lower—we only had one complete group of seven students in each of the two courses. This mortality between the two phases suggests that any difference between the phases can be a result of selection bias, rather than learning that occurred in the two courses and/or due to the repetition of the experiment. Token investments in Phase 2 are depicted in Figure 6.2. However, we address here some elements of cooperation in phase 2 that are worth noting. The most important source of difference is round 5 in the second phase in both courses. While in-class discussions after rounds 2 and 3 indicated that many students understood the group optimum level of investment (9 tokens) and the individual optimum level (20 tokens, with others at 9 tokens), we only see convergence to 9 token investments in round 5. Knowing about the optimum level was not enough for groups to converge toward this level of investment. It was the ability to learn who the members in the group were and talk to them face-to-face that enabled students to devise the cooperative strategy. Putnam (1995) also noted that the face-to-face encounter is important to building social capital. In this case, the personal interactions gave students an opportunity to reflect on their strategies, share ideas for achieving the common goal, and create new ways to meet that goal. This impact of face-to-face discussion within the group was noticed in both courses.

There was one difference between the two courses that may be puzzling for the reader. While the Science group remained at the group optimum level in rounds 5 and 6, the Cooperation course group diverted in round 6. Unfortunately we did not record the discussion in this group verbatim. We have noted, however, that this group had an explicit discussion of inter-round equity. Rather than simply discussing the cooperative level of investment for the remaining two rounds, the Cooperative course group at the end of round 5 decided to share information about each individual's token orders in earlier rounds. They identified a group member who had been investing at very low levels in earlier rounds. The group then committed to stay at the group optimum level of investments

Cooperation Course

Science Course

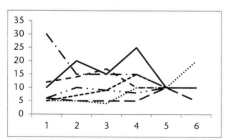
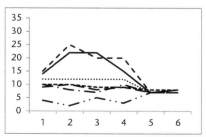

FIGURE 6.2 Individual Token Investments in a Group, Phase 2

and encouraged the low investor to invest 20 tokens (the individual level optimum) in round 6. As a matter of fact, the group member who suggested this compensation strategy offered to reduce his investment to 5 tokens to get the rest of the group to agree. While we cannot attribute this concern for the inter-round equity to the curriculum in cooperation, we note here the different type of conversation in this group.

The experiment also partially confirmed a finding in earlier experimental literature on types of individuals and their social value orientations (Casari and Plott, 2003; Kurzban and Houser, 2005). As depicted in Table 6.1, some individuals are predominantly non-cooperative, no matter what others do. For example, student 1 in the Science course and students 1 and 3 in the Cooperation course were above the group optimum token investments for most rounds with investments between 10 and 30. We also had a cooperative student whose investments were around the group optimum no matter what others did (student 2 in the Science course). A majority of the students, however, seemed to be varying their token investments between 5 and 25.

Discussion

We presented here theoretical and empirical reasons for employing a common pool resource experiment. Participation in such experiments builds a better understanding of the moral and intellectual difficulties individuals face when interacting in groups. Students used creativity, analysis, communication, and reflection skills to learn about and practice key concepts related to social capital and explore the logic of interdependence.

While experiments and simulation games have been historically used in courses in microeconomics or business, our results suggest that this experiment can be used in any course. Specifically, we administered the experiment in two substantially different freshman courses: a social science course focused on cooperation, competition, and conflict and a course focused on scientific methods. Our results indicate comparable levels of cooperation in both courses. The results also suggest substantially higher levels of cooperation in the experiment that allowed students to identify other members in the group and engage in face-to-face conversations. Therefore, we recommend that all six rounds be administered and conversations between rounds carefully documented. The information on token investments by individuals in groups, without revealing the identity of the individuals, and the records of conversations in the class or in the groups between rounds should then be reported back to the students in a follow-up session. This allows students to identify strategies that were adopted and their effectiveness.

The literature on the use of simulation games has argued that they work best for students who don't like learning by themselves and who like engaging in discussions with others. Increasingly, however, we educate *quiet introverts*, who frequently have excellent solutions to problems but prefer not to participate in large class discussions and, therefore, do not influence the rest of their class (Monahan, 2013). We argue that such experiments also provide introverted students to be engaged in a smaller group and contribute to the whole group's understandings. An experiment like the one reported in this chapter provides such students with time to first analyze the situation by themselves and then engage in conversation with peers around very specific issues.

Students across both courses exhibited learning about the importance of social capital through this creative process. Irrespective of disciplinary training, once given the opportunity to communicate with other students in their group, they were able to identify the group optimum levels of fishing and develop an agreement that each individual will invest only at that level. In addition, creative abilities (e.g., imagining, exploring, synthesizing, connecting, and adapting) are used and strengthened by this experiment. Our results suggest that this approach can be successfully administered in a social science course, a quantitative reasoning course, or in a science course to provide students with opportunities to practice cooperation.

Note

1. We thank the Teaching and Learning Center and the Center for Undergraduate Studies, University of Washington, Bothell, for their financial support. We also wish to thank Charles Jackels, Professor Emeritus, for allowing us to administer the experiment in his science course.

Bibliography

Ahn, T. K., Ostrom, E., & Walker, J. M. (2010). A common-pool resource experiment with subjects from 41 countries. *Ecological Economics, 69*(12), 2624–2633.

Astin, A. W. (1987). Competition or cooperation?: Teaching teamwork as a basic skill. *Change: the Magazine of Higher Learning, 19*(5), 12–19. http://dx.doi.org/10.1080/000 91383.1987.10570152

Axelrod, R. (1984). *The evolution of cooperation.* New York: Basic Books.

Blumenfeld, P. C., Marx, R. W., Soloway, E., & Krajcik, J. (1996). Learning with peers: From small group cooperation to collaborative communities. *Educational Researcher, 25*(8), 37–40.

Casari, M. & Plott, C. R. (2003). Decentralized management of common property resources: Experiments with a centuries-old institution. *Journal of Economic Behavior and Organization, 51,* 217–247.

Dewey, J. (1916). *Democracy and education: An introduction to the philosophy of education.* New York: Macmillan.

Dolšak, N. & Ostrom, E. (Eds.). (2003). *The commons in the new millennium: Challenges and adaptation.* Cambridge, MA: The MIT Press (2nd Print).

Dorn, D. S. (1989). Simulation games: One more tool on the pedagogical shelf. *Teaching Sociology, 17*(1), 1–18.

Dudley, R. L. & Gitelson, A. R. (2002). Political literacy, civic Education, and civic engagement: A return to political socialization? *Applied Developmental Science, 6*(4), 175–182.

Dugatkin, L. A. (1997). The evolution of cooperation. *Bioscience, 47*(6), 355–362.

Easton, D. & Hess, R. (1962). The child's political world. *Midwest Journal of Political Science, 6*(3), 229–246.

Fan, C. (2000). Teaching children cooperation—An application of experimental game theory. *Journal of Economic Behavior and Organization, 41*(3), 191–209.

Freeman, S., Eddy, S. L., McDonough, M., Smith, M. K., Okoroafor, N., Jordt, H., & Wenderoth, P. M. (2014). Active learning increases student performance in science, engineering, and mathematics. *PNAS2014, 111*(23), 8410–8415.

Gillies, R. M. (1999). Maintenance of cooperative and helping behaviors in reconstituted groups. *The Journal of Education Research, 92*(6), 357–363.

Holtzman, M. (2005). Teaching sociological theory through active learning: The irrigation exercise. *Teaching Sociology, 33*(2), 206–212.

Jackson, N. (2008). *Tackling the wicked problem of creativity in higher education.* Background paper for a presentation at the ARC Centre for the Creative Industries and Innovation, International Conference Brisbane. http://imaginativecurriculumnetwork.pbworks.com/ f/WICKED+PROBLEM+OF+CREATIVITY+IN+HIGHER+EDUCATION.pdf

Johnson, D. W. & Johnson, R. T. (2009). An educational psychology success story: Social interdependence theory and cooperative learning. *Educational Researcher, 38*(5), 365–379.

Kolb, A. Y. & Kolb, D. A. (2005). Learning style and learning spaces: Enhancing experiential learning in higher education. *Academy of Management Learning & Education, 4*(2), 192–212.

Kramer, R. M. & Brewer, M. B. (1984). Effects of group identity on resource use in a simulated commons dilemma. *Journal of Personality and Social Psychology, 46*(5), 1044–1057.

Kurzban, R. & Houser, D. (2005). Experiments investigating cooperative types in humans: A complement to evolutionary theory and simulations. *PNAS, 102*(5), 1803–1807.

Lipkus, I. & Peters, E. (2009). Understanding the role of numeracy in health: Proposed theoretical framework and practical insights. *Health Education & Behavior, 36*, 1065–1081. http://dx.doi.org/10.1177/1090198109341533

Marks, M., Lehr, D., & Brastow, R. (2006). Cooperation versus free riding in a threshold public goods classroom experiment. *The Journal of Economic Education, 37*(2), 156–170.

Monahan, N. (2013). Keeping Introverts in mind in your active learning classroom. *Faculty Focus.* October 28, 2013. http://www.facultyfocus.com/articles/teaching-and-learning/keeping-introverts-in-mind-in-your-active-learning-classroom/ Accessed on September 28, 2015.

Niemi, R. G. & Junn, J. (1998). *Civic education.* New Haven, CT: Yale University Press.

North, D. C. (1990). *Institutions, institutional change and economic performance.* Cambridge, UK: Cambridge University Press.

Nowak, M. A. (2006). Five rules for the evolution of cooperation. *Science, 314*(5805), 1560–1563.

Nye, P. & Hillyard, C. (2013). Personal financial behavior: The influence of quantitative literacy and material Values. *Numeracy, 6*(1), Article 3. http://dx.doi.org/10.5038/ 1936-4660.6.1.3

Ostrom, E. (1990). *Governing the commons.* Cambridge: Cambridge University Press.

Ostrom, E. (1996). Civic education for the next century: A task force to initiate professional activity. *PS: Political Science and Politics, 29*(4), 755–758.

Putnam, R. D. (1995). Bowling alone: America's declining social capital. *Journal of Democracy, 6*(1), 65–78.

Putnam, R. D., Leonardi, R., & Nanetti, R. Y. (1993). *Making democracy work: Civic traditions in modern Italy.* Princeton, NJ: Princeton University Press.

Stone, C., Henig, J., Jones, B., & Pierannunzi, C. (2001). *Building civic capacity: The politics of reforming urban schools.* Lawrence, KS: University Press of Kansas.

Torney-Purta, J., Lehmann, R., Oswald, H., & Schulz, W. (2001). *Citizenship and education in twenty-eight countries: Civic knowledge and engagement at age fourteen.* The International Association for the Evaluation of Educational Achievement. http://www.iea.nl/fileadmin/user_upload/Publications/Electronic_versions/CIVED_Phase2_Age_Fourteen.pdf

7

TOWARD MINDFUL ASSESSMENT IN HIGHER EDUCATION

A Case Study in Contemplative Commentary on Student Work to Promote Creative Learning

Linda S. Watts

As higher education shifts its focus from 'what is taught' to 'what is learned,' a number of provocative assessment questions arise: What does mindful practice offer to this paradigm shift within assessment of creative learning? How might course learning goals and objectives reflect an emphasis on contemplative practice? In particular, how does such an approach inform strategies for evaluating, responding to, and redirecting student writing? How do metacognition and mindfulness interact within higher education? With this brief case study, I seek to share my current (best-so-far) practice with regard to each of these issues. The hope is that some aspects of this discussion will prove relevant across levels of study, fields of study, and institutional contexts.

What Does Mindful Practice Offer to This Paradigm Shift Within Assessment of Student Learning?

The featured course, "The Beholding 'I': Social Observation as Contemplative Practice in the Helping Professions," addresses the nuanced work conducted by such figures as teachers, health care professionals, and social workers. This course was influenced by previous efforts such as Robert Coles's Harvard course, "A Literature of Social Reflection." Coles (2010) calls upon us to consider the compelling power of humanistic inquiry in addressing issues surrounding central practices throughout the helping professions: observation, description, narrative, commentary, advocacy, and intervention.

I wanted to engage class members in exploring and contributing to the literary and journalistic documentary tradition of social observation. In so doing, I recognized that we would be posing questions regarding the complex relationships generated through acts of social observation:

To what degree are we responsible for what we see?

What do we notice and why? What does that say about us, or others?

How do we think about the stories of others, and about our own stories?

Is it most important that we emphasize our commonalities with others or identify our differences from others, or is there a third option?

Is there an ethics of reading?

In what ways are we accountable for what we write? Are we duty bound to act upon the social phenomena we observe, read about, and write about?

What does it mean to help? What does it mean to serve?

How are we to understand the dynamic of empathic connection?

What is the quality of compassion, and what are its optimal results?

How do we strive for reciprocity in human relationships?

At its best, what might creative coexistence look, feel, and sound like?

What role does literature play in human rights and human thriving?

How does language contribute to creating a more peaceful and just world?

In what sense are all of these issues critical to arriving at a professional identity informed by reflective practice?

How Might Course Learning Goals and Objectives Reflect an Emphasis on Contemplative Education?

Beyond raising those questions, I wanted students enrolled in the class to consider how to sustain both themselves and their practices in the helping professions. That intent caused me to delve into the literature regarding mindfulness in education. In addition to assigning students to read examples of the literature of social observation, I found myself developing assignments to promote skills, awareness, and capacities needed for helping professionals and for their clients.

On this basis, invoking a premise Grant Wiggins and Jay McTighe (1998) call 'backward design' of curriculum, I moved from thinking about the course assignments as a series of traditional student essays to a suite of activities that might more vividly cultivate and demonstrate these emerging competencies in students. That meant that while students would still write some essays, they would also engage in contemplative photography assignments and learn (or develop) practices such as meditation and guided visualization. That is, students would have some assignment options through which to customize their selections of contemplative activities to suit their own professional interests, constituencies, and needs.

As a result, my approach to framing course learning outcomes changed considerably. As navigational tools, the goals and objectives became more layered and decidedly plural. Here is an excerpt from the course syllabus in which I address these assessment complexities:

> What are the course learning goals and objectives? The usual answer instructors provide to this question deals mostly with content. To be sure, you will come to understand more about literature and the helping professions. As importantly, you will be challenged to learn some lessons that transcend topic. This course, like many you have taken or will take, interlocks several sets of objectives:

Humanistic Content This Course Will Ask You to Discover

- Bringing thoughtful and purposeful attention to the conditions of people's lives;
- Deepening understanding of the perils and possibilities of conducting engaged and examined lives in the company of others;
- Engaging productively with complexity, conflict, paradox, and ambiguity;
- Sustaining lifelong inquiries into shared meaning and action;
- Exploring personal meaning through experience and reflection.

Specific Skills the Course Will Invite You to Build

- Dispositions associated with mindful practice (nonjudging, nonstriving, nonattachment, acceptance, patience, trust, openness, curiosity, letting go, gentleness, nonreactivity, loving-kindness);
- Acuity of vision as relevant to mindful practice (beholding, noticing thoughts, noticing feelings, noticing gaps, seeing dispassionately);
- Relational abilities associated with the helping professions (witnessing and welcoming, being present, deep listening, attunement, connection, empathy, compassion);
- Familiarity with techniques associated with mindful practice (mindful breathing, mindful movement, body scan, sitting meditation, walking meditation, walking with words);
- Awareness of methods for self-care in the helping professions (introspection, self-awareness, values clarification, gratitude, distress tolerance).

Translatable Abilities the Course Will Help You Cultivate

- Public speaking
- Dialogue/discussion
- Analysis/interpretation/critical thinking
- Writing
- Productive engagement with complexity
- Inquiry—posing, refining, and responding to compelling questions.

Lofty Aspirations for Students in This Course

The course is designed to help you become a more critical, creative, and contemplative practitioner in the helping professions. Throughout our study you will both respond to and generate texts (mostly visual or verbal) that attempt to convey the richness and complexity of people's lives. You will also engage in activities, assignments, and exchanges designed to:

- Widen, strengthen, and render more nimble your capacities for observation;
- Enhance your ability to use both language and image to convey insights into complexities of the human condition;
- Sharpen and render more incisive your skills for refining, revising, and reframing verbal or visual observations—including your individual efforts, your collaborative efforts, and efforts made by other observers;
- Become more acute in introspective, reflective, and prospective domains.

Earthly Aspirations for Students in This Course

By the end of the course, students will demonstrate *improved ability* to perform in the following tasks as a self-directed and integrative learner:

1. Effectively select and develop examples of life experiences, drawn from a variety of contexts (e.g., family life, artistic participation, civic involvement, work experience) to illuminate concepts/theories/ frameworks of fields of study [*connect relevant experience and academic knowledge*]. This learning also supports student growth in IAS Core Learning Objective: Interdisciplinary Research and Inquiry, and UWB Undergraduate Learning Goals II and III.
2. Adapt and apply skills, abilities, theories, or methodologies gained in one situation to new situations to solve problems or explore issues [*transfer*]. This learning also supports student growth in IAS Core Learning Objective: Critical and Creative Thinking, and UWB Undergraduate Learning Goals I and V-Creative Thinking and Problem Solving.
3. Fulfill assignment(s) by choosing a format, language, or visual representation to connect content and form explicitly, demonstrating awareness of purpose and audience [*integrated communication*]. This learning also supports student growth in IAS Core Learning Objective: Writing and Communication, and UWB Undergraduate Learning Goals II and V-Communication.

4. Evaluate changes in own learning over time, recognizing complex contextual factors (e.g., works with ambiguity and risk, deals with frustration, considers ethical frameworks) [*reflection and self-assessment*]. This learning also supports student growth in IAS Core Learning Objective: Collaboration and Shared Leadership, and UWB Undergraduate Learning Goal I.

These learning objectives are informed by and adapted from the Valid Assessment of Learning in Undergraduate Education (VALUE) rubrics, generated through the Association of American Colleges and Universities (see Rhodes. 2010). Those wishing to know more about the course structure may consult the planning calendar in the chapter appendix.

How Does Such an Approach Inform Strategies for Evaluating, Responding to, and Redirecting Student Writing?

To demonstrate the way mindful practice has modified my approach to assessing student work, I will focus on a given assignment within the course/case study described. Within this assignment, class members were asked to make and explore connections among course materials, featuring two or more items (of which at least one should be a reading selection from one of our required texts, Adam Davis's anthology *Taking Action: Readings for Civic Reflection*) (Davis, 2012). Within the course, the Davis book was used in combination with volumes by Snel (2013) and Zehr (2005). Here is the assignment prompt:

> Some of my favorite (and most memorable) moments as an undergraduate involved the optimal experience Mihaly Csikszentmihalyi describes as 'flow': a state of deep enjoyment, creativity, and a total involvement with life and learning. Your challenge in these weekly writings is to convey your moment of 'flow' in a way so vivid and compelling that readers find it irresistible (Csikszentmihalyi, 1990, p. 6).
>
> As a purposeful attempt to cultivate such connections and to explore them as they occur, you will write weekly discovery-based writings in which your chief objective is to feature one insight (one you either have or wish to approach more closely), and in specific, an insight possible only through responding to the course materials and experiences *in combination*.
>
> As acts of communication, these writings speak most immediately to their audience (the instructor and class members) when featuring elements in common, such as the literary selections. That helps others 'enter' your essays and think/feel/sense with you. Do not assume that we have interpreted the literary texts as you have, though. Instead, help us see where and how you have made sense of them. Link the literature to other course

components, such as discussions, assignment options, and the like. Again, remember to be a good companion to your reader, who may not share your exact experience and perspective but wishes to understand.

Above all, help us join in your sense of new or renewed understanding. Make sure you—and your readers—sense why the insight you have achieved matters so much.

The literary cluster associated with this particular assignment carried the theme "Here and Now," which bridged beautifully among the three key course components (literature, helping professions, and mindfulness practice), particularly as they intersect through the act of social observation. The items included in this literary cluster were Constantine Cavafy's "The City," Pablo Neruda's "I'm Explaining a Few Things," Gwendolyn Brooks's "kitchenette building," Adrienne Rich's "What Kind of Times Are These," Ahmad Faraz's "Don't Think," Naomi Shihab Nye's "Trying to Name What Doesn't Change," Tony Hoagland's "America," and Adam Zagajewski's "Try to Praise the Mutilated World." Davis groups these selections through a shared set of concerns around time consciousness and, in particular, the notion of mindfulness as an openness and curiosity about one's experience in the present moment, sometimes referred to as 'presence.'

In responding to this issue of the "Here and Now," both as articulated in the readings from the Davis collection and as addressed in other course elements (viewings, screenings, activities, discussions, and the like), students found an opportunity at approximately the midpoint of the academic term to reexamine the interstices of the literature of social observation, the helping professions, and mindfulness practice. They found opportunities to deepen their sense of this interplay, to challenge the ways these course materials speak (and speak to one another), and to extend that study in ways that would not have been possible if the materials had been encountered separately. Responses to this assignment are kept intentionally concise (a page or less), and are reviewed in terms of the student writer's demonstrated ability in three areas: (1) thoughtful engagement with the course materials, (2) purposeful exploration of a meaningful point of contact (whether it be one of accord or friction) among course materials, and (3) compelling insight into the implications of such a (dis)juncture, and of noticing it in this fresh way.

In other words, I wanted to apply mindfulness principles to the evaluation of, and feedback on, student writing. Here are some central commenting strategies I employed in responding to submission for this assignment, each accompanied by a sample comment:

1. **Begin with acknowledgement**. Devote first attention to those aspects of the student piece that seem most effective and engaging. Make sure that the student understands both the fact that these attributes are valued, and the reasons why they matter so much. Not only does this approach affirm the

student's effort, it also assists the student in identifying what characteristics of the piece prove most powerful for actual respondents.

Sample Comment

I enjoyed getting this window into your experiments in reading and response through these weekly writings. I think your 'text only' (rather than context) approach offers a distinctive perspective on the literary selections. It likely focuses our attention more closely both on the language and on its relevance across life circumstances. I am glad to learn that "The City," while not an easy encounter for you, proved relevant to your current situation. Ultimately, I regard it as a hopeful poem in the sense that we cannot have a hope of changing behavioral or attitudinal patterns until we recognize them (and their effect on our experience and outlook). How did it prove helpful to you in this specific instance?

2. **Engage with ideas/hypotheses before commenting on the manner of their statement**. By addressing oneself to the specific insights/ intuitions a student advances, it becomes apparent that their work has been engaged with both close and individual attention. Student thoughts must be taken seriously, and it is helpful to mark that fact in the narrative comments devoted to student work.

Sample Comment

I appreciate the way you look closely at structure within the Neruda poem. I think you are on to something with your hypothesis about structural shifts within the text bearing some connection to time frame. That is where I think you are at your best within this piece. A next step would be to do a bit more to help your reader discern the flow among the pieces to which you refer (Neruda, Rich, and Hoagland), and to detect— especially at the end, what you would have readers notice about the texts as a set. What do we understand or notice only when the texts are viewed in combination?

3. **Wherever possible, read student work generously**. If a student is on the cusp of an achievement, it may make sense to credit the individual with that attainment. Comments can detail the nature and importance of that progress, so that the learner can find satisfaction in the growth (even if it is still a work in progress).

Sample Comment

There is so much for a reader to notice within your piece. I am especially delighted to see your deft interpretation of "Don't Think," in which you capture the tension between the two figures within the scene depicted there. While some readers tend to take the poem literally ('don't worry, be happy'), it seems more likely to me that the poem portrays the struggle each of us faces in attending to the world without becoming immobilized by those acts of attention. I suspect mindfulness is about a balancing of attention—a recalibration of sorts.

4. **Serve as a respondent rather than as an editor.** If learning is a dialogue, then instructor comments represent an important component of that conversation. If a teacher falls into the habit of 'correcting' errors or omissions in student work, particularly if that appears to the student to be the teacher's primary contribution, the dialogue can quickly deteriorate. Instead, proceed from engagement with the questions the student's work raises (even if they remain unresolved), leaving line-level redirection to a later time or to last remarks, as comparatively lower order concerns.

Sample Comment

I appreciate your point about the benefits to be found in not *always* staying in the here and now.

For me, the final cluster of readings from the Adam Davis book helps create a productive tension between mindfulness and its counter-energies/practices.

I can readily see, however, how that could prove confusing. In some ways, it is the most elusive or advanced set of companion concepts we will encounter this term: being intentional and staying receptive, cultivating calm without becoming subdued, directing energy without wielding it against others, intervening in injustice without getting lost in judgments of others, and—ultimately—realizing that the present has importance largely in its relationship to both the past and the present. The present is born in the past, and the future is born in the present. Their meanings are interdependent. It might help to think of mindfulness as an effort to right or restore a balance (rather than to replace one outlook or state of mind with another).

I also value your point about the importance of "appreciative living in the here and now, for its duration of presence is unknown." How do you go about doing that in your own life, and how do these readings help you approach that balance anew?

5. **Venture something of yourself, not as a definitive authority, but as someone engaged in shared inquiry.** Students grow, both in capacity and motivation, through a learning environment in which their teachers help them extend or sustain a point's exploration.

Sample Comment

As I read this piece, I find you engaging closely with this literary cluster (along with its relationships to previous readings, such as Shao Yanxiang's "My Optimism"). I take your point about a somewhat more solemn tone prevailing in this section of the Davis book. It is as if he, as editor, wants to avoid any too-bright, too-cheerful concluding messages about what it means to 'take action' in a complicated time such as this one. In that sense, his way of invoking 'here and now' is rather less blissful than some of the mindfulness folks, yet—I suspect—still not too bleak, just reality-transacted. In part, I suspect that is why he ends with Adam Zagajewski's "Try to Praise the Mutilated World," whose final words hold out some genuine promise, with its final reference to "the gentle light that strays and vanishes and returns."

6. **Focus prospective feedback around one pivotal advancement the student stands poised to make**. Rather than meeting the student's work with a barrage of corrections and items of advice, it may be at least as effective to concentrate instructor commentary around a single step ('next step') a student might take in order to reach a greater level of insight, proficiency, or expression. In this way, students can readily identify what area, and what action in regard to it—at least in the teacher's view—holds highest priority for building success either in revision of the current piece or approaching subsequent work. Invoking this strategy also challenges an educator to consider what learning intervention might make the most positive difference for a student.

Sample Comment

I appreciate the way your discussion of Cavafy and Hoagland turns our attention to the prisons we make for ourselves (through unexamined habits of feeling, thought, or behavior). A next step would be to link that textual pair a bit more closely to the point you seek to make regarding Neruda. I suspect that the implicit connection has something to do with a common need to direct our attention in productive ways to realistic possibilities (rather than to get lost in nostalgia about the past or idealism about the future).

7. **Where practical, comment in a manner that acknowledges that/ how learning is a relationship (not just between a student and a teacher, but also between a student and a form of inquiry)**. This approach might mean something as simple as observing a student's strongest moments within a given piece (where 'you are at your best'), and helping make it ever clearer how the student might leverage those moments. In other

instances, it might involve comments that promote the learner's engagement with that inquiry, such that the relationship deepens.

Sample Comment

There is much to admire here, and I believe you are at your best when you say: "I wonder at what point we start carrying our worries around with us. It seems so funny the practice of mindfulness initially feels so foreign when that is where we started out." This outlook on mindfulness helps us imagine the possibility that we are recovering an awareness lost through living. At least for some folks, I think this makes mindfulness a more approachable matter, an inborn capacity rather than an elusive attainment. I hope you encounter many more opportunities to—as you say—exist, create, and be present.

8. **Greet with enthusiasm all student attempts at innovative perspectives, new connections, integration of source materials, application of terms/concepts, and synthesis of understandings**. Otherwise, students may not appreciate the value of such steps. Even when imperfectly attempted (for who, after all, is perfect?), these student glimpses at systems thinking or integrative learning are critical moments in a student's journey of understanding.

Sample Comment

I like the way in which your piece problematizes the notion of 'here and now.' Just as it would be impossible to always be mindful, it would be as unhelpful to be locked in the present as it would be to be stuck in the past or the future. I also value the way you bridge to the language of recovery, which recognizes the way we frequently recreate dynamics in our lives (wherever we go, whenever we go there). While that might initially sound grim as a realization, it is in fact a source of hope and renewal—if only we can recognize and reckon with that reality.

9. **Use comments to nudge students toward enhanced balance and proportion (whether between theory and application, argument and counterargument, and so forth)**. Teachers play an important role in helping students recognize and respect complex relationships of balance, whether in their work, their learning, their experiences, and/or their lived worlds.

Sample Comment

I enjoy the way you frame this discussion of 'here and now' with a keen understanding that mindfulness (or presence) is not a preoccupation with the present so much as it is a rebalancing of our energies across the domains of past, present, and future. I think you are at your best when you say: "How we react and respond to the pain is what shapes our present, for our choices are crucial." It is the difference between seeing time as something that happens to us, or a field of possibility within which we act daily through choices, whether conscious ones or not.

10. **Keep the dialogue ongoing and the inquiry sustained**. I find it useful to conclude comments on student work with next-round considerations, which often include posing a question or dilemma suggested by the work submitted.

Sample Comment

Your central idea here, about the hazards of holding onto things too tightly, offers a good point of access to the issue of 'here and now.' Sometimes we labor under the illusion that by changing external things (like location or station), we can transform our lives. More often and more likely the 'change of scenery' we seek involves, at least in part, internal changes or movements. How has this been true for you?

These response strategies, as applied to commenting on student work, serve to blend my previous efforts to emphasize metacognition with my current attempts to introduce mindfulness in the assessment of student learning in higher education.

How Do Metacognition and Mindfulness Interact Within Higher Education?

The discourse of mindfulness as applied to higher education is new enough that the relationship of such practice to metacognition is still taking shape. Some scholars regard the two as distinct, others as overlapping (Jankowski and Holas, 2014). In this regard, I find most helpful the work of educator Nora Mitchell (1999). In the context of a book chapter focused on the teaching of poetry, she characterized two distinct ways of knowing: apprehension and comprehension.

According to Mitchell, these words describe a dialectical relationship between two forms of human knowledge. She writes:

These two ways of grasping do not coexist comfortably; the conflict between them must be resolved as one learns. Apprehension is registrative, affective, sensory, engaged, intuitive, appreciative, subjective, personal, timeless, global, tacit. Comprehension, on the other hand is interpretive cognitive, conceptual, distanced, reflective, critical, objective, social, linear, analytical, articulate. . . . Although they are not neatly opposed, these two sets of processes clearly exist in tension.

(Mitchell, 1999, p. 143)

Class members were quickly engaged by this juxtaposition between apprehension and comprehension, applying it to the patterns of their prior and current educational experiences. We also found it helpful to examine particular forms of study through this lens. Discussion questions included:

- In terms of reading literature, how are these forms of knowing distinct?
- How do helping professionals draw from either/both of these ways of knowing?
- Within your mindfulness practice, do both apprehension and comprehension play a part?

Additionally, the context of the featured course afforded an opportunity to affirm the complementarity of these distinct ways of knowing. Among the questions considered were:

- What happens when one of these forms of knowing exists in the absence of the other?
- Are there situations where both kinds of knowing are helpful, or even necessary?
- If so, how do we work toward a balance between the two kinds of knowing?
- What insights or new understandings might a balanced approach make possible?

This conversation also gave us a chance to discuss that/why apprehension tends to be less prominent than comprehension within higher education assessment models. In this regard, we posed several questions:

- Would you say that the words typically more closely associated with apprehension and comprehension receive greater attention and/or are assigned higher value within colleges and universities? Why or why not?
- Is one of these forms of knowing easier to measure and document than the other? Why or why not?
- Do apprehension and comprehension require separate evaluation, or are they interdependent educational abilities to be assessed in tandem?

Ultimately, class member responses to these questions followed a pattern. Most students felt that higher education success required attributes associated with both apprehension and comprehension. Still, they indicated that comprehension was emphasized more within their undergraduate course of study, and was markedly more prominent within the evaluation techniques and assessment measures employed within their higher education experience. By striving to promote both apprehension and comprehension within this course's design, delivery, and assessment, it was more possible for students to build their capacities within both ways of knowing in a synergistic manner. As students sought ways to link literature, helping professions, and mindfulness, they came to regard apprehension and comprehension as a productive tension to engage creatively rather than as a binary opposition to resolve through reason alone.

Bibliography

Coles, R. (2010). *Handing one another along: Literature and social reflection: On character, courage, and compassion.* New York: Random House.

Csikszentmihalyi, M. (1990). *Flow: The psychology of optimal experience.* New York: Harper Perennial.

Davis, A., ed. (2012). *Taking action: Readings for civic reflection.* Chicago: Great Books Foundation with Center for Civic Reflection.

Jankowski, T., and Holas, P. (2014). "Metacognitive Model of Mindfulness." *Consciousness and Cognition* 28, 64–80.

Mitchell, N. (1999). "But I Don't Read Poetry: Relearning to Read Literature," in Steven Schapiro, ed., *Higher education for democracy: Experiments in progressive pedagogy at Goddard College* (pp. 131–146). New York: Peter Lang.

Rhodes, T. (2010). *Assessing outcomes and improving achievement: Tips and tools for using rubrics.* Washington, DC: AAC&U.

Snel, E. (2013). *Sitting still like a frog: Mindfulness exercises for kids (and their parents); Simple mindfulness practices to help your child deal with anxiety, improve concentration, and handle difficult emotions.* Boston: Shambhala.

Wiggins, G., and McTighe, J. (1998). *Understanding by design.* Alexandria, VA: Association for Supervision and Curriculum Development.

Zehr, H. (2005). *The little book of contemplative photography: Seeing with wonder, respect, and humility.* Intercourse, PA: Good Books.

APPENDIX

Course Planning Calendar

Week One

3/30—Term begins

4/3—Post to the "Getting Acquainted" discussion board on Canvas, due at 8:30 a.m. (post to Canvas)

4/3—Familiarize yourself with our Canvas page, particularly the syllabus and planning calendar, due at 8:30 a.m. (nothing to submit, but bring any questions to Face-to-Face Session 1)

4/3—*Face-to-Face Session 1*, 8:45 a.m.–1 p.m.

Recommended: Read something about the lives and contributions of one of these writers. How does such information shape your response as a reader?

Note: If you are uncertain how to work with literary texts, may I suggest Janet E. Gardner's *Reading and Writing About Literature: A Portable Guide*, Third Edition (New York: Bedford/St. Martin's, 2012). It includes tips for reading various literary genres as well as techniques for responding to literature, such as annotating or journaling.

Week Two

4/7—Read section from Davis titled "Need and Care" (pp. 1–47), due at 8:30 a.m. (nothing to submit, but reading notes advised)

4/10—*Weekly Writing*: Need and Care, due at 8:30 a.m. (submit via Canvas)

Recommended: Try out one of the optional discussion boards associated with our course on Canvas, such as "Café Questions" or "Water Cooler."

Week Three

4/14—*Submission 1*: Contemplative Photography or Mindfulness Exercise, due at 8:30 a.m. (submit via Canvas)

[Choose ONE of the following TWO options]:

> *Contemplative Photography Option*: Read Zehr, Chapter 1 ("Getting Started"), and complete "I See/I Feel/I Think" activity
> OR
> *Mindfulness Exercise Option*: Read Snel, Chapter 1 ("Introduction to Mindfulness"), conduct Exercise 11 ("Sleep Tight"), and complete corresponding journal entry

4/17—Read section from Davis titled "Serving and Protecting" (nothing to submit, but reading notes advised)
4/17—*Weekly Writing*: Serving and Protecting, due at 8:30 a.m. (submit via Canvas)
4/17—*Face-to-Face Session 2*, 8:45 a.m.–1 p.m.
Recommended: Try out one of the Guided Visualizations available to you as an audio recording on Canvas.

Week Four

4/21—*Submission 2*: Contemplative Photography or Mindfulness Exercise, due at 8:30 a.m. (submit via Canvas)
[Choose ONE of the following TWO options]:

> *Contemplative Photography Option*: Read Zehr, Chapter 2 ("Changing Our Lens"), and conduct "Photographing Without a Viewfinder" activity
> OR
> *Mindfulness Exercise Option*: Read Snel, Chapter 2 ("Parenting With Greater Mindfulness"), conduct Exercise 5 ("The Pause Button"), and complete corresponding journal entry

4/24—Read section from Davis titled "Teaching and Learning" (pp. 83–136), due at 8:30 a.m. (nothing to submit, but reading notes advised)
4/24—*Weekly Writing*: Teaching and Learning, due at 8:45 a.m. (submit via Canvas)
Recommended: Try out one of the Mindfulness Resources available to you as an audio recording on Canvas.

Week Five

4/28—*Submission 3*: Contemplative Photography or Mindfulness Exercise, due at 8:30 a.m. (submit via Canvas)
[Choose ONE of the following TWO options]:

> *Contemplative Photography Option*: Read Zehr, Chapter 2 ("Changing Our Lens"), and conduct "Receiving an Image" activity
> OR

Mindfulness Exercise Option: Read Snel, Chapter 3 ("Attention Starts With the Breath"), conduct Exercise 3 ("Attention to the Breath"), and complete corresponding journal entry.

5/1—Read section from Davis titled "Difference and Connection" (pp. 49–82), due by 8:30 a.m. (nothing to submit, but reading notes advised)

5/1—*Weekly Writing*: Difference and Connection, due at 8:30 a.m. (submit via Canvas)

5/1—*Face-to-Face Session 3*, 8:45 a.m.–1 p.m.

Recommended: Try out one of the Contemplative Practices available to you as audio recordings on Canvas.

Week Six

5/5—*Submission 4*: Contemplative Photography or Mindfulness Exercise, due at 8:30 a.m. (submit via Canvas)

[Choose ONE of the following TWO options]:

> *Contemplative Photography Option*: Read Zehr, Chapter 3 ("Practicing Mindfulness"), and conduct "Exploring the Ordinary" activity
> OR
> *Mindfulness Exercise Option*: Read Snel, Chapter 4 ("Training Your Attention Muscle"), conduct one of the green box activities included in the chapter, and complete corresponding journal entry

5/8—Read section from Davis titled "Actions and Outcomes" (pp. 165–198), due at 8:30 a.m. (nothing to submit, but reading notes advised)

5/8—*Weekly Writing*: Actions and Outcomes, due at 8:30 a.m. (submit via Canvas)

Recommended: Find out about Adam Davis, the editor of *Taking Action*.

Week Seven

5/12—*Submission 5*: Contemplative Photography or Mindfulness Exercise, due at 8:30 a.m. (submit via Canvas)

[Choose ONE of the following TWO options]:

> *Contemplative Photography Option*: Read Zehr, Chapter 3 ("Practicing Mindfulness"), and conduct "Break the Rules" activity
> OR
> *Mindfulness Exercise Option*: Read Snel, Chapter 5 ("Out of Your Head and Into Your Body"), conduct Exercise 4 ("The Spaghetti Test"), and complete corresponding journal entry

5/15—*Weekly Writing*: Here and Now, due at 8:30 a.m. (submit via Canvas)

5/15—Read section from Davis titled "Here and Now" (pp. 199–218), due at 8:30 a.m. (nothing to submit, but reading notes advised)

5/15—*Face-to-Face Session 4*, 8:45 a.m.–1 p.m.

Recommended: Research the backstory (context) for your tentative reading selection to feature in the Proposal for an Essential Reading Assignment.

Week Eight

5/19—*Submission 6*: Contemplative Photography or Mindfulness Exercise, due at 8:30 a.m. (submit via Canvas)

[Choose ONE of the following TWO options]:

Contemplative Photography Option: Read Zehr, Chapter 4 ("An Attitude of Wonder"), and conduct "Exploring Abstraction" activity

OR

Mindfulness Exercise Option: Read Snel, Chapter 6 ("Weathering the Storm Inside"), conduct Exercise 7 ("A Safe Place"), and complete corresponding journal entry

5/22—Begin looking for potential readings to feature in your Proposal for an Essential Reading Assignment for the "Beholding 'I,' " due at 8:30 a.m. (nothing to submit)

5/22—*Face-to-Face Session 5*, 8:45 a.m.–1 p.m.

5/22—*Reflective Activity*, conducted during Face-to-Face Session 5 (submit in class)

Recommended: Try out one of the Mindfulness Resources available to you as an audio recording on Canvas.

Week Nine

5/26—*Submission 7*: Contemplative Photography or Mindfulness Exercise, due at 8:30 a.m. (submit via Canvas)

[Choose ONE of the following TWO options]:

Contemplative Photography Option: Read Zehr, Chapter 4 ("An Attitude of Wonder"), and conduct "Finding Mystery in the Familiar" activity

OR

Mindfulness Exercise Option: Read Snel, Chapter 7 ("Handling Difficult Feelings"), conduct Exercise 6 ("First Aid for Unpleasant Feelings"), and complete corresponding journal entry

5/29—Finalize your reading selection to feature in your Proposal for an Essential Reading Assignment for the "Beholding 'I,' " due at 8:30 a.m. (nothing to submit)

Recommended: Prepare a discussion guide for the reading selection you have chosen to feature in your Proposal for an Essential Reading Assignment.

Week Ten

6/2—*Submission 8*: Contemplative Photography or Mindfulness Exercise, due at 8:30 a.m. (submit via Canvas)
[Choose ONE of the following TWO options]:

Contemplative Photography Option: Read Zehr, Chapter 7 ("Making Meaning"), and conduct "Where Is the Energy" activity
OR
Mindfulness Exercise Option: Read Snel, Chapter 8 ("Sitting Still Like a Frog: Mindfulness Exercises for Kids [and Their Parents]"), conduct Exercise 10 ("The Secret of the Heart Chamber"), and complete corresponding journal entry

6/5—Post to the "Staying Acquainted" discussion board on Canvas, due at 8:30 a.m. (post to Canvas)
6/5—*Submission 9*: Contemplative Photography or Mindfulness Exercise, due at 8:30 a.m. (submit via Canvas)
[Choose ONE of the following TWO options]:

Contemplative Photography Option: Read Zehr, Chapter 7 ("Making Meaning"), and conduct "Disciplined Seeing" activity
OR
Mindfulness Exercise Option: Read Snel, Chapter 10 ("Patience, Trust, and Letting Go"), conduct green box activity ("The Wishing Tree"), and complete corresponding journal activity

For all to do before the evaluation time window closes (watch your email for details): Please complete online course evaluation
6/5—Last day of classes for the term
Recommended: Try out one of the Guided Visualizations available to you as an audio recording on Canvas.

Week Eleven

6/9—*Submission 10*: Contemplative Photography or Mindfulness Exercise, due at 8:30 a.m. (submit via Canvas)
[Choose ONE of the following TWO options]:

Contemplative Photography Option: Read Zehr, Chapter 8 ("The Little Book of Contemplative Photography: Seeing with Wonder, Respect, and Humility") and conduct "Taking Stock" activity
OR
Mindfulness Exercise Option: Reread your favorite chapter from Snel, repeat your favorite mindfulness exercise, and complete the corresponding journal entry

6/9—Complete your Proposal for an Essential Reading Assignment for the "Beholding 'I,'" due at 8:30 a.m. (submit via Canvas)

Course Grading in Brief:

Course Contributions 140 points (throughout)
(includes face to face sessions as supplemented by—but not substituted for—activity on Canvas)

Face-to-Face Session 1, 4/3, 8:45 a.m.–1 pm.
Face-to-Face Session 2, 4/17, 8:45 a.m.–1 p.m.
Face-to-Face Session 3, 5/1, 8:45 a.m.–1 p.m.
Face-to-Face Session 4, 5/15, 8:45 a.m.–1 p.m.
Face-to-Face Session 5, 5/22, 8:45 a.m.–1 p.m.

Weekly Writings to Make Connections 120 points (as specified)

Weekly Writing: Need and Care, 4/10, 8:30 a.m.	20 points
Weekly Writing: Serving and Protecting, 4/17, 8:30 a.m.	20 points
Weekly Writing: Teaching and Learning, 4/24, 8:30 a.m.	20 points
Weekly Writing: Difference and Connection, 5/1, 8:30 a.m.	20 points
Weekly Writing: Actions and Outcomes, 5/8, 8:30 a.m.	20 points
Weekly Writing: Here and Now, 5/15, 8:30 a.m.	20 points

Contemplative Photography or Mindfulness Exercises 200 points (as specified)

Submission 1, 4/14, 8:30 a.m.	20 points
Submission 2, 4/21, 8:30 a.m.	20 points
Submission 3, 4/28, 8:30 a.m.	20 points
Submission 4, 5/5, 8:30 a.m.	20 points
Submission 5, 5/12, 8:30 a.m.	20 points
Submission 6, 5/19, 8:30 a.m.	20 points
Submission 7, 5/26, 8:30 a.m.	20 points
Submission 8, 6/2, 8:30 a.m.	20 points
Submission 9, 6/5, 8:30 a.m.	20 points
Submission 10, 6/9, 8:30 a.m.	20 points

Reflective Activity   120 points

While there is nothing to prepare in advance for this activity, make certain to bring all your work from the course with you to this session.
Conducted during Face-to-Face Session 5, 5/22

Writing Assignment:
Proposal for an Essential Reading for the "Beholding 'I'"   120 points

Begin looking for potential readings to feature, 5/22, 8:30 a.m.
Finalize your reading selection to feature, 5/29, 8:30 a.m.
Complete your proposal, 6/9, 8:30 a.m.

Total Available Points for Course = 700

You can convert your points to the 4-point scale mathematically. For example, 525 points would be a 3.0, 350 points would be a 2.0, 175 points would be a 1.0, and so on. Questions? See me.

8

PLAY AND 3D ENQUIRY FOR STIMULATING CREATIVE LEARNING

Alison James

Introduction

As an early computer programmer and long-serving (female) US naval officer, Rear Admiral Grace Hopper was no stranger to breaking new ground. She is famous for observing: "Humans are allergic to change. They love to say 'We've always done it this way.' I try to fight that. That's why I have a clock on my wall that runs counter-clockwise" (as cited in Scheiber, 1987). Another popular saying, attributed diversely to Henry Ford, Mark Twain and others, reminds us "If you always do what you've always done, you'll always get what you've always got." Both of these statements point toward the spirit of creativity: breaking away from the usual in order to extend knowledge, vision and capabilities.

Their words set the tone for this chapter, which is organized in two parts. The first scopes out the features and practices of learning creatively, compares creative arts learning to traditional academic study and introduces play and three-dimensional approaches. It suggests, drawing on Claxton (2006), that creative learning is a matter of developing habits of mind, culture and community, as well as trying out techniques. The second part focuses on my educational use of LEGO® SERIOUS PLAY®,[1] a method which takes building bricks out of the toy box and employs them to explore deep issues. While discussion centres primarily on this use within creative arts, design and media degrees in the UK, the techniques and principles outlined are transferable and interdisciplinary. Throughout the chapter the positives of creative learning are celebrated, and play and playful*ness* revealed as essential partners of this process. Examples show how play and creativity are strongly rooted in pedagogic theory and mobilize learning dispositions more fully than some traditional approaches. There are inevitably challenges within creative learning which are also highlighted; individuals may have fears about their own creative identity or be suspicious of play and innovation, while institutional structures and beliefs can hobble their freedom to be creative. Ways of minimizing such concerns and increasing the benefits of creative engagement are emphasized within the LEGO SERIOUS PLAY case study.

Creativity, the University and Creative Learning

The literature on creativity reveals multiple definitions of this word, with meanings that vary according to context and perspective. Williams defines creativity as a 20th-century term, with general meanings of originality and innovation, as well as "an associated special sense of productive" (2014, p. 79). For Robinson (2011), creating results in things which are new and have value, whether they are exceptional or everyday, new to the world, or just to the individual. They might start with finding solutions to small problems, which go on to have a greater impact than intended: Art Fry (with the help of Spencer Silver) invented the Post-it Note when trying to make a sticky bookmark for his hymnal (Bellis, n.d.). The creative process can generate feelings of timelessness (Csikszentmihalyi, 1998) or joy (Gauntlett, 2007, 2011), and is not limited to the gifted, but is open to everyone. Claxton (2006) even reassures us that being creative is not wacky, and you do not have to dress weirdly to do it. Such observations, and those which follow, are important for two reasons: they offer a glimpse into the complex and varied nature of creativity while also suggesting that it can be a personal and subjective experience.

In terms of higher education as a sector, Barnett's (2015) research into new models of the university in the 21st century shows creative conceptualizing at work. His literature review challenges the characterization of the university today as largely entrepreneurial by finding variants such the ecological, theatrical or borderless university. He cites Kavanagh's (2012) conception of the university as "Fool": the jester who speaks the truth to the king through antic behaviour when no other courtier would dare. For Kavanagh, the Fool is always allied to a sovereign institution and "has many faces; he is a shape-shifter, a chameleon, a trickster, always open to the possibility of transformation" (2012, p. 101). Any sinister connotations to this character notwithstanding, universities too operate in relation to major societal bodies. In addition, the ability to shape-shift and to transform is certainly essential to UK universities in the present climate. Opportunities to freely and safely explore predetermined or open-ended outcomes, test scenarios and build new kinds of reality as part of such change are all enhanced by creativity and play.

Across disciplines, including the arts, design and media, although creativity is associated with making something physical it is also cognitive and conceptual. It is as much about up-ending thinking processes (de Bono's lateral thinking, Eno's Oblique Strategies) as it is about drawing, cutting, sticking or building. Creativity is performative as well as kinaesthetic and multisensory, therefore some of the ways in which it can be nurtured involve movement and space. An obvious example of this is theatre work, while another is the upsurge in the use of labyrinth walking for learning, teaching and contemplation. At the University of Kent in England, the geometric and symmetrical features of the labyrinth have inspired mathematics teaching, concerts have been held within its confines, and creative writing and reading performed while walking (James and Brookfield, 2013, 2014; Sellers, 2013). The multisensory and visual nature of such approaches has significant resonance for extending creative learning to other disciplines, as it involves all dimensions of the body, not just the brain.

Learning creatively happens, therefore, when inventive, imaginative and physical methods are used to explore a subject and harness its practices to new partners. Robinson defined teaching creatively in primary school as "using imaginative approaches to make learning more interesting and effective" (1999, p. 89, cited in Jeffrey and Craft, 2004, p. 1), while Jeffrey and Craft (2004) argue that teaching *for* creativity and teaching creatively are interrelated. However, Claxton (2006) notes that one can be done without the other, and as teachers we can all think of times when we have done neither. Sometimes we stick to expected formulae or the tried and tested as safe options when the time to design inventive ones is lacking (James, 2015b).

In our book *Engaging Imagination: Helping Students Become Creative and Reflective Thinkers* (James and Brookfield, 2014), Stephen Brookfield and I explore how creativity in teaching can deepen and sustain student reflection. Figure 8.1 combines the qualities of creativity outlined here with those of imagination and play. Although they are separated into columns, the connections between the three of them are easy to deduce and help develop creative learning. Before exploring them in relation to LEGO SERIOUS PLAY, it is useful to consider how creative learning is understood in the arts and design.

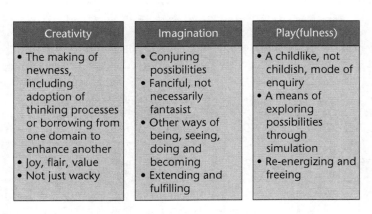

Creativity	Imagination	Play(fulness)
• The making of newness, including adoption of thinking processes or borrowing from one domain to enhance another • Joy, flair, value • Not just wacky	• Conjuring possibilities • Fanciful, not necessarily fantasist • Other ways of being, seeing, doing and becoming • Extending and fulfilling	• A childlike, not childish, mode of enquiry • A means of exploring possibilities through simulation • Re-energizing and freeing

FIGURE 8.1 Essential and Interrelated Elements of Creative Learning

'Creative' Versus 'Academic' in the Arts and Design

Creative practice is fundamental to the arts and design—this much is obvious. However sometimes students separate out the 'creative' from the 'academic' in their minds, although their tutors may see these as much more closely integrated. Students view as academic or intellectual anything resembling traditional modes of learning—essay production, lectures, reading, writing, formal examinations. Creativity for them is located in making, designing and conceiving, as indicated earlier. Furthermore, their strengths may lie in visual and productive modes of self-expression, not necessarily writing. As Line, a Scandinavian student with excellent English, reflected:

> It feels like when I put down my thoughts on paper and try to fit them into the structures and rules of academic writing, my own thoughts become alien to me and I no longer understand them or see the logic of them in the same way.

This sense of alienation from ways of working make it essential that different pedagogic approaches are adopted, not out of student deficit, but because alternative modes of engagement will stimulate richer thinking, expression, engagement and understanding.

A common myth for arts students which needs dispelling is that theoretical, social and cultural analysis is 'intellectual' and separate from their creative practice. This is easily challenged—just think of the political messages of propagandist art, gender and identity issues in fashion, social discourses informing films. Nevertheless, making things is primarily what arts students have come to do. They immerse themselves in it physically and visually, not just cognitively; they engage in hands-on, exploratory, imaginative, rule-breaking, all-encompassing ways. By associating intellectual and academic with written, traditional modes of learning, they sometimes fail to recognize how those two elements are present within the physical forms of practice.

Somehow the academic and creative have to become close friends to ensure that the gap is bridged between practice and subjects that students perceive to be external or secondary to it. Engeström (1999) is one who argues that using mediating artefacts helps stimulate dialogue, share ideas and develop understanding. In the fields of cultural and historical studies and museum curation this is already happening extensively and successfully. Objects and artefacts are being used to illustrate issues such as gender, politics, identity, style and subculture, and personal tastes. To illustrate, in an introduction to cultural theory at the London College of Fashion, students are invited to analyze and decode their tutor's clothing from such perspectives; Prown's work (1982) on material culture analysis is invaluable for this. Acknowledging and understanding the depth and complexity of factors at work within some artefacts is essential, otherwise they may appear only to have shallow meaning or value. Using playful, multisensory, and three-dimensional approaches to unite diverse aspects of the curriculum is one way of building this bridge.

How Can I Teach My Subject Creatively?

While many guides to cultivating creative thinking and doing exist, none of them offers the 'right' or 'only' way to nurture creative learning. Furthermore, creativity by itself it is not automatically a good thing; its value depends on how and where it is used, and by whom. It is for the lecturer (and student) to decide what works best in a disciplinary context. Some attempts to stimulate creativity are "copy-this-and-make-one-yourself" approaches (home styling, crafts, the perfect Victoria sponge), which may offer a point of awakening. However deep creativity goes beyond mimicry or reproduction into generation of the unique, quirky or different. To illustrate, Storey and Ryan's ground-breaking catalytic clothing project takes jeans beyond being archetypal daywear and makes them a means of purifying the air around us.

Storey and Ryan's union of science and fashion is one example of unexpected alliances which add new dimensions to experiences and to subject knowledge. Others may be less serious, but thought-provoking nonetheless. This can be seen in the case of UK brewing company Theakstons, sponsor of a high profile crime-writers festival for over a decade. In conjunction with this, their traditional brown ale, Theakston's Old Peculier, often carries a ten-word crime story, printed on the bottles. An example is "The Case of the Killer Cliché" by Simon Beckett: " 'Good grief!' exclaimed Bertie. 'The butler really did do it!' " ("Win VIP Access," 2010). The creative challenge is the combination of minimal language form and genre, while the unexpected presence of the story offers entertainment for the drinker and raises awareness of the festival.

Breaking new ground on any scale involves investing the self, experimenting and venturing. It is uncertain and it is risky. It can become highly personal and often bound up with considerations of identity. Teaching creatively therefore has to allow for individual strengths, preferences, and interests to be developed at a suitable pace. Student learning dispositions also need to be attended to. Are they excited or fearful about this label 'creative'? Do they fear having too much freedom or too little freedom in which to explore their ideas? (Some of these fears manifest themselves as 'stuckness' in learning, and in LEGO workshops students have often constructed and narrated their sense of paralysis when they are out of ideas.) Are they fixating on 'what is allowed'? Have they permission to experiment, make something random, fail? Do they have too little confidence in their abilities or too much? Setting up an environment in which students can air such questions and work out their own answers to them is essential to creative learning.

Building a Creative Learning Culture

Fostering a creative culture involves finding out how to know, do, be and live together—the elements enshrined in the Four Pillars of Learning (Delors, 1996). This, along with motivating students and attending to individual needs, has become harder to achieve as university class sizes have risen and time and resources reduced. However, as Thomson et al. argue (2012) pedagogy is more than method, curriculum and assessment: it encompasses relationships, dialogue and learning to be in a disciplinary context. Gauntlett (2011) and Vygotsky (1978) also stress the importance of connecting and interacting with others; creative encounters provide rich terrain for this to happen.

As Claxton (2006) asserts, fostering a creative culture and habits of mind takes time and involves more than just having awaydays or stand-alone sessions. His CREATE mnemonic suggests six factors which are needed for a creative mentality to flourish. These are Curiosity, Resilience, Experimenting, Attentiveness, Thoughtfulness and Environment-setting. In addition to these, he suggests that the individual needs to take pleasure in and be willing to endure the states of frustration that accompany a creative process. Part of being creative involves helping students believe they are capable of developing these features: all are addressed within the LEGO SERIOUS PLAY case study discussed later.

Despite the distinctiveness of arts learning flagged up by Claxton, the arts are not always valued as highly in educational terms as other subjects. Robinson (2010, 2011) suggests this is because models of education in the UK have 19th-century roots and are outdated. Reading/writing, logico-deductive reasoning and mathematics are still viewed as superior to other subjects and forms of engagement. The arts, instead, are often dismissed as merely 'vocational' subjects, the poorer relative of traditional academic study, when they simply operate on a different basis of practice and enquiry.

Arnheim argues for the importance of visual thinking to be reappraised because "unless the stuff of the senses remains present the mind has nothing to think with" (1969, p. 1). Reasoning, inferring, evaluating, deducing, connecting, analyzing—all of these higher order practices need sensory involvement to complete or enrich them. This is where object-based activities such as those using LEGO come into their own. Prophetically, Arnheim also wrote: "As the ruling disciplines stress more rigorously the study of words and numbers, their kinship with the arts is increasingly obscured and the arts are reduced to a desirable supplement" (1969, p. 3). This is a situation all too readily recognized in creative circles in the UK today.

So far this chapter has considered the nature of creativity within and outside the arts, and the benefits and challenges of fostering a creative learning culture. The focus now shifts to the scientific argument for creativity, and also for play, in order to herald the LEGO case study.

Play: The Partner of Creative Learning

Perhaps the first question to ask in relation to this bold assertion is, "What do you mean, play?" Play can fall into all kinds of categories: activity free from any agenda or predetermined purpose; for relaxation and amusement; competitive or goal-oriented; bound by rules and conventions or unfettered by any. In recent years, appreciation of play as a significant means of deepening knowledge and building relationships has grown. Play has been promoted on a large and small scale, from Kane's radical manifesto for the rethinking of society as a whole (2004) through to competitions, outdoor challenges and games. Some of these—such as sheepdog handling classes to develop self-awareness and reflection (Petts, 2015)—transport participants into strange situations to find new ways of addressing familiar problems. Rafts are built in groups to navigate rivers and test teamworking; competitions modelled on the *Dragons' Den* or *The Apprentice* television shows test skills and nerve in pitching business ideas; the principles of gamification are becoming integrated into all kinds of activities, with incentives to reward persistence.

Play may involve creativity, and creativity may be playful, however they are not synonymous. Higher education is more welcoming, perhaps, of creativity than it is of play, which is often dismissed as low-level or frivolous activity. Advocates of play, however, are united in the opinion that play is not something that you grow out of after a certain age. Psychiatrist and play researcher Stuart Brown explains why it is important: "Three-dimensional play fires up the cerebellum, puts a lot of impulses into the frontal lobe—the executive portion—and helps contextual memory be developed" (2008).

When people play they are unpressured, in charge, liberated, following their hearts and interests, both escaping and re-energizing. As guest editors of *Creative Academic* magazine (2015), Chrissi Nerantzi and I wanted to see where these feelings and behaviours were at work in higher education. We had already found powerful praise for play: as the highest form of research (Einstein); as the fertilizer of the brain (Brown); as one of ten central human capabilities (Nussbaum); and in the suggestion that you can learn more in an hour of play with someone than in a year of conversation (Plato) (as cited in Nerantzi and James, 2015, p. 4). In response to our call for evidence of play in higher education, more than thirty contributors from diverse fields came forward. Each emphasized the higher order nature of play and creativity and the way they were intertwining to enrich the student's grasp of and enthusiasm for learning. Cases included the Friday experiment, or "What will happen if I do this?" (Smith); using dance and performance to teach business skills (Kiviaho-Kallio); creating games based on novels (Josephson Abrams); making and wearing masks for brainstorming (Jackson); and using Play-Doh to visualize concepts or practice (Stead, Jenkins). All enhanced student independence, motivation and engagement by

- Surprising and intriguing students;
- Relaxing and absorbing them in the activities;

- Allowing for ownership, choice and decision-making;
- Edging them away from regulation and convention ("what we have to do in this situation");
- Enhancing participation and a sense of belonging;
- Extending their belief in what is possible.

Such outcomes synthesize the features of creative learning, the need to connect and to overcome fear described thus far, and can all be found when working with LEGO.

Creative Learning and LEGO SERIOUS PLAY

The LEGO SERIOUS PLAY methodology was created in 1996 as a creative thinking process to enable companies to tackle complex issues or tired business practices. Its clients have included major corporations such as Google, eBay, NASA and the International Red Cross. The brand name LEGO is a conflation of the first two letters of each of the Danish words 'leg godt,' meaning 'play well.' The LEGO SERIOUS PLAY process has been fully described elsewhere (Gauntlett, 2007, 2011; Nolan, 2010; James and Brookfield, 2014; Kristiansen and Rasmussen, 2014; Nerantzi and Despard, 2014; James, 2015a, 2015b) and will be outlined here for brevity. To learn its methods enthusiasts can either train as accredited facilitators or use a guide (Gauntlett, 2010), available online through a 'community approach' model of access.

Through the LEGO SERIOUS PLAY process participants can investigate complex issues of any nature, shape, size or scale. These might include fleshing out top-level strategy, conducting a successful project, gathering a rich understanding of a topic, evaluating own learning, or finding out what people think (James, 2014, 2015b). While the method is playful, the intent is serious, as the name suggests. It works by taking three-dimensional toy components and using them to create symbolic, metaphorical structures which embody intangibles (thoughts, emotions, relationships) as well as more concrete elements. Nets and webs might evoke a cluttered mind or frustrated efforts, and skeletons exhaustion, fear or hidden secrets. Its applications can gently coax individuals to find points of commonality and consensus, or generate unforeseen and divergent solutions to problems (see Figure 8.2).

Frank Wilson's book, *The Hand* (2000), is dedicated to a forensic scrutiny of how the hand is at the core of all human functioning. In it he emphasizes the centrality of the hands to constructionist learning (Papert and Harel, 1991), as the nerve receptors in the fingers send electrical codes to the brain via the central nervous system. Wilson argues that we think through our fingers, through a concept he defines as 'hand knowledge,' and that these digits send messages to our brain rather than simply waiting for the brain to tell the hand what to do. LEGO SERIOUS PLAY (in keeping with other playful and creative methods) is constructionist in ethos and nature. Through the method, students learn by

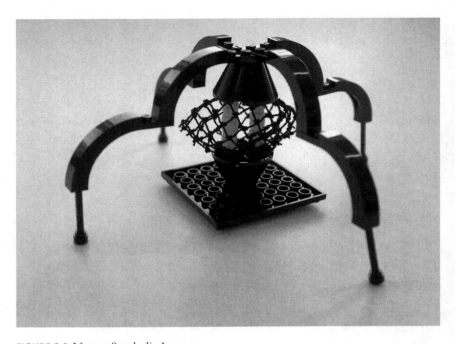

FIGURE 8.2 Nets as Symbolic Imagery

Source: By kind permission of Graham Barton. All rights reserved.

doing and making, and in creating something they produce two outcomes. One is an actual item, and the other is new knowledge, relating to relationships and self-discovery as well as to the subject. Papert viewed "concrete thinking/ hands-on thinking not as a stage that children outgrow, but rather as a style of thinking that has its benefits and uses, just as logical or formal thinking has its benefits and uses" (Kristiansen and Rasmussen, 2014, p. 87). It therefore has just as much place in higher education as other modes of enquiry.

While it is predominantly used in corporate settings, LEGO SERIOUS PLAY (and variants that draw heavily on its principles) is being used effectively in higher education contexts. Participants in sessions work uniquely with the bricks, their attention undisturbed by pens, paper and digital devices, which are forbidden (the latter only permitted to photograph models). Building activities are individual and collaborative, and sharing, discussing and reflecting underpin the process. Models can be adjusted, added to and connected to others, and thus whole landscapes are created. Furthermore, these can be reconfigured to allow participants to test out the impact and consequences of factors, actions and decisions in an array of possible scenarios (see Figure 8.3).

Builders decide what their models mean, and no one has the right to interpret or impose their own view. They can, however, question, observe or comment,

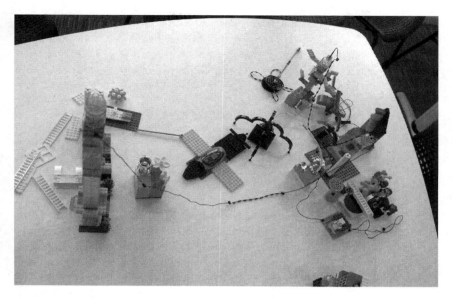

FIGURE 8.3 Landscape and Connections Between Models

in the best traditions of collaborative learning. Interactions are democratic and egalitarian, following a rule that everyone builds, everyone shares and everyone speaks. As the bricks themselves are easy to connect to each other, participants can succeed quickly; in addition, the colour, shape, and texture of the materials make symbols, elements, options and decisions visually memorable. The senses are drawn in, through touch and sight, while the memory is stimulated by the visual imagery, inventiveness and humour of individual stories and constructions.

Entering a workshop where assortments of LEGO are set out on tables and participants are invited to express themselves through such media can energize or unnerve. Students (and staff) are either intrigued by the unconventional set-up or wary of what they might be asked to do. Both of these relate to their perception of the appropriacy of play at an advanced level of study. Such assaults on their mindset create a state of alertness—taking students away from the humdrum or known and forcing them to reassess what is going on around them. Whatever their reservations, they are usually reassured by two aspects of the process. One is that they are in charge of what they construct and what it means— there is no external interpretation to be made of what they are building beyond their own. The second is that it becomes quickly apparent that while the medium may be a children's toy, the tasks are anything but childish.

> The LEGO SERIOUS PLAY session was an extremely different experience I have ever had in a workshop. The entire process and idea of the session

was so innovative that at first it sounded a little silly and I was confused by how we can learn from playing with LEGO . . . On the outside, it all looks and sounds like a random and fun session to play with LEGO but after experiencing it, one would understand how something that looks so plain and easy can actually demonstrate a whole new level of meaning.

(Student)

While playing with an array of bricks can be hugely entertaining, the conversations they provoke, not the materials, are the most important part of the process. These are triggered using questions that are likely to be highly generative and inclusive, described in workshops by master trainer Per Kristiansen as 'low threshold, high ceiling.' This means ones which everyone can answer easily but which allow for rich and deep elaborations. A question like "What affects your motivation to learn?" can evoke in response intrinsic and extrinsic factors, personal preferences, things which help or get in the way, areas for development. While building may start with one simple question, many others are then asked which can help challenge, probe and extend understanding. Although there is a structure to the workshop, participants have plenty of freedom to build as they wish. As there are no right answers, there is also scope for unpredictability, which can be both unsettling and generative.

An important difference between learning conventionally and using this three-dimensional approach lies in the means of communication. The first part of a class is dedicated to acclimatizing students to the notion of metaphorical building. If students played with LEGO when they were little, their creations were most probably literal: a house was a dwelling, a dog was a pet, a train was a form of transport. With LEGO SERIOUS PLAY the accent is on the symbolic meaning (not the surface meaning), informed by the work on metaphor by Lakoff and Johnson (1980). Instead, a house might embody security; a dog a threat or devotion; a train a journey, the speed of progress or an unstoppable person—the only limit being the person's imagination and ability to make associations through, and with, the model.

Various examples illustrate this: threshold concepts to do with ergonomics have been expressed in the shape of a shark, symbolizing a flawlessly designed creature; staff and student feelings at the end of the academic year have been evoked through dangling white skeletons. The vagaries of project management have been represented as flailing monkeys (Nolan, 2010), while the student-tutor relationship in Figure 8.4 was notably captured as a zookeeper riding a tiger cub—with much debate as to who was who. The student was, in fact, the tiger—grateful for guidance but feeling weighed down nonetheless by pressure and expectation emanating from what they thought their tutor wanted. The green plants are the student's sense of imagination and potential, and the subtly hidden black chain lying among them the feeling of being pinned down and held back. The face of the tiger cub says it all.

FIGURE 8.4 Student Model of Their Relationship With Their Tutor

Source: By kind permission of Graham Barton. All rights reserved.

These examples give a tiny flavour of the extent to which the means of expression is playful, symbolic and memorable. The next student story takes a familiar metaphor which, in straightforward creative terms, might be dismissed as a cliché. The originality of the metaphor is not of prime importance, rather it is about the student finding the most powerful visual symbol to voice how they have viewed an action, decision, event or other.

> I made a structure with two tiers; the bottom is a zigzag path that represents the path of my life, which is not straightforward and a future that is unpredictable. Constructed with curved pieces joined together, the top represents the winding journey of getting through the obstacles in my life. The metaphor for my structure is that my road towards success is narrow, complicated and unexpected. The height between the two tiers symbolizes the fact that failure is a long way down and the struggle to keep staying up is the essence.
>
> *(Student)*

Exercises loosen up students' thinking to enable them to come up with many more possibilities than the immediate or obvious and have transferable value. These might involve passing an abstract brick, animal, or colour around a group to generate the maximum possible number of associations that could be linked

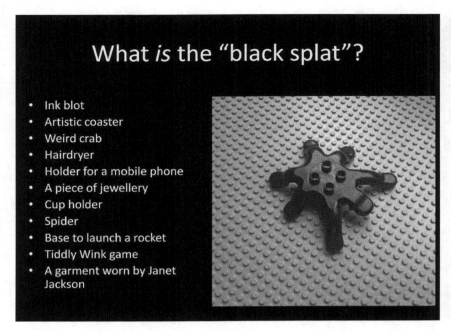

What *is* the "black splat"?

- Ink blot
- Artistic coaster
- Weird crab
- Hairdryer
- Holder for a mobile phone
- A piece of jewellery
- Cup holder
- Spider
- Base to launch a rocket
- Tiddly Wink game
- A garment worn by Janet Jackson

FIGURE 8.5 Diverse Interpretations of "the Black Splat"

to it. Figure 8.5 illustrates a few of the meanings ascribed to the 'black splat' (actually a Duplo ladybird base), used as an abstract trigger for associations during warm-up activities. Insisting that the LEGO piece is passed around the group numerous times is a simple but effective means of moving students away from sharing easy, surface allusions that spring to mind; waiting patiently for participants to dig deeper into the well of their associations means they come up with more thoughtful and unusual contributions than the first ones.

As noted earlier, Wilson's notion of hand knowledge is fundamental to LEGO SERIOUS PLAY; this is because rummaging and sifting through the bricks stimulates the sending of messages to the brain via nerve endings in the fingers. This partly explains why participants often say that they are surprised by what they have built, as they have not planned it out first in their head. In addition, mood, the appeal of the materials, and what is on their mind, will affect what students construct in response to a question, and will vary from day to day. These factors, on top of the method and focus, mean that working with bricks is something that they can do regularly as part of their learning repertoire, not just as a one-off experience or light relief from 'proper' study.

LEGO SERIOUS PLAY can be used to address any question to which the answers are not obvious, or may be many. A purist LEGO SERIOUS PLAY approach will limit workshop numbers to ten to twelve people and typically lasts a day, which feels like something of a luxury in most UK universities. In my own teaching and staff development, the majority of my sessions last between two and four hours, although some of the most valuable insights occur the longer and deeper participants explore. Gauntlett (2008) led the way in using these techniques in large lecture activities, building models of learning with 160 students. This can work well, although the outcome and the depth of enquiry may vary from the more intimate groups. It can also be useful to have additional helpers to support the work, roaming the room and asking questions of their own. Figure 8.6 shows some of the contexts in which the methods have been used (see also James, 2013; James and Brookfield, 2014; James, 2015b).

Here are five examples which illustrate this further:

1. In personal and professional development workshops students reflect on their learning throughout the year, building their strengths, weaknesses, attributes, realizations, areas for development and next steps. They note each others' development needs and build for a partner.
2. As part of a PhD induction programme (Barton and James, in press). Students build models embodying how they feel about embarking on their PhD, what they want their research to look like and achieve, and what their fears and expectations are around the experience.
3. In short courses running before the start of the university year to enable new students to make the transition to undergraduate study. Some may be the first in their families to go to university and are unfamiliar with and unconfident about what it involves. The process can help allay any fears and encourage them to identify what they are bringing to the experience.
4. Students use LEGO SERIOUS PLAY to monitor the design and completion of a consultancy project working for an external client: considering feasibility, relationships, factors affecting progress, and how to ensure success.

Author uses of LEGO SERIOUS PLAY in HE

- To explore identity – of a team, a role, an individual
- For student reflection
- To think about 'big topics': student engagement, sustainability, threshold concepts, aspects of the disciplines, research ideas
- For evaluation and monitoring, e.g. of academic or departmental progress and planning, annual course review

- To build community, capture all voices and share ideas
- To establish trust & connections between people
- As part of academic support, sharing ways of tackling difficulties and motivating learning
- For professional development outside the university/abroad

FIGURE 8.6 Themes and Contexts of LEGO SERIOUS PLAY Use in Higher Education

5. In workshops (Barton and James, in press) on 'stuckness,' students from all levels of study explore the internal and external blocks to their learning. They also build solutions for each other's problems.

> The LEGO session was surprisingly very beneficial to me. I went in not knowing what to expect and came out having a different perspective. Although it was only the beginning of the project I was overwhelmed with the quantity of work expected and so found myself in a rut. This session taught me how to approach the project from multiple different perspectives and helped to reignite my passion for my theme.
>
> *(Student)*

How LEGO SERIOUS PLAY Supports Creative Learning

Zepke and Leach (2010) outline ten proposals for enhancing student engagement: nearly all ten are at work in this process, while the first five are of particular relevance. These are to:

1. Enhance students' self-belief
2. Enable students to work autonomously, enjoy learning relationships with others and feel they are competent to achieve their own objectives
3. Recognize that teaching and teachers are central to engagement
4. Create learning that is active, collaborative and fosters learning relationships
5. Create educational experiences for students that are challenging, enriching and extend their academic abilities.

(Zepke and Leach, 2010, p. 169)

Proposals 1, 2, 4 and 5 are all made visible in the examples of creative learning offered in this chapter, while the importance of proposal 3 and the teacher's capabilities in orchestrating creative experiences cannot be understated. This is not to say that students have no role to play in co-constructing them, or even setting up their own, however teachers need to model the practices and lead the way.

The benefits of three-dimensional, playful approaches can be mapped out against the CREATE framework referred to earlier which Claxton (2006) offers as a means of developing creativity in education:

Curiosity: Students need to formulate their own questions as part of developing their own creativity. The whole LEGO SERIOUS PLAY process is predicated on formulating good questions and its materials and techniques very different from traditional university approaches. Models are often surprising to the person who has built them, but also to their fellow participants in terms of the ideas visualized.

Resilience: Being creative is neither easy nor always enjoyable. Building what you believe about a difficult or complex subject in LEGO is not easy either, but time is allowed for participants to realize that valuable insights can result from persisting.

Experimenting: New materials and metaphorical expression engender fresh perspectives and unlock intuition, insight and solutions: "You can do so much with just a handful of bricks" (Student).

Attentiveness: The quality of student attentiveness, supported by a ban on electronic devices and the need to be fully 'present' is noticeably higher than in other forms of tuition. A student with attention deficit disorder remarked that if she had been in a seminar with PowerPoint she would have been "crawling the walls," but "when my fingers are busy I'm golden," thus emphasizing the power of the hands-on and the three-dimensional for capturing student focus.

Thoughtfulness: This involves all kinds of thinking, concentration, flow and focus, and has to do with developing 'mental suppleness' (Claxton, 2006, para. 18). Thoughtfulness is particularly noticeable in the ways students attend to others' stories: "My classmate constructed a little LEGO jetpack that symbolizes the help and support that will guide me through my journey and not to be afraid of failure" (Student).

Environment-setting: The process can be conducted anywhere there is room to build (preferably on big tables or a shared surface, including the floor) and space, height and distance can all be invoked. The freedom to use physical space and have plenty of bricks to stir the imagination is a distinctive departure from traditional modes of learning and is central to the generation of rich ideas.

An element of surprise plays a major part in the CREATE framework—not least in terms of curiosity, motivation, and engagement as it keeps students interested and focused. It also helps build understanding, bond connections and enable participants to reassess impressions or assumptions: "I was pleasantly surprised how Legos [*sic*] could represent people's accomplishments, strengths and weaknesses" (Student).

In addition to the features of CREATE, the following remarks have been made by staff and students:

- The techniques are simple to acquire and inclusive, and there is no right or wrong way to build, which builds capability and self-belief: "I left [the workshop] with optimism and I gained skills that made me communicate confidently" (Student).

- Once the principles have been acquired, students can apply them to their own contexts and interests, such as research and consultancy projects (or, in my case, writing a book, as illustrated on the Engaging Imagination website).
- The process is founded on the premise that the answers lie within the system, therefore students have the power to solve their own issues and plot fresh courses of action.
- As the participants decide what their model stands for, this helps with trust, ownership and agency. Having their stories heard, models and ideas admired, and solutions accepted enables participants to realize the value of their own contributions.
- Building together boosts participation, peer assistance, and collaboration; supporting each other through enquiring, not telling or critiquing. People get to know each other quickly, connect through the sharing of models and through building for each other: "It helped me build a closer bond with my classmates and so it helped me feel I wasn't the only one [to] struggle with the project" (Student).
- The process fosters three kinds of thinking: creative (how to embody thinking in a physical form), reflective (the extent to which activities so far have been successful/need work/need rebalancing) and critical (hunting down and challenging assumptions, deepening analysis of issues and drilling into specifics).
- It underlines the importance of process, not just product, in powerful ways. In many other forms of teaching students are expected to show their workings, explain a method, or justify conclusions; here those processes become three-dimensional. As part of critical reflection on own learning this is often an essential step in moving students away from dull diarizing to effective analysis of progress.
- The point of building is not to make a visually pleasing model (though this often happens), but to articulate and clarify thoughts which are important to the builder. As it is not possible to walk in after a workshop and instantly know what a model might stand for, it emphasizes the importance of full participation and contribution in learning.

Conclusions

This chapter has sought to do three things: explore the complex nature of creativity and its relevance to arts, and non-arts, education; examine and make explicit the pedagogic and scientific foundation for creative approaches to learning, in particular those adopting three-dimensional techniques; and issue a small, heartfelt battle cry for the value of creative arts learning. These three objectives have been discussed separately and brought together within the LEGO SERIOUS PLAY case study. In collating diverse positions on creativity these are seen to house and express higher order thinking in new and surprising forms. The chapter has also emphasized that interpretations of creativity are not limited to the production of artefacts or items, but also cover the conceptual, abstract and cerebral. Hand in hand with this is the understanding that the cerebral, conjured in terms such as academic, intellectual and cognitive, is not purely evoked through text or traditional modes of learning but through non-textual forms. Playful, three-dimensional practices bring to life key theoretical and practical aspects of learning a subject and can help bridge gaps between the two.

Moreover, creativity is seen as playing a fundamental role in generating and maintaining a rich learning culture. This is partly possible because the creative learning approaches discussed allow students to have some ownership and control of the processes and outcomes; there is room for choice and subjective engagement without having to be right or wrong. Such activities are highly inclusive, allowing voices from all cultures and backgrounds and maximizing engagement by students with diverse histories and learning preferences. They also serve to democratize learning encounters in that all voices are equal in a LEGO SERIOUS PLAY workshop. They can also bring learners together.

Furthermore, allowing students to play and be creative as part of their decision-making can boost motivation, confidence and autonomy. Overcoming any sense of block, burden or incapacity is essential to fostering the creative capability of an individual in any subject. Such personally defined and expressed creativity allows for engagement which enables students to make choices and decisions that stretch and challenge them. This is a multilayered endeavour, involving skill acquisition, metacognitive development, knowledge expansion, culture generation and identity work. The interpretation of objects, or creation of models, make possible the physical embodiment of ideas, which brings new perspectives to discussion. This has been demonstrated most specifically in the profile of LEGO SERIOUS PLAY. The often witty, imaginative and surprising character and appearance of models enables understanding of and strengthens connections between those building. The way that visual and kinaesthetic dimensions enrich understanding and make learning memorable has been emphasized through the consideration of neuroscience and constructionism.

The approaches discussed can be applied to the consideration of any complex issue to which there is no straightforward answer. They are already being used to challenge ways of conceiving of intelligence and attainment and beliefs about what constitute appropriate modes of learning at university. Going forward, perhaps they should be applied to addressing emerging and existential questions about the purpose and nature of higher education today.

Note

1. LEGO® and LEGO SERIOUS PLAY® are trademarks and/or copyrights of the LEGO Group. The author has no commercial affiliation with either LEGO® or LEGO SERIOUS PLAY®.

Bibliography

Arnheim, R. (1969) *Visual thinking.* Berkeley and Los Angeles, CA: University of California Press.

Barnett, R. (2015, April) *Believing in the University.* Paper presented at the PedRIO Conference, University of Plymouth, England.

Barton, G., and James, A. (in press) Threshold Concepts, LEGO® SERIOUS PLAY® and systems thinking: towards a combined methodology. *Practice and Evidence of the Scholarship of Teaching and Learning in HE.*

Bellis, M. (n.d.) *Post it note.* Retrieved from http://inventors.about.com/od/pstartinventions/a/post_it_note.htm

Brown, S. (2008) *Play is more than just fun.* Retrieved from https://www.ted.com/talks/stuart_brown_says_play_is_more_than_fun_it_s_vital?language=en

Claxton, G. (2006) Cultivating creative mentalities: a framework for education. *Thinking Skills & Creativity,* 1, 57–61. Retrieved from https://www.researchgate.net/profile/Guy_Claxton/publication/222545047_Cultivating_creative_mentalities_A_framework_for_education/links/0046352b80ddae3710000000.pdf

Csikszentmihalyi, M. (1998) *Finding flow: the psychology of engagement with everyday life.* New York: HarperCollins.

de Bono, E. Personal website of Edward de Bono. http://www.edwdebono.com

Delors, J. (1996) *Learning: the treasure within.* Report to UNESCO by the International Commission on Education for the 21st Century. Paris, France: UNESCO.

Engeström, Y. (1999) Activity theory and individual and social transformation. In Y. Engeström, R. Miettinen & R.-L. Punamäki (Eds.), *Perspectives on activity theory* (pp. 1–16). Cambridge: Cambridge University Press.

Gauntlett, D. (2007) *Creative explorations: new approaches to identities and audiences.* London and New York: Routledge.

Gauntlett, D. (2008) *Building models of learning in LEGO.* [YouTube video]. Retrieved from Cambridge University Press: https://www.youtube.com/watch?v=3bVox3Yp-cQ

Gauntlett, D. (2010) *Open-source introduction to LEGO® SERIOUS PLAY®.* Retrieved from http://davidgauntlett.com/wp-content/uploads/2013/04/LEGO_SERIOUS_PLAY_OpenSource_14mb.pdf

Gauntlett, D. (2011) *Making is connecting: the social meaning of creativity, from DIY and knitting to YouTube and Web 2.0.* Cambridge: Polity.

Jackson, N. (2015) Do most attempts to teach for creativity involve some form of play? In C. Nerantzi & A. James (Eds.), Exploring Play in Higher Education, *Creative Academic Magazine,* 2B, 42–45. Retrieved from http://www.creativeacademic.uk/

James, A. (2013) Lego Serious Play: a three-dimensional approach to learning development. *Journal for Learning Development in Higher Education,* 6. Retrieved from http://www.aldinhe.ac.uk/ojs/index.php?journal=jldhe&page=article&op=view&path%5B%5D=208

James, A. (2014) Learning in three dimensions: using Lego Serious Play for creative and critical reflection across time and space. In P. Layne & P. Lake (Eds.), *Global innovation of teaching and learning in higher education: transgressing boundaries* (pp. 275–294). London: Springer. http://dx.doi.org/10.1007/978-3-319-10482-9

James, A. (2015a) Developing leadership through play. *Developing Leaders Quarterly,* 19, IEDP. Retrieved from http://www.iedp.com/magazine/2015issue19/index.html#22

James, A. (2015b) *Innovating in the creative arts with LEGO.* Innovative Pedagogical Practices Report for the Higher Education Academy, England. Retrieved from https://www.heacademy.ac.uk/innovating-creative-arts-lego

James, A., and Brookfield, S. (2013) The Serious use of Play and metaphor. *International Journal of Adult and Vocational Education and Technology*, 4, 3. ISSN: 1947–8607.

James, A., and Brookfield, S. (2014) *Engaging imagination: helping students become creative and reflective thinkers.* San Francisco: Jossey-Bass. Website http://www.engagingimagination. com

Jeffrey, B., and Craft, A. (2004) Teaching creatively and teaching for creativity: distinctions and relationships. *Educational Studies*, 30, 1, 77–87. Available from http://oro. open.ac.uk/425/2/CT-TFC-Final-Ed_Studies.pdf

Jenkins, E. (2015) Playdoh fashion. In C. Nerantzi & A. James (Eds.), Exploring Play in Higher Education, *Creative Academic Magazine*, 2A, 30. Retrieved from http://www. creativeacademic.uk/

Josephson Abrams, D. (2015) Play: much more than purposeless activity. In C. Nerantzi & A. James (Eds.), Exploring Play in Higher Education, *Creative Academic Magazine*, 2A, 24–25. Retrieved from http://www.creativeacademic.uk/

Kane, P. (2004) *The Play ethic: a manifesto for a different way of living.* New York: Macmillan.

Kavanagh, D. (2012) The university as fool. In R. Barnett (Ed.), *The future university: ideas and possibilities* (pp. 101–111). New York: Routledge.

Kiviaho-Kallio, P. (2015) Beam me up for business: Porvoo campus playground. In C. Nerantzi & A. James (Eds.), Exploring Play in Higher Education, *Creative Academic Magazine*, 2A, 17–18. Retrieved from http://www.creativeacademic.uk/

Kristiansen, P., and Rasmussen, R. (2014) *Build a better business with the Lego Serious Play Method.* New Jersey: Wiley.

Lakoff, G., and Johnson, M. (1980) *Metaphors we live by.* Chicago: University of Chicago Press.

Nerantzi, C., and Despard, C. (2014) Do LEGO® models aid reflection in learning and teaching practice? *Journal of Perspectives in Applied Academic Practice*, 2, 2, 31–36.

Nerantzi, C., and James, A. (2015) A waterfall of questions or can we afford not to play in HE? In C. Nerantzi & A. James (Eds.), Exploring Play in Higher Education, *Creative Academic Magazine*, 2A, 4–5. Retrieved from http://www.creativeacademic.uk/

Nolan, S. (2010) Physical metaphorical modeling with Lego as a technology for collaborative personalised learning. In J. O'Donohue (Ed.), *Technology supported environments for personalised learning: methods and case studies* (pp. 101–111). Hershey, PA: IGI Global.

Papert, S., and Harel, I. (1991) *Situating constructionism.* First published in Papert, S. and Harel, I. (1991) *Constructionism.* Norwood, NJ: Ablex. Retrieved from http://www. papert.org/articles/SituatingConstructionism.html

Petts, A. (2015) Working like a dog. In C. Nerantzi & A. James (Eds.), Exploring Play in Higher Education, *Creative Academic Magazine*, 2A, 10. Retrieved from http://www. creativeacademic.uk/

Prown, J. (1982) Mind in matter: an introduction to material culture and method. *Winterthur Portfolio*, 17, 1, 1–19. University of Chicago Press.

Robinson, K. (2010) *Changing education paradigms.* [RSA Animate video on YouTube] Retrieved from https://www.youtube.com/watch?v=zDZFcDGpL4U

Robinson, K. (2011) *Out of our minds: learning to be creative.* Chichester, UK: Capstone.

Scheiber, P. (1987) The wit and wisdom of Grace Hopper. *The OCLC Newsletter*, March/April, 1987, No. 16. Retrieved from http://www.cs.yale.edu/homes/tap/Files/hopper-wit.html

Sellers, J. (2013) Quiet time, quiet space: a labyrinth for your university or college. In R. Sewell, J. Sellers & D. Williams (Eds.), *Working with labyrinths: paths for exploration* (pp. 41–54). Iona, UK: Wild Goose.

Smith, D. (2015) Play: the path to discovery. In C. Nerantzi & A. James (Eds.), Exploring Play in Higher Education, *Creative Academic Magazine*, 2A, 13–14. Retrieved from http://www.creativeacademic.uk/

Stead, R. (2015) Trivial pursuits in Playdoh? Perhaps not! In C. Nerantzi & A. James (Eds.), Exploring Play in Higher Education, *Creative Academic Magazine*, 2B, 38–41. Retrieved from http://www.creativeacademic.uk/

Storey, H., and Ryan, T. *The Catalytic Clothing Project*. Retrieved from http://www.catalytic-clothing.org/home.html

Thomson, P., Hall, C., Jones, K., and Sefton-Green, J. (2012) *The Signature Pedagogies Project: final report*. Newcastle: Creativity, Culture and Education.

Vygotsky, L. S. (1978) *Mind in society: the development of higher psychological processes*. In M. Cole, V. John-Steiner, S. Scribner & E. Souberman (Eds.), (A. R. Luria, M. Lopez-Morillas & M. Cole [with J. V. Wertsch], Trans.). Cambridge, MA: Harvard University Press. (Original manuscripts [ca. 1930–1934]).

Williams, R. (2014) *Keywords* (4th ed.). London: Fourth Estate.

Wilson, F. (2000) *The hand*. New York: Vintage.

"Win VIP Access to Theakstons Old Peculier Crime-Writing Festival." (2010, February 18) *The Guardian*. Retrieved from http://www.theguardian.com/books/competition/2010/feb/18/theakstons-old-peculier-crime-competition

Zepke, N., and Leach, L. (2010) Improving student engagement: ten proposals for action. *Active Learning in Higher Education*, 11, 3, 167–177. http://dx.doi.org/10.1177/1469787410379680

9

THE DYNAMICS OF CREATIVE LEARNING

A Case Study in Best Practices in Public Urban Higher Education

Gina Rae Foster

The STAR Model and Resiliency Principles

The current receptivity to interdisciplinary teaching and learning in higher education has sparked the design of multiple innovative models of creativity as applied to learning. Creativity, the highest level of the Revised Bloom's Taxonomy, might also be considered through cognitive scientist Daniel T. Willingham's definition of thinking as "problem-solving" (2009) in a context of appropriate challenge (Willingham states that humans think or problem-solve most effectively when problems are neither too difficult nor too simple for the thinker to address). This chapter will present a case study of the STAR Model (Foster, 2008) and Resiliency Principles (Foster, 2009), which I have developed in a public urban university in New York City to address the difficulties "unprepared" as well as "exceptional" students face in problem-solving across disciplines and cultural contexts.

The STAR Model and Resiliency Principles emerged from research and practice in international trauma and resiliency theory, project management principles, facilitation practices, ontological ethics, and constructivist pedagogy and have developed further with contributions from cognitive science learning research and social media. The STAR Model offers students and faculty the opportunity to consider and construct creative solutions to problems through various combinations of the dynamics of goals, time, communication, processes, and resources, each of which may be interpreted differently depending on disciplinary and cultural norms. For example, time and goals may vary widely between cultures that value punctuality as part of achieving goals within a set beginning and ending period, and cultures that value group participation and shared communication occurring to the satisfaction of all or most team members.

The Resiliency Principles (stability, capacity, flexibility, and community) extend creative learning to considering the larger social context in which problems occur, heightening the levels of critical thinking for more advanced learners. Both models have been developed and tested primarily in hard science and business courses (biology, chemistry, mathematics, physics, psychology, and accounting) with undergraduates and have also been introduced to faculty teaching college and master's level courses in English composition and literature, health sciences, nursing, social work, and theatre. The STAR Model has been recognized as a "best practice" by the US Department of Education and has gained international attention in conference presentations and trainings. The following case study describes the effects of these models on the creative learning of the student support service providers, who exhibited increased capacities for problem-solving similar to and at times greater than observed in the students they assisted. It was hoped that the design of allowing peer leaders to become assistant supervisors and then assistant coordinators would develop a sustainable program over time; however, the continuing economic crisis in higher education, particularly public urban higher education, proved stronger than internal efforts toward stability.

Creative Problem-Solving

Problem-solving within a discipline requires an understanding of that discipline's traditional and non-traditional approaches to resolving questions. This understanding must be paralleled by extensive practice in disciplinary problem-solving, including multiple opportunities to fail so as to deepen comprehension about what does and does not function well for different processes (Willingham, 2009). The combination of content and skills connected to extended practice would seem, on the surface, to be delivered fairly easily through lectures and demonstrations that students could mimic in their development of mastery.

However, student success data and the personal professional experiences of many educators indicate this is not the case. Students do not automatically understand problem-solving directions or modeling (Willingham, 2009). Information literacy in terms of being able to read a question and identify its intent and appropriate scope of response seems to be poorly represented across institutions of higher education (Kolowich, 2011). The ability to separate content and skills and then recombine these in meaningful and productive ways also seems lacking for many students (Ambrose et al., 2010; Walsh & Sattes, 2011). To ask learners to transfer problem-solving skills across disciplines seems unrealistic if not inappropriate.

This suggests that problem-solving skills are difficult both to teach and to learn. These difficulties are not limited to STEM disciplines but can be observed across the social sciences, arts, and humanities, within and between fields of study. As Daniel T. Willingham (2009) notes, "People are naturally curious, but we are not naturally good thinkers; unless the cognitive conditions are right, we will avoid thinking" (p. 3). He equates thinking with problem-solving rather than with conscious perception or reflection. For cognitive conditions to be right, Willingham explains, the problems to be resolved must be neither too difficult nor too easy for the thinker. This means that an appropriate level of challenge must be offered in order for effective problem-solving to take place (2009). This is in line with Lev Vygotsky's "zone of proximal development," in which learning occurs when and where the learner is located near his or her limits of being able to learn unassisted (McLeod, 2012).

In public urban colleges and universities, how to teach problem-solving is an increasingly urgent question, as many students enter these institutions underprepared in terms of literacy, numeracy, and basic reasoning skills. Problemsolving, as noted earlier, is an activity often avoided due to the existence of inappropriate cognitive conditions, and such conditions are prevalent for students who have little experience in creating and maintaining their own optimal learning environments. Diversity in cultural assumptions, economic status, and family educational history further complicates efforts to teach problem-solving as expectations for both process and result—expectations that may differ widely from those of the institute providing the educational opportunities. Additionally, government mandates for improved assessment and evidence of improved academic success firmly attached to the availability of federal funding place stress on educators to produce effective problem-solvers without necessarily addressing the gaps in preparation and expectation experienced by students. Ideal learning environments include attention to prior knowledge and misconceptions as well as course climate and knowledge organization—a combination of factors difficult to provide when set learning objectives may be beyond the current capacities of many students in a class. If the convergence of so many challenges that seem inappropriate to the perfect cognitive conditions for thinking lies here, then creative learning in terms of creative approaches to problem-solving and to teaching problem-solving may be one place of productive response.

For students and faculty already entangled in personally and sociopolitically traumatizing environments, the addition of shared learning can deeply challenge resilient responses to change factors regardless of commitments and intentions. The problem then set before higher education is one of supporting resiliency both inside and outside the classroom/website so that each can better inform and develop the other in ways that support lifelong learning and social justice. The alternative is to continue to view students as underprepared and faculty as overworked, both located in a context that is poorly resourced and structured. This alternative provides little promise for positive change and supports a culture of both student and instructor burnout.

At Lehman College/CUNY, a public urban college in the Bronx, New York, William Bosworth reports that the student population is one of the most diverse and most traumatized of any population in the country (http://www.lehman.

edu/deannss/bronxdatactr/discover/bxtext.htm). Students who attend Lehman rely largely on financial aid and balancing work, family, and studies in hopes of achieving their long-term professional goals and, in many cases, improving their economic status. Unfortunately, the uneven academic preparation many of these students experience in their secondary schools leads to high failure rates in the prerequisite courses for pre-professional major courses necessary to pursue such fields as business, nursing, and medicine. Additional factors in student success that weigh heavily in an public urban higher education context are student motivation and course climate, as Ambrose et al. (2010) emphasize: a lack of belief in one's own capacity for achievement, reinforced by overt and covert messages from instructors and peers, is linked to high failure rates and lack of persistence.

This combination of under-preparedness with economic and human rights challenges is not unique to Lehman; many of our national colleges and universities share similar concerns with their students. Various approaches to student academic support have been the source of interventions and research studies: at Lehman, these interventions included the establishment of a Supplemental Instruction program supported by a Title V Department of Education grant. Title V grants are federal grants designed to support sustainable improvements at Hispanic-serving institutions (HSIs) of higher education. The program was introduced in 2007; limitations were identified in this intervention, however, and a revised model was developed and implemented over subsequent years.

The STAR Model

The STAR Model (Figure 9.1) and Resiliency Principles (Figure 9.2) developed out of and in response to gaps in traditional Supplemental Instruction (SI) that I noticed both during the University of Missouri at Kansas City (UMKC) Supplemental Instruction trainings and over time in conducting Lehman's SI Program, specifically:

1. A lack of development of means for training peer coaches in emphasizing facilitative approaches versus those of traditional lecturers;
2. A lack of active supervision, mentoring, and professional development of individual SI Leaders (peer coaches offering SI-focused review sessions to fellow students);
3. A lack of attention to learning objectives and self-assessment in planning tools;
4. A lack of discussion of time management and resource identification and development related to SI Leader responsibilities.

Other programs with UMKC-based SI services may have addressed one or more of these in their own development: at Lehman, all four of these gaps catalyzed a transformation from peer academic support closely linked to tutoring to peer academic support closely linked to resiliency.

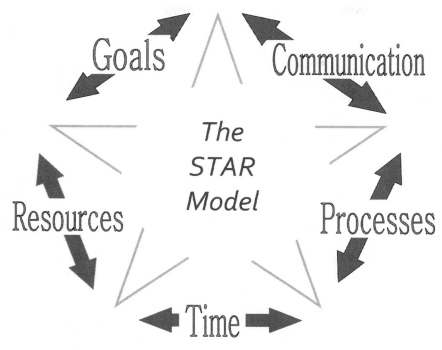

FIGURE 9.1 The STAR Model

Source: Foster (2008).

Regarding the first gap, in addition to the pedagogical theory and study strategies offered during the two UMKC trainings I noted multiple references to facilitation as a peer coaching skill. However, facilitation theory and practice were not actually developed in training SI Supervisors or SI Leaders or emphasized in communication and process assessment.

Another gap noted was that of active supervision, mentoring, and professional development. Again, these were cited in the UMKC training as positive and frequent outcomes of SI programs and were not included in examples or lists of expectations for SI Supervisors. This seemed to miss the importance of connecting professional development to service: if the work did not challenge its providers to learn and expand themselves, the energy brought to the work would dwindle, and the vision guiding the work would often be lost.

After the first year of managing the Title V SI Program, it was clear that SI Leaders were capable of taking appropriate class notes and identifying the main points of lectures, but were not necessarily aware of an instructor's learning objectives and able to convey these in their sessions. The SI Leaders also demonstrated a tendency to avoid self-reflection and self-assessment of their review session planning and implementation.

Time management, along with resource identification and development, are common gaps in many offices and businesses. In the early years of the Title V SI Program, the supervisors of SI Leaders in our program had difficulty keeping their supervisees (and themselves) on task and predicting what would be needed in completing their own projects. Clearly, a change in training focus and mission focus was needed.

Each of these four areas pointed to deficits in problem-solving and provided opportunities for interventions. In terms of the first gap, in pedagogical theory and strategies, an understanding of the SI Leaders themselves proved essential. Our first set of students-as-leaders-as-students included two graduate students, three advanced undergraduate students, and one sophomore, all preparing to offer support for students taking college algebra. Except for the sophomore student, the group shared an understanding and practice of mathematics far advanced from even intermediate studies: they studied number theory, linear algebra, and probability. Several had forgotten the rudimentary steps to solve introductory algebra problems, and we noted that arithmetical skills were at times less than perfect. These were A students recommended by mathematics faculty: the perception that these students would be excellent peer instructors underlined the misperception that expertise is linked to an automatic ability to convey information and assist learners in their first problem-solving and concept-attaching steps.

One of my first approaches to breaking down this misperception was to introduce the apparent dichotomy between teaching and facilitation. Traditional teaching is an approach that SI and constructivist theories define as lecturing rather than discussing the information to be learned. In traditional teaching, knowledge is transmitted from the expert lecturer to the novice listener, who takes notes and relies on memory rather than practice to retain and reproduce the information presented. Facilitation, in contrast, prioritizes group discussion, group consensus, and the effacement of the facilitator as leader. The facilitator guides and supports rather than instructs and disciplines. Although there may be times to indicate the accuracy of one answer or approach over another to the group or a group member, in general a facilitator works to encourage the group to find and verify problem solutions and strategies so that they can integrate the gained knowledge as part of their own practice.

Two non-pedagogical sources further extended understandings of effective practice. Gary Klein's (1999) *Sources of Power: How People Make Decisions*, describes instinctive problem-solving; Malcolm Gladwell's *Outliers: The Story of Success* (2008) argues that high-stakes decisions tend to be made based on experience, and that experience must be repetitive rather than singular. Learning, as evidenced by decisions that demonstrate an integration of skills, content, and choice, emerges from practice. That practice must be so engrained as to have automated much of its iteration so that the skill or content that forms the current decision is part of chunked memory rather than conscious, isolated information (Willingham, 2009).

Thus, creating a model that could then be iterated to the point of automating certain types of decision-making became one objective in creative learning and program quality control. The repeated issues with time management, goal-setting, and resource engagement at all levels of staffing, in combination with varying competencies with communication and process skills, seemed to address our project management and professional development limitations and offer a concrete set of practices around which to focus trainings, supervision, and assessment. I termed these five areas "dynamics" to underline the mobility and activity inherent in each, and challenged our team to investigate the different ways in which each dynamic might be understood on its own and in partnership with the others: goals, communication, process, time, and resources.

The STAR dynamics then created a context to address the second gap, the need for more active supervision, mentoring, and professional development. From the beginning of the Title V SI/STAR Mentoring & Coaching Program, the focus was to keep the SI Leaders and STAR Coaches as well as their supervisors and mentors, self-identified as students rather than instructors. Leading group review sessions for introductory courses requires an ability to communicate with students at that introductory level, which is difficult for knowledge experts and particularly difficult for those with intermediate knowledge mastery (Ambrose et al., 2010; Willingham, 2009). The SI Leaders and STAR Coaches were meant to be "peer" leaders and guides with these introductory translation-of-knowledge capacities; in fact, these student and recent graduate employees possessed levels of expertise in the content and skills knowledge of the courses targeted for academic support that placed these leaders and coaches in non-peer identities and roles. As intermediate learners, their internal senses of their own abilities tended to translate into knowledge transmission rather than novice learner knowledge transformation. This misalignment needed to be addressed if peer (or near-peer) learning was to take place. Drawing from personal teaching experience and observations as well as research into liberatory teaching practices, I formed the base assumption that maintaining the "freshness" of the learning experience would translate into increased empathy for the students ultimately being served, and increased skills in identifying and implementing appropriate learning strategies in review sessions.

In response to the third gap, self-reflection and self-assessment, the UMKC SI review session planning tool was redesigned to include identification of learning objectives and to provide summary opportunities for self-assessment in terms of facilitation skills and study strategies used as well as successes, failures, and unanticipated occurrences during the sessions. SI Assistant Supervisors then used this planning and summary form in the weekly supervision meetings to improve job performance and increase self-assessment skills. Self-assessment surveys were given to both SI Assistant Supervisors and SI Leaders each term; these were discussed during professional review meetings for those employees who wished to return to work for the program. Professional reviews provided opportunities to reflect on problem-solving capacities and how these had or had not developed over the previous term.

In the sixth year of the program, which was now called the STAR Mentoring & Coaching Program, the Acting STAR Coordinator and an Associate STAR Mentor developed an observation tool with Likert scales to reflect observers' impressions of STAR Coaches' (formerly SI Leaders') abilities to demonstrate the skills emphasized in formal trainings. The RSORS (Review Session Observation Rating Scale) and a companion self-rating tool became standard assessment and self-assessment activities for the remaining two and a half years of the program (Schmalstig & Peart, 2013).

Finally, I addressed the fourth gap, time management and resource development, with the introduction and development of the STAR Model. In developing the STAR Model as a visual model and also interactive set of problem-solving practices, I drew partially from Roger Schwarz's Group Effectiveness Model (2002), which contains three areas: group structure, group process, and group context. Past research and fieldwork in trauma studies, project management, and pedagogy extended and enriched the model for use in a public urban higher education context. According to the 2014 Center for Collegiate Mental Health Report (2014), students in public urban universities typically self-report high levels of trauma and stress in their personal lives, the effects of which can be seen in students' struggles to support families on poverty-level incomes and to function as caretakers to ill and injured family members, to live with racism and other forms of identity-based oppression, and to function with current and past experiences of violence embedded in their lives. Including trauma studies with pedagogical and project management theory seemed essential to increasing empathy and effectiveness in our SI Program employees.

Each dynamic of the STAR Model can be considered independently and in combination with the other dynamics, dependent on problem need and context. For example, "goals" can be explored as an isolated concept with students in terms of setting achievable goals, establishing priorities, methods of planning goal attainment (linear, networked, backwards planning, for example), and assessment of goals both reached and unrealized. Goals can also be explored in terms of assessing and applying appropriate amounts and kinds of time, effective processes, relevant and effective communication, and identifying, developing, and using resources to assist in successful goal completion.

Lehman's SI Leaders first engaged with the STAR Model in spring 2008 during a day of midterm training designed to provoke self-assessment and reinforce program skills and concepts. The STAR Model quickly became the rubric by which SI Leaders and SI Assistant Supervisors assessed each of their activities; many of our team members reported applying the dynamics to their own personal lives and finding success in improving problem-solving with time management, goal-setting, communication, process, and resource skills. However, it soon became evident that our SI Assistant Supervisors were eager to increase their mentoring skills beyond the project management skills they were beginning to master. The Resiliency Principles (Figure 9.2) were introduced in 2009 and became an integral part of SI Assistant Supervisors (and later, STAR Mentor) training and practice.

The Resiliency Principles

As stated earlier, public urban higher education students engaged in cross-cultural learning environments report high rates of trauma in their personal and professional lives. Lehman College's former interim associate provost, Paul Kreuzer (personal communication, September 1, 2015), advocates that "resiliency is at the heart of the cross-cultural learning problem and at the heart of the need to recognize the difficulty of developing appropriate problem solving skills." The STAR Model addresses creative problem-solving in its application to specific challenges; a need to address trauma through creative approaches to resiliency seemed an important framework to provide the supervisors of peer academic coaches interacting with traumatized learners (and interacting with their own traumatic learning as well).

Resiliency has been defined as the ability of an entity to recover its form and substance following change (Dictionary.com, 2015). In trauma studies, resiliency

Resiliency

Community

Flexibility

Capacity

Stability

FIGURE 9.2 The Resiliency Principles

Source: Foster (2009).

can be applied to both individuals and groups, which I would argue holds true for those engaged in learning. In some ways, the challenges of learning can create mental and emotional states similar to trauma as assumptions and misconceptions are threatened and dismantled in the process of creating what Willingham (2009) calls the appropriate "cognitive conditions" for acquiring new knowledge. To be a resilient learner would mean to possess the capacities for recovering one's sense of consistency and stability as a learner within the community of learners. Resilient learning would also indicate the possession and demonstration of flexibility that is neither hyper-mobile (excessively flexible, accepting all ideas as equally valid, and unable to set priorities or evaluate performance) nor rigid (unable to take in new information or try new approaches to problem-solving).

Lehman College participates in the Penn State annual Center for Collegiate Mental Health reporting and asks students to self-report their exposure to stress and trauma (Center for Collegiate Mental Health [CCMH], 2014). Among the students enrolled at institutions providing data for this report, Lehman's students self-report two standard deviations away from their peers in terms of traumatic experience (Norma Cofresi, personal communication, November 26, 2012). This would seem to indicate a need on the part of the college to assess student resiliency and to offer resiliency interventions to support academic and professional success.

Each Resiliency Principle presents a continuum along which one can locate resilient and non-resilient expressions. Stability ranges from rigidity to limpness, and capacity from limitation to openness. A person or group can be hyper- or hypo-mobile: easy or difficult to move in response to catalysts. Community, as seen in recent international events involving internally displaced peoples and refugees, can be welcoming and inclusive or hostile and isolated. When located on resilient parts of the continuum for each principle, problem-solving is supported by a context of motivation and persistence. When located on non-resilient parts of the continuum, problem-solving becomes difficult and obstructed because the context is unreliable and uncertain.

Stability forms the roots of the Resiliency Principles. Judith Herman (1997) and Bessel Van Der Kolk (2014) have demonstrated that stability is the first step in trauma healing and recovery for those suffering from complex post-traumatic stress disorder: drawing from Vamik Volkan's (2004) work on large group identity one can argue that stability is a core principle for traumatized groups as well. Stability may be understood as having one's primary needs met and having a sense of consistency in one's assessment of self as well as in daily living activities. In terms of education, stability might be considered in the context of prior knowledge and assumptions (Ambrose et al., 2010). This might include the student's own knowledge and skill set before attempting a course as well as the information provided in the syllabus and the instructor's activities in the first weeks of class to establish common assumptions, practices, and shared facts.

Once one has established sufficient stability in self and in learning, other qualities can be developed that demonstrate resiliency. Capacity is a principle I have considered at some length in *Lyric Dwelling: The Art & Ethics of Invitation & Occupation* (Foster, 2012).

> Capacity is a term of both openness and limitation. A capacity is perhaps best considered as the environment in which an individual (whether a being, a concept, a set or group or beings or concepts which self-identifies or that self-identify) can move without the individual's exceeding the reach of that which constitutes its identity. This exceeding can be understood as that which, if achieved, would cause the individual to cease to be what it is, through fragmentation or transformation. A capacity is both the conceptual and physical temporo-spatiality in which an individual can be itself and the limits of the conceptual and physical temporo-spatiality in which an individual can remain itself as currently self-identified.
>
> *(pp. 62–63)*

Capacity in terms of problem-solving and creative learning, based on this definition, means transforming identity and reconsidering both motivation and persistence. A student's motivation for learning and justification for persistence can be redirected from beliefs in whether one is capable of solving the problems at hand to beliefs in what capacities are indicated by the problems to be solved and what capacities may be opened by reaching the problem-solving skills called for rather than focusing solely on arriving at the solutions.

The combination of stability and capacity creates opportunities for considering multiple responses to problems while maintaining connections to prior learning. There is a spiral sense to learning when students engage in problem-solving from internal senses of stability and capacity. The concepts underlying many discipline-based inquiries exhibit continuity in their tested applications over time; the capacities inherent in many concepts to hold true for a variety of solutions bring learners to heightening levels of return in their development.

Traveling along the spiral begun with stability and capacity indicates a need for flexibility, being able to respond to changes without breaking or losing internal and external rigor. To be flexible means to be responsive rather than reactive, to bend without losing control. Recent hurricanes and typhoons have shown the limits of natural flexibility; for a flexible learner, responding accurately to problems worded differently yet asking for the same solution process demonstrates mental flexibility as much as responding to a request to explain different perspectives on a political or social issue. Students with rigid rather than rigorous thinking lack the resilient flexibility to problem-solve creatively because they cannot consider different alternatives; students who are caught in relativist thinking may be too flexible and unable to call on a control of approaches and choices in their work.

However, individual approaches to problem-solving show limitations over time, particularly as students advance in learning and the complexity of required tasks. Basic coding projects may be mastered by novice students; advanced software design requires a team of experts and mentored intermediate learners to analyze, plan, and execute the final product. An increase in necessary connections to address problems effectively calls for an increase in an effective community.

Students live in communities in their personal and academic lives: communities are based on sharing of objectives, resources, processes, and/or traditions. The resiliency of community can be fixed or fluid, depending on group identity and group resources as well as aims and methods (Volkan, 2004). Students living with broken or frozen community identities may bring these senses of disconnection to their academic work; students in classrooms that fail to function as resilient communities may also find problem-solving increasingly difficult. This is borne out by the research into peer academic work that demonstrates the higher success rates of students who form study groups outside of class over those who choose to approach their studies alone (Arendale & Hane, 2014).

Creative Learning Through Shared Problem-Solving

> What started out as an experiment to improve student learning in difficult courses, became a development of a method for inculcating creative thinking in the staff of the program with a supplemental effect of improving learning in the originally targeted students.
>
> *(Paul Kreuzer, personal communication, September 1, 2015)*

The intent of the changes in the Title V SI and STAR Mentoring & Coaching Programs was to foster increased capacities for creative problem-solving. As we continued program development and services, this intent was supported by all roles in the programs. STAR course instructors reinforced the STAR Dynamics and Resiliency Principles throughout the courses, trainings, supervision and mentoring meetings, and observations. Program management supported this reinforcement by practicing and describing these two models in daily and long-term activities—for example, timesheets; loans of textbooks, chalk, markers, and erasers; use of laptops and mobile devices; logic models; and data collection were all spoken of using STAR Dynamic or Resiliency Principle "tags."

SI Leaders, STAR Coaches, SI Assistant Supervisors, and STAR Mentors were informally and formally observed for progress in creative problem-solving through applying training content and skills to their review sessions. Additionally, these program "students" created and maintained ePortfolios that included regular posting of work product and ongoing training discussions: the ePortfolio work was reviewed weekly and discussed during weekly supervision and mentoring sessions. Our program students received frequent constructive feedback on their development; the feedback was "tagged" with references to the STAR and Resiliency Principles both as reinforcement and as progress markers so that our students could integrate this external awareness with their own internal awareness of capacity development.

Through this reinforcement of program models and flexible approaches to problem-solving, employees/students were able to work together across cultural and other differences (gender, age, economic status, even educational levels) to the point that the exceptions stood out vividly. Even those whose large group identities placed them at traditional odds with one another (for example, tribal and religious feuds) found ways to work together productively and positively when the STAR and Resiliency Principles underlaid the work they were assigned. By using these two models as methods and as rubrics, we were able to redirect energies toward tasks and thus able to facilitate some rational, pragmatic outcomes.

As further evidence of creative problem-solving and capacity development, there are multiple success stories related to the STAR Model and Resiliency Principles and their use with the STAR Mentoring & Coaching Program as well as trainings and presentations in other venues. One of these events involved the use of the STAR Model for an all-day staff retreat at the Joseph S. Murphy Institute for Worker Education and Labor Studies. Staff members were taken through a series of exercises designed to clarify expectations, support teamwork, and address concerns that had been voiced to the retreat planning team. The results were telling: teamwork and communication showed clear improvements through the day as well as in the months following, as reported by participants in post-surveys and informal conversations. However, the effects of the training also included several staff members reporting discoveries that they were ready to move on to other employment as their individual senses of goals, communication, processes, time, and resources differed irreconcilably from those of the management team.

In the STAR Mentoring & Coaching Program itself, professional development was frequently dramatic. "I'm not creative!" was a frequent objection to early stage training activities. One to two academic terms later, this self-perceived lack of creativity would be replaced with suggestions for new problem-solving strategies that made use of the STAR Dynamics and Resiliency Principles, either to improve student success or professional development. One former physics SI Leader studying for actuarial examinations repeatedly expressed his skepticism regarding self-reflective activities (yet stayed with the program) and was known to respond as briefly as possible to ongoing training prompts and to say "I don't know" reflexively when asked a critical thinking question. After being promoted to SI Assistant Supervisor and STAR Mentor, he responded to the Resiliency Principles with great attention. As he became responsible for mentoring and training others who had been in his position, he became more passionate about learning and leadership. His skills and commitment proved so valuable that he was promoted to Associate Mentor and finally to Acting Coordinator of the program. During his leadership of the STAR Mentoring & Coaching Program, he co-designed observation assessment tools, implemented advanced social media strategies, and redesigned trainings and evaluations. His rise in the program could be directly connected to the development of his capacities for self-reflection, his increased flexibility in thinking and problem-solving, and his expanding sense of community among the STAR Coaches, students, faculty, and staff.

Each of the six Acting Coordinators of the SMC Program showed similar professional growth. Many of the SI Leaders, STAR Coaches, SI Assistant Supervisors, and STAR Mentors who did not progress toward leading the program moved into other professional successes: medical and nursing school programs followed by residencies and entry-level positions, full-time teaching positions in higher education, and mid-level managerial positions in corporate and non-profit organizations. Each credited the STAR Model and Resiliency Principles with improving their professional skills and helping them focus their efforts more effectively toward achieving their goals.

Conclusions

During eight and a half years of program operations, 4,561 students participated in review sessions offered by 134 SI Leaders and STAR Coaches. Approximately 125 instructors and 50 SI Assistant Supervisors and STAR Mentors provided mentoring, training, and supervision to these SI Leaders and STAR Coaches, which in turn was passed on to the students learning creative methods of problem-solving in classes and review sessions. We coined a term, "reciprocal mentoring," to describe the multidirectional nature of engaging with and disseminating the assumptions and methods of the STAR Model and the Resiliency Principles.

These numbers do not include the external institutions and programs who received STAR Model and Resiliency Principle training or were exposed to the models through other venues, and they do not reflect the training and problem-solving efforts of the Transfer Coaching Program at Lehman College, which also used the two models. It is likely that more than 10,000 people have been exposed to the STAR Model and Resiliency Principles in the past seven years. At Lehman, at least forty countries were represented among those engaged with the models. Therefore, one conclusion that could be drawn from the participation data was that the number of direct and indirect exposures to our models has been high enough to observe patterns of problem-solving that may have been influenced by our approaches to creative learning.

In some senses, nearly any model with sufficient structure and simplicity would be successful when used by those who believed it would be successful. The human tendencies to adapt and problem-solve, combined with the tendencies to depend on perceived authority/expertise and to use what resources are made available tend to invest self-development strategies with more efficacy than these perhaps warrant taken on their own, apart from personal investment. However, the power and efficacy of any model also rely on its iterative and adaptive capacities. The STAR Dynamics and Resiliency Principles are easily iterated, based on their simplicity, and easily adapted, based on their range of interpretation and ease of recombination.

The simplicity of the models bears repeating: the models are both simple to see and remember, with one-word labels for each dynamic or principle. The dynamics can be combined or ordered as needed: combinations and orders are elicited by the problems to be solved rather than superimposed. This maintains the integrity of the context or problem. And yet, the dynamics themselves remain consistent in name and area of influence yet malleable in application.

The principles, in contrast, do have a hierarchy or progression to maintain. Again, the consistency in name area contains the malleability of the application; again, the context or problem owns its identity separate from efforts to resolve. It is the encounter between the principles and the problem that allows the continua of the Resiliency Principles to come into play and assist in reinterpreting the problem so that it may better be addressed.

And yet, one of the limitations common to qualitative problem-solving methods is that many problems contain within themselves areas of dependency subject to external circumstances beyond the influence of individuals or small groups. As it was dependent on external funding and institutional support, the STAR Mentoring & Coaching Program at Lehman College came to an abrupt end in July 2015. Although the program had been institutionalized as part of a federal grant, budget and administrative concerns were cited as reasons for effectively terminating the program. Over the program's years of operation, changes in leadership were frequent and budget shortages were common. Clearly, sufficient funding and consistent leadership are essential for such a program to be sustainable.

Somewhat surprisingly, student participation in SMC review sessions stayed consistent; student success rates in most SMC supported courses were on average 10% higher for those who engaged in the review sessions four or more times per term. Students who credited their success in SMC-supported courses to SMC review session participation became new SMC Coaches and Mentors, thus providing a shifting yet strong base for program continuity and quality maintenance. Student success rates reflect national and international SI success rates for programs based on the UMKC SI model.

What seems to differ between the Lehman programs and other SI-based support services are the professional skills and leadership developed in those who worked for both the Title V SI and STAR Mentoring & Coaching Programs: although we do not have comparison data for professional success with other programs, the post-program placements in graduate and professional programs as well as entry-level positions in desired fields seem remarkable. Several of our program "graduates" used evidence of their work and growth with us to support job and graduate/professional school applications. These include community college mathematics teachers, nurses, MD/PhD students, physicians' assistants (PAs), program administrators, and human resource specialists. Anecdotal data suggests that these young professionals are introducing and applying the STAR Model and Resiliency Principles in their new work and study environments, influencing colleagues and clients to experience these as development and problem-solving opportunities similar to those experienced in our programs.

Creative learning, as indicated earlier, occurs when non-traditional approaches are taken to solve traditional problems, or stated another way, when the potential dynamics and principles at stake in a given context are combined and recombined in unexpected ways to address complex questions. The creative learning that took place during the eight and a half years of developing, refining, and reinforcing the STAR Model and Resiliency Principles was not primarily confined to a single discipline or set of skills or group of participants. Students, faculty, program employees, and program leaders all contributed to identifying dynamics and principles particular to problematic situations, whether these included course assignments and exams or study skills and professional development challenges. Rather, these models assisted students and employees in learning about learning and in acquiring transferable problem-solving skills.

Creative learning can be interpreted in many ways. From a holistic standpoint, creative learning engages all participants in creative thinking, methods, and solutions. However, it is one thing to ask teachers and learners to think creatively; it is quite another to train teachers and learners in creative thinking. The practice and exposure of self-reflection to peers lies at the heart of creative problem-solving: one must be vulnerable and humble in examining one's assumptions and areas for growth while maintaining sensitivity and integrity in responding to others' sharing of their self-reflective discoveries. The ePortfolios offered our program participants a safe place for these self-reflections, as did the weekly mentoring and supervision meetings.

Clearly, providing sufficient structure while maintaining sufficient space and time to explore multiple options is one of the primary challenges in designing and assessing a creative learning environment. Another challenge is to attach meaning to the learning experience; what holds a personal importance in terms of values, objectives, or connections will motivate and sustain teachers and learners through complex problem-solving and capacity building.

The STAR Model and Resiliency Principles correspond well to these challenges by offering simple, flexible rubrics open to multiple attachments of values, objectives, and connections that are context-dependent. These models do not replace disciplinary content and skills learning methods but rather encompass these methods to establish a sense of stability in approaching new ideas and situations that allows for appropriate and perhaps more effective risks to be taken in trying out unfamiliar strategies.

If creativity is indeed the highest level of critical thinking, as the Revised Bloom's Taxonomy presents, then models that integrate the previous levels of remembering, understanding, applying, analyzing, and evaluating will most successfully support this outcome. The STAR and Resiliency models can be considered at each level, as was briefly demonstrated earlier. Improvements in goal-setting and assessment, time management, appropriate selection and application of communication skills and problem-solving processes, combined with identification and development of appropriate resources form a foundation and framework for creative learning.

Questions

As mentioned earlier, one of the successes of the STAR Model and Resiliency Principles has been to train students and recent graduates in developing the professional and academic skills indicated by the dynamics and in transferring these skills to their coursework and to the self-regulation of their own professional lives. With the cessation of training and services based on these models, the questions that remain are both present and future oriented: Which, if any, of these skills and strategies are program and college graduates continuing to apply in their early professional lives? Has the training and practice in creative learning transferred to new areas of problem-solving? Finally, are the capacities of our learners increasing and changing to expand their resiliencies and opportunities beyond those they themselves anticipated before encountering the models?

Early evidence suggests that those pursuing teaching as a career are engaging their students at local community colleges and schools in some strategies and concepts related to the STAR Model and Resiliency Principles. Former SI Leaders and STAR Coaches studying medicine have reported setting up peer study groups on their own initiative and using the STAR Model in their discussions. Former program participants are applying the STAR Dynamics to academic and career preparation. Former SI Leader and STAR Coach nursing students are using communication and process skills in their entry-level positions in hospitals and home health care programs.

In this moment of transition between programs ending and new projects beginning, the question I would most like to explore is this: what creative learning might be applied to the STAR Model and Resiliency Principles to improve both their theoretical bases and applications? If these models outlast the projects for which they were initially designed, perhaps the flaws inherent in any model will be identified and addressed with positive implications for nurturing new generations of creative learners and problem-solvers.

Bibliography

Ambrose, S. A., Bridges, M. W., DiPietro, M., Lovett, M. C., & Norman, M. K. (2010). *How learning works: 7 Research-based principles for smart teaching.* San Francisco: Jossey-Bass.

Arendale, D. R., & Hane, A. (2014). Holistic growth of college peer study group participants: Prompting academic and personal development. *Research and Teaching in Developmental Education, 31* (1), 7–29.

Bosworth, W. (2015, May). *Discovering the Bronx: Using census data to highlight social problems and achievements in a major urban area.* Retrieved September 26, 2015, from Discovering the Bronx: Using Census Data to Highlight Social Problems and Achievements in a Major Urban Area: http://www.lehman.edu/deannss/bronxdatactr/discover/bxtext.htm#S2013

Center for Collegiate Mental Health (CCMH). (2014). *Center for Collegiate Mental Health (CCMH).* Retrieved September 26, 2015, from Penn State News: http://news.psu.edu/photo/343725/2015/02/05/center-collegiate-mental-health-2014-annual-report

Dictionary.com. (2015). *Resilience or resiliency.* Retrieved September 26, 2015, from Dictionary.com: http://dictionary.reference.com/browse/resiliency?s=t

Foster, G. R. (2008). *The STAR model.* New York: Lehman College, City University of New York.

Foster, G. R. (2009). *Resiliency principles.* New York: Lehman College, City University of New York.

Foster, G. R. (2012). *Lyric dwelling: The art & ethics of invitation & occupation.* Dresden: Atropos Press.

Gladwell, M. (2008). *Outliers: The story of success.* New York: Little, Brown and Company.

Herman, J. (1997). *Trauma and recovery: The aftermath of violence from domestic abuse to political terror.* New York: Basic Books.

Klein, G. (1999). *Sources of power: How people make decisions.* Cambridge, MA: MIT Press.

Kolowich, S. (2011, August 22). *What students don't know.* Retrieved September 26, 2015, from Inside Higher Ed: https://www.insidehighered.com/news/2011/08/22/erial_study_of_student_research_habits_at_illinois_university_libraries_reveals_alarmingly_poor_information_literacy_and_skills

McLeod, S. A. (2012). *Zone of proximal development.* Retrieved December 15, 2015, from http://www.simplypsychology.org/Zone-of-Proximal-Development.html

Schmalstig, M., & Peart, M. (2013). Review Session Observation Rating Scale (assessment tool). New York: Lehman College, City University of New York.

Schwarz, R. (2002). *The skilled facilitator: A comprehensive resource for consultants, facilitators, managers, trainers, and coaches.* San Francisco: Jossey-Bass.

Van Der Kolk, B. (2014). *The body keeps the score: Brain, mind, and body in the healing of trauma.* New York: Viking.

Volkan, V. (2004). *Blind trust: Large groups and their leaders in times of crisis and terror.* Charlottesville, VA: Pitchstone.

Walsh, J. A., & Sattes, B. D. (2011). *Thinking through quality questioning: Deepening student engagement.* Thousand Oaks, CA: Corwin.

Willingham, D. T. (2009). *Why don't students like school?* San Francisco: Jossey-Bass.

PART III
Enhancing Creative Learning
Essays

10

CREATIVE APPROACHES TO STIMULATE CLASSROOM DISCUSSIONS

Stephen Brookfield

When I began my teaching career I was committed to the use of discussion. My instincts and training told me that discussion should be my 'go to' method, partly because I felt it would be more engaging for the students I was teaching and partly because it seemed to me inherently democratic. I was a poor student myself and was bored stiff throughout my own schooling. The curriculum had nothing I could get passionate about and the pedagogy was, to be generous, unimaginative. So, as I approached my own first class as a teacher at a technical college in south-east London (UK) I was determined to avoid the teacher-dominated, passive pedagogy I had been subjected to as a learner.

My first weeks and months, indeed that whole first year, were pretty demoralizing. I would assign creative pre-reading and bring to class what I thought were interesting discussion questions. But student silence and non-compliance were very effective in sabotaging me, rendering me powerless. No matter how provocative the topic, and no matter how artfully I phrased my questions, the discussions were mostly lifeless.

My response to this situation was to force myself to get out of bed every morning and take the subway to what I knew was going to be another joyless day. But one optimistic thought kept recurring. I told myself that if I could stick it out I would gradually learn from experience how to adjust, improvise, bob and weave (pedagogically speaking), and pick up the emotional rhythms of the students. As I got better at discerning how the class was feeling and at knowing what activities would be likely to engage them, I saw myself becoming a sort of discursive jazz musician able to riff and extemporize in the moment. Students' comments and the subtle clues of their body language would be quickly analyzed and lead me to make instantaneous decisions that would light the fires of student enthusiasm.

In this imagined narrative of my future practice I trusted that I would learn creativity in my handling of discussion. To some extent this was accurate. I do believe that 45 years later I exercise a much greater degree of improvisation and extemporaneous decision-making in the middle of class. But what I had omitted from my first year of practice was any attention to how students could learn to engage in discussion through the use of specific exercises and protocols. The creativity I had imagined characterizing my future classrooms was all centered on me, not my students.

Over the years I have come to understand that it is students who learn creativity, not just the teacher. In this chapter I want to present nine of the most successful techniques and approaches that have helped students broaden the ways they participate in discussion, learn a range of different discussion behaviors and activate their visual, dramatic, poetic, and musical creativity. All nine exercises are designed to democratize classroom participation, to address multiple learning preferences, and to bypass the privileging of speech.

Holding Silent Discussions

Silence is usually something teachers feel should be avoided at all costs in most classrooms. Typical constructions of silence are that it indicates confusion; hence, when teachers ask questions and are met with silence, the inference is that students can't answer because they don't understand the question or lack the information or reasoning skills to provide an answer. Alternatively, silence is read as a sign of truculence, an intellectual strike by students whose refusal to say anything effectively disempowers the teacher.

But in discussions silence is a necessary interlude that allows for the processing of information. Students from Asian cultural backgrounds, indigenous students, introverts, and students for whom English is a second language all value the time for reflection, cognitive connection, and rehearsal that periods of silence provide. Student feedback on classroom process often highlights intentional silence as an engaging moment in class sessions. So, simply beginning a discussion exercise with the announcement that students should take a minute to think quietly about a question before starting to talk is mentioned in classroom evaluations as a helpful instructional act. It's the public intentionality of silence that's crucial. Naming silence as important, saying why a moment of silence is being requested, and building opportunities for silent participation into any rubrics for class participation are all important elements in socializing students to accept silence as a necessary part of conversational rhythm.

Silence in Discussion: Chalk Talk

A very adaptable activity, *Chalk Talk*, was developed by Hilton Smith (2009) of the Foxfire Fund in Appalachian schools. It's conducted in silence and is very brief—typically no more than ten minutes. This is a great way to get a quick visual and graphic representation of where a group is on an issue. This exercise unearths the concerns of students and shows how well students understand an issue or topic. Here's how the process goes:

- The teacher, facilitator, or leader writes a question in the center of a black or white board (or electronically) and circles it. In auditoriums or classrooms I have sometimes had to cover several walls with blank sheets of newsprint for groups of people to write on. Multiple markers or chalk sticks are placed by the board so lots of people have the chance to write simultaneously.
- Everyone is invited to come and stand by the board to participate in the activity. The leader explains that for about five minutes people should write responses to the question on the board. The group maintains silence as this is happening so that people can focus entirely on the written dialogue.
- Several people usually get up immediately and start writing at different parts of the board. There are also frequent pauses between postings.
- Those who are not writing at any point are asked to observe what's being posted and to draw lines between comments that appear to connect in some way. If they have questions or responses to a posting, they also write that on the board.
- The facilitator also participates by drawing lines connecting comments, by writing questions, by adding her own thoughts, and so on.
- The facilitator closes the silent part of the exercise when the board is so full that posting new comments is difficult or when there's a distinct lull in posting.
- The facilitator and the group then talk about the graphic that has been produced. They identify clusters of common responses, questions that have been raised, and different analytical perspectives. Outlier comments are also noted.
- The leader invites people to take out smartphones, tablets, and laptops to snap photos of the *Chalk Talk* board, and asks volunteers to post these to a group website.
- If this exercise is used in an organizational setting, the group then identifies issues emerging from *Chalk Talk* that will be addressed by teams that people volunteer for. These teams then develop these issues into new organizational agendas.
- If this exercise is used in an academic class to introduce a new topic, the instructor alerts students to her plan to return regularly to themes and questions noted in the graphic.

This is a very adaptable exercise and I've used it in a wide range of academic classrooms, professional development activities, staff training, and community meetings. One advantage is that it secures a much higher rate of participation than typically happens in speech. If I pose a question to a group in class and then take ten minutes to have people respond to it by raising hands or shouting out responses, I get a response from maybe 10% of students. And I always feel obliged to add a comment or two in response to each student's contribution just to show the class that I am paying attention and earning my paycheck. By way of contrast, *Chalk Talk* typically secures at least a 60% participation rate.

This technique also develops students' visual capabilities. For those who already gravitate to visual and graphic ways of communicating and learning, this is a welcome alternative to speech-based modes of discussion. For those who rely on verbal modes of communication and who have been schooled to think this is the only way discussions happen, *Chalk Talk* opens up the possibility of experimenting with visual communication. In particular it trains people to look for connections and contradictions using visual scanning. As students see multiple postings appear, they are enjoined to draw lines connecting posts that appear on different parts of the board. This inevitably heightens their awareness of the importance of synthesis to good discussions. It's hard for many students to recognize connections amid a flurry of words when earlier comments are forgotten. With *Chalk Talk* every comment is recorded on the board and becomes part of the permanent record. This means that a comment made in the first minute of the exercise can be addressed in the seventh or eighth minute. Finally, this exercise is well suited to introverts, second-language speakers, and reflectively oriented group members who need time to think and process before contributing something.

Silence in Discussion: Bohmian Dialogue

People often assume that a good discussion is one without awkward pauses, where participants are eagerly and quickly initiating new comments, responding to previous ones, and lining up to be next to speak. But this image doesn't match how people typically process information. To think through the meaning of a startling new comment or to respond to a provocative yet complex question often requires substantial thinking time. Physicist David Bohm (1996) has developed a process for getting groups to talk and think together more deeply and coherently about difficult issues. The purpose of his dialogic model is to create a flow of meaning among dialogue participants designed to help groups think more effectively together about seemingly intractable problems.

The process has a few simple ground rules:

• Participants gather to consider an issue or topic of mutual interest. They form a circle and the convener explains the meaning of dialogue—it's the creation of a flow of meaning among the participants, there are no winners or losers and no attempt to persuade or convince. The focus is on understanding what people actually say without judgment or criticism, and the object is to develop collective thinking. People have radically different opinions that should be expressed as precisely that; as different 'takes' or perspectives prompted by a contribution.

- One person speaks at a time, and while that person is speaking people listen intently.
- The convener participates by making contributions, and steps in to remind people of the ground rules when participants start trying to convince or rebut each other, or when the conversation turns into a debate. Optimally, everyone takes on that responsibility.
- Bohm recommends talking about dialogue itself when people first come together through questions like "What makes dialogue on this issue so difficult?" or "What conditions foster good dialogue about racial tension?"
- There is no pressure to respond to the opening question immediately. People are encouraged to be silent and to speak only when they have something to say or a thought prompted by another's comment. Silence indicates that people are actually thinking. If it's helpful, participants can close their eyes or look at the floor, though some prefer to give non-verbal support and eye contact.
- This process continues for as long as seems optimal. Bohm recommends two hours, but I have used briefer chunks of time.
- The process concludes with participants sharing what they came to understand more deeply.

The long silent pauses between contributions are often frustrating for people used to the 'discussion as animated speech' model. So an initial uncertainty, even hostility, about the process is normal and to be expected. The facilitator should not stop this discomfort being expressed but also should not back down from the process too quickly. The facilitator should keep reminding people that the looseness of the process is designed to release imaginative thinking and foster careful listening. Bohm (1996) recommends a group size of forty members so the group represents the diversity of experience and opinion that often undermines dialogue. I have sometimes adapted this process to smaller groups of fifteen, twenty, and twenty-five. For me the process works best where groups are struggling with contentious issues such as race.

Despite the unfamiliarity of this process people often express their gratitude after the discussion. Slowing down the process means each person's contribution to the whole is fully heard and the absence of competition and one-upmanship bypasses the temptation to rebut or proselytize. In Bohmian discussion facilitators step in if they have something to say, but there is no pressure to do so. Their most important role is to intervene to make sure the few ground rules are observed. So if they hear someone judging or criticizing a comment, or if they see an interaction becoming a debate, they remind people of the ground rules.

Participating in the process requires a leap of faith not only on the part of facilitators but also from students. After all, you're asking people to talk in a specific way that is experienced as strange and unsettling. So, this activity should be reserved for times when a group has enough faith in you as its leader that they will trust in embarking on this journey with you. The activity also illustrates the role of facilitator power. People often assume that in a good discussion the facilitator becomes part of the furniture—an unnoticed fly on the wall. I believe the opposite is true. In a good discussion the facilitator models his or her commitment to the process by asking good questions that draw people out, linking different comments together, expressing appreciation for people's specific contributions, pausing to think silently before answering a question, making sure that quieter people get the chance to speak, and so on. When a process like Bohmian dialog occurs, the facilitator has the responsibility to point out when the process is going astray by reminding people that the ground rules are being contravened.

Incorporating the Visual

For a text- and word-based teacher like myself, visual elements are something I need to strive to incorporate in classroom activities. Since so much assessment and testing is conducted through text, it's not surprising if visual communication is undervalued if not overlooked entirely by many instructors, particularly in discussion. The typical image of a good discussion is of people talking animatedly. There is little silence, people are making lots of enthusiastic eye contact, talk flows seamlessly and uninterruptedly, and important things are said. When you announce to students that you're going to hold a discussion, they don't usually think of people drawing.

Visual Discussion: Drawing Discussion

Drawing Discussion, like *Chalk Talk*, emphasizes visual and graphic ways of 'talking' to each other and is appreciated by those who process information spatially and communicate ideas visually. I use it to ensure that as wide a variety of participants as possible can feel engaged in a class, workshop, or meeting. The process involves the following;

- A question or problem is posed, such as: What does a good discussion look like? How do we know when a theory has explanatory power? How can photosynthesis be explained visually? What is a moral action? What constitutes a proof?
- Each participant is given a sheet of paper and a few markers to create a drawing or collage that addresses the question. Highly abstract designs with no attempt at representation are fine. People work by themselves for about ten minutes.

- Participants then convene in small groups and each person explains their drawing to the other group members.
- The group discusses how the individual images connect or contradict each other and works to produce a final group visual incorporating some aspect of each individual's composition. One member takes notes regarding what the group is attempting to communicate.
- Once the group pictures are completed, each is displayed on a wall around the room and a blank sheet of paper is placed next to each.
- People are invited to tour the gallery of visuals and provide comments, questions, and reactions on the blank sheets. They are encouraged to do this using images rather than words.
- The whole group reconvenes and participants can ask different groups about their postings. The member who took notes as the group visual was developed takes the lead in responding to questions posed about a group's drawing or collage.

This is a refreshing change in settings where there's a strong and habitual reliance on the spoken and written word. The energy unleashed in this technique often gets people to relate to each other more casually and amiably. *Drawing Discussion* is an opportunity to flex creative muscles and explore issues with a new freedom and intellectual abandon.

Making Visual Discussion Safer: Collaging Discussion

If you use the word 'drawing,' people (and by that I mean me!) are often immediately beset by fear and embarrassment regarding their lack of artistic talent. But tell people they are going to be working on a collage and all that goes away. With collage you work from ready-made images in magazines, newspapers, flyers, your own photographs, downloaded images, or small objects that can be glued onto a poster. You don't need to be an 'artist' to make a collage, or to be good at graphic design or draftsmanship; all you need are magazines, glue, and a pair of scissors. In this approach, provide the group with magazines, fabric scraps, and glue and ask them to create a group collage incorporating each of their individual responses.

As Simpson's (2009) account of her participation at a workshop for cancer patients illustrates, the freedom collage affords can be galvanizing and meaningful. She describes how, when participants were working on collages,

> the workshop was alive with color, cutting, and pasting, tears, laughter, a buzz of emotion, depth of understanding, optimism, and hope. THIS creative energy was exactly what I wanted to surround myself with. And this particular art form was clearly accessible to everyone in the room regardless of age, life place, previous creative experience, or artistic skill.
>
> *(pp. 78–79)*

Cranton (2009) offers a similar verdict on using the method with vocational trades instructors at a Canadian community college. Teaching a unit on learning styles, she asked these instructors to create collages to illustrate the different learning styles they felt they exhibited. She recounts how

> both the process of finding or creating images and the creation of the collage itself led to a deeper examination of learning style, and the ensuing discussion in the whole group led us to question the premise of the concept of learning styles and challenge the idea of creating teaching methods to support each learning style.
>
> *(p. 186)*

One of the most powerful illustrations of collage is in Grace and Wells's (2007) description of their work with sexual minority youth. To illustrate the way people's identity became separated from their external presentation of self, participants worked with old school lockers to create an in/out representation of how they felt about themselves as compared to the way they were seen by the world. On the outside of the lockers were stereotypical depictions of lesbian, gay, bisexual, and transgendered people, representing how participants felt they were viewed by teachers, parents, classmates, and communities. The inside of the lockers contained images, collages, and dioramas that depicted the inner selves they kept hidden from families, friends, and teachers. One participant combined shards of broken glass and fragments of a smashed mirror with disembodied and scratched-out photographs, with the phrase 'running scared' written amid pairs of eyes watching the viewer.

Incorporating Body Movement and Classroom Geography in Discussion

In American college classrooms discussion is usually done sitting down. Students remain static, seated in a particular place. They display animation by hand motion, swiveling heads, or nods, but typically don't get up and start wandering around in the middle of a discussion. Indeed, a student who suddenly started to walk to different corners of the classroom in the middle of a discussion would typically be regarded as disruptive, even deviant. The only permissible time to get up is for classroom breaks and sometimes to move chairs into arrangements for small groups. Because discussion is a teaching method we use to introduce complexity to students, promote an active engagement with material, and encourage intellectual flexibility, there should be a role for body movement to be incorporated into these processes.

Stand Where You Stand

The *Stand Where You Stand* exercise deliberately incorporates kinetic elements and body movement to represent students' cognitive functioning. Its logic is that as students acquire new information and develop new understanding they move to different physical spaces in the classroom. In *Stand Where You Stand*, a discussion is held in which the purpose is to introduce students to three or four distinct perspectives that can be applied to understanding a new concept. The technique invites students to move to different stations in the room that represent each of these perspectives as their discussion of them persuades students of the relative merits of each.

I learned this exercise from Joan Naake of Montgomery College in Germantown, Maryland. I like how it teaches people about the complexities of an issue using physical movement and how it opens up the possibility of changing one's mind. Here's how it works:

- The facilitator identifies an issue of importance to a community, class, or organization.
- Before a group meets, participants are asked to read material that provides relevant information on the issue and explore it from different viewpoints.
- When people gather together, the facilitator begins by stating an opinion or making a claim about the issue the group has examined in the pre-reading.
- Participants spend two to three minutes individually writing down all the reasons why they agree or disagree with the statement just made.
- While people are writing the facilitator posts four signs around the room reading "Strongly Agree," "Partly Agree," "Partly Disagree," and "Strongly Disagree."
- When the individual writing time is up, participants are asked to stand underneath the sign that most closely approximates their position on the claim or statement.
- In pairs or trios, people at each station state the reasons for their choice of position.
- People at the different stations then share with the whole group their reasons for agreeing or disagreeing with the statement.
- As these arguments are shared, people are free to move to another sign at any time if the arguments they hear convince them to change their position.
- When all four viewpoints have been heard, the group reassesses the numbers of people who support the four positions. Those who have moved during the exercise are asked to share what convinced them to go to a different sign.
- Finally the whole group assesses which position secures the most agreement, if other information is needed, next steps, and any subtleties and nuances revealed.

One of the chief reasons people respond well to this is because of the physical exercise entailed by moving their body around the room as a way of expressing the development of their viewpoints. It helps keep up energy during lulls and provides a physical representation of how a group's thinking on an issue changes and evolves. It also underscores that changing your mind because of new data or a better argument is a sign of strength, not weakness.

Introducing Rhythmic and Musical Elements in Discussion

Rhythmic and musical analogies abound in discussion. We have crescendos of conversation when multiple voices are speaking followed by softer interludes, solo voices make arguments interspersed with choruses of affirmation or disagreement, themes of point and counterpoint interweave as arguments are made and rebutted, and improvisations are made on a theme as new points are raised. Adapting this language, it's not the stretch it might at first seem to incorporate musical elements into discussion.

Musicalizing Discussion

In this technique a wholly different set of capabilities is involved, sometimes using words (as in adapting well-known songs with new lyrics or creating new songs on the spot) but at other times using pure sound. Having a discussion in musical form may seem outrageous to many educators and is something that will be harder to adapt to some questions or topics rather than others. But, as with the previous exercises, the intent is to release creative energy by inviting people to communicate understanding using an unfamiliar modality. Here are the instructions people follow:

- Small groups of six to eight members are given kazoos, tambourines, harmonicas, ukuleles, triangles, and any other small, inexpensive instruments so everyone has something to play.
- The group's assignment is to create a musical composition of up to a minute that uses instruments and voices to capture the dynamics of a problem, issue, or experience.
- Members are told to keep in mind the possibilities of:

  ○ Moments of harmony and dissonance;
  ○ Periods of silence, loudness, crescendo, and decrescendo;
  ○ Solos interspersed with ensemble playing;
  ○ Variations on a theme;
  ○ Different musical sounds connecting and responding to each other;
  ○ Conflict that may or may not be resolved harmonically;
  ○ Compositions that emphasize balance and symmetry;
  ○ Compositions that emphasize chaos and disorder.

- Facilitators briefly demonstrate how they might musicalize some of the bulleted examples to represent their understanding of a specific topic.
- Groups disperse for twenty to thirty minutes to create their compositions.
- When ready, groups return and each performs its composition.
- The whole group reconvenes to discuss what different compositions conveyed and any new insights gained as a result.

Once the initial discomfort has worn off and people start to work in groups, many participants, especially musicians and other artists, appreciate the recognition that communicating through music is a way to make sense of the world. This exercise frees people up to try out new ideas and communicate in a novel way, and it tends to build relationships in a way different from how that happens through the formality of speech. I have found it a good way to infuse new energy into a series of classes, meetings, or workshops where energy is declining and a sense of staleness has crept in. I would not advocate trying this out early on in a group's existence, but it has been very successful in re-energizing groups that are falling into lulls.

Incorporating Theatrical Elements Into Discussion

Most classroom activities have some degree of theatricality built into them. This is probably seen most evidently in lecturing where hand gestures, eye contact, the raising and lowering of one's voice, walking around the room, and using dramatic pause for effect are used to emphasize important points, signal changes in direction, and introduce multiple perspectives. Classroom discussions can also benefit from introducing dramatic elements to structure a discussion.

As is the case with other artistic modalities, incorporating theatrical elements is intended to unleash a group's creative energy and to introduce a sense of play into classroom and organizational routines. It draws on improv theater in particular (McKnight and Scruggs, 2008) and theater of the oppressed (Boal, 2002, 2006), asking groups to respond to a question or address a problem by staging a short skit whose progress can be interrupted, or outcome altered, through the spontaneous intervention of audience members. In this regard Boal's work on using theater with revolutionary social movements, peasants, and grassroots groups has been particularly influential and been widely used around the globe, and not just with adults. A recent volume (Duffy and Vettraino, 2010) provides accounts of theater of the oppressed being adopted in early childhood classrooms, elementary education, high schools, Israeli-Palestinian encounters, and with incarcerated youth. In India, (Ganguly, 2010) estimates that Boal's methods have been used extensively for the past thirty years to reach over a quarter of a million villagers in West Bengal alone.

Bringing the body into learning is for many a powerful experience (Snowber, 2010). Getting the body up out of a chair to illuminate or express an idea is usually remembered much more clearly than an explanation from an instructor, no matter how lucid. But the degree to which participants are pushed is a matter of judgment. At its extremes, the use of theater is disturbing and upsetting.

A good example of how the dangerous and discomforting nature of theater can be used to shake up discussion is Butterwick and Selman's (2003) account of a series of workshops among feminist groups in Vancouver. The project, titled *Transforming Dangerous Spaces*, was intended to explore conflicts and tensions common to feminist coalitions. Butterwick recalls a scene where Subha (a pseudonym)—a woman of color—played a White woman and asked Butterwick to play a woman of color. Butterwick was somewhat intimidated by this prospect but agreed to go along with the exercise. Subha then stood on a chair and asked Butterwick to sit in front of her on the same chair. Subha talked loudly and forcefully while pressing her hands down on Butterwick's head, forcing her to bend to her knees. Butterwick eventually found herself folded in half struggling to breathe.

Butterwick recalls the debriefing of the scene:

> I spoke of how powerful the scene was—of my deeper and embodied appreciation of White privilege and racial domination. I also expressed my fears of playing a woman of color, of stereotyping and essentializing. Sheila (the facilitator) asked why I had agreed to play the character. In my response, I said that I had deferred to the request—sensing the scene would be risky but important. Sheila challenged me, noting that deference can be a form of racism.
>
> *(Butterwick and Selman, 2003, p. 14)*

Scenes like this one are indeed dangerous educational spaces to create, and they need skilled facilitators and willing participants to engage in them. In the *Transforming Dangerous Spaces* project, the participants were experienced and committed feminist activists. As such, there was a readiness to take much greater risks than would be the case in, say, a required college preparation program or a freshman orientation institute. As Butterwick and Selman (2003) note,

> a power and danger of drama process is that it can trigger participants in unexpected directions, and they can find themselves exploring, experiencing, and processing emotions, memories, and other aspects of themselves that were previously unknown or private. The results can surprise, shock, and reveal the unexpected.
>
> *(p. 14)*

In Forum Theater, derived from Boal's work, a community watches a scripted scene in which a typical kind of oppression is acted out. So, for example, a group of adult illiterates watch a job interview in which the applicant tried desperately to hide his inability to read or fill in a required form. The 'Joker' (a key actor in Forum Theater) then asks the audience to suggest different ways the actor experiencing oppression could have responded to the situation. As alternatives are suggested, the Joker entices audience members to come in and play the scene using the different alternatives they have suggested. Different audience members suggest different ways of confronting the oppression, and after each replaying of the scene everybody discusses what happened and what might be changed.

Forum Theater can be used in multiple settings where people feel they are being pushed around. A good example of its adaptability is Tania Giordani and Mike Brayndick's Forum Theater piece titled "The End Game at Jansen School." Dr. Giordani is a parent of school-age children in Chicago. In 2010 she conducted interviews with parents and students faced with a round of public school closings, and then developed a Forum Theater script designed to animate discussion about ways local communities could mobilize to fight these closings. The script has been performed in multiple settings: at a Midwest Title I conference with parents from Milwaukee, Detroit, and Chicago; at Francis W. Parker School in Chicago; and sometimes with students as young as fourth grade being involved. This last iteration was particularly powerful, according to Giordani:

> Students thanked me at the end for including them in the conversation about what was happening at their own school. That was pretty powerful because as parents we tend to want to protect our children from what is going on, especially as we fight with hope against the school closures. Through the plays and discussion, we (parents) are realizing, we should invite our children to join the conversation and fight. The dialogues after the performances are so intense and engaging, we are always going over our 2 hour time.
>
> *(Giordani, personal communication, 2012)*

The idea of Forum Theater is that it is a rehearsal for life. It provides a relatively safe space for people to try out different approaches to confronting power and pushing back against it. Of course it's not totally safe, because people take a risk to get up and try out their suggested alternatives. For people unused to performing or theater, that can be intimidating. But it is safe in that there are no political consequences to their improvisations.

Image Theater is the use of the body to create images of oppression and is meant to be physically as well as intellectually liberating. For example, contorting the body into shapes that represent how oppression feels, or arranging several bodies that demonstrate the interaction of cells, is something that does not come easily to academic classrooms. So a crucial element in the use of Image Theater is teachers' readiness to risk looking weird or foolish by themselves being willing to contort their own bodies. As explained by Williams (2010), "the body is liberated from unconscious movement, routine movement resulting from socioeconomic exploitation, and from the reduction of the body into an automaton" (p. 272).

In her adaptation of Image Theater, Lawrence (Butterwick and Lawrence, 2009) describes how a gay male participant created a sculptured image of how he had experienced oppression using his and other learners' bodies. He placed his body in the middle of the sculpture holding his head to ward off blows in a schoolyard bullying and placed a circle of people gathered round him pointing, jeering, and raining blows on him. The audience did not know he was being beaten because he was gay, since no talking is allowed during this kind of sculpting.

After the sculpture was 'unfrozen,' the gay participant playing the oppressed and those playing the oppressors discussed how they had experienced the situation. The oppressed revealed his gay identity as the cause of the beating and those playing oppressors spoke about their discomfort in that role. The discussion was then broadened to include learners not in the sculpture who had been observing it. The exercise ended with people suggesting alternative ways of staging a sculpture. In one, a person playing the role of the gay student held his head high with a confident expression on his face as those playing oppressors turned away from him. In another he was leaning forward with a finger pointing out addressing the oppressors who were listening attentively. A third scenario had two former oppressors recast as allies to the gay student, with the three of them challenging the other oppressors.

Dramatizing Discussion

I use a stripped-down dramatic exercise that incorporates some of the elements discussed earlier that runs as follows:

- Small groups of six to eight members are given thirty minutes to discuss a question or analyze a text.
- Each group then spends another thirty minutes creating a brief skit that they believe captures the content, agreements, and disagreements of their discussion.
- Each skit is then presented to the large group.
- Any members of the large group may interrupt the skit at any time, as new characters who introduce new plot elements or take skits in new directions.
- The group originating the skit can choose to follow the lead of the interrupter or continue their skit according to their initial plan.
- After all skits are presented, participants discuss how they captured the issues discussed in groups and any new insights raised.

Not surprisingly, dramatizing discussion often works well with groups sharing a creative or artistic orientation, such as community arts organizations or museums. Instead of just talking about how things might be different, dramatizing discussion involves people using their minds and bodies to enact a different future. This builds momentum for change and provides an empowering glimpse into how a constraining situation can be altered.

Although improvising is something people do in everyday life, and particularly in conversations, converting this improvisational instinct into constructing a meaningful skit is a stretch for most of us. So dramatizing discussion greatly benefits from someone with improv training. Groups sometimes get stuck at the halfway point when they have to develop a skit, and if that happens it may be helpful to reconvene the whole workshop or class and take a few minutes to brainstorm suggestions for specific skits.

Using Social Media

The last creative technique I wish to present emerges from the explosion of social media tools in the 21st century. Instead of trying to ban smartphones, laptops, tablets, and other devices from the classroom, my strategy is to incorporate their use into classroom activities. Of course, any time students are allowed to use devices there is the chance that they will abuse the privilege as they text, check Instagram or Facebook, shop online, or catch up with Twitter. But it's not as if wandering minds or diversionary tactics are only evident in the digital era. I have brought copies of music magazines like the *New Musical Express*, *Spin*, or *Mojo* to lectures so I could read them unobserved under the desk in the back row of an auditorium. Friends of mine used to draft their English soccer or cricket teams during class discussions. I still like to slip sarcastic notes to neighbors in large meetings or conferences, an antediluvian form of texting. So a wandering mind or inability to concentrate is hardly the province of millennial students.

My approach is to embrace technology rather than fight it and to use it (as far as I can) to stimulate and deepen discussion. I am always interested in securing the widest possible participation in discussion and to encourage students who find it hard to jump into the hurly-burly of cross talk. I want to make sure that difficult questions are raised rather than being skirted around or passed by quickly. I want to serve introverts, people for whom English is not a first language, and those who, like me, need time to process and mull over and rehearse before speaking. For me the incorporation of anonymous social media tools is a highly effective way of pursuing all these purposes. If a permanent social media channel is open throughout a discussion, and if the instructor constantly checks the feed for questions, comments, overlooked points, and reactions to specific prompts, this is a way to democratize the classroom and widen participation. It also allows for the raising of contentious issues that people feel too afraid to speak for fear of the reactions they will provoke.

Today's Meet

I particularly like to use the *Today's Meet* tool (https://todaysmeet.com/) as an electronic way of getting immediate and anonymous input from group members, to structure discussion, check for understanding, and generate new questions. It can be used with any group size from team meetings or classes of ten to fifteen people right up to town hall meetings, conference keynotes, workshops, or classes of several hundred students. Here's how it works:

- As facilitator you pull up the *Today's Meet* website on a screen everyone can see.
- You show them how you create a unique page for the session, giving it a specific name (for example, for a session on anti-racism your page might be titled http://www.todaysmeet.com/antiracism; for a class on photosynthesis it might be http://www.todaysmeet.com/photosynth).
- Then you enter your fictional identity for the day. I often use 'Scouse,' an English slang term for someone born in Liverpool.
- Participants then access the *Today's Meet* home page on their phones, tablets, or laptops and create a fictional identity so they can enter comments anonymously.
- You encourage people to use *Today's Meet* to ask questions, give reactions, provide critiques, raise issues, and suggest new directions for the discussion whenever these occur to them. You explain that you will pull up the feed on a screen every fifteen minutes so everyone can see what's been posted. Of course, anyone who is logged in can also view the feed on his or her device.
- At fifteen-minute intervals you address the comments people have posted. You respond to questions, note suggested new directions, deal with criticisms, and ask the group if they would like to respond to anything on the screen.
- Another use for this tool is to ask small groups to use *Today's Meet* to summarize the main points they discussed or the key questions they raised. Everyone can then review the postings on the screen in lieu of a series of spoken reports.
- Finally, a third option is to pose a question to a large group. Then, instead of hearing people speak their responses (which privileges the confident extroverts), everyone posts their responses to the question on the *Today's Meet* page you've created. If you ask for a minute or two of silence while people are doing this you will get far greater participation than if you'd gone straight to speech.

Millennial students like this tool because they are so used to texting as a medium of communication. But even for digital immigrants there are several clear benefits. People have the opportunity to ask questions or make points whenever these occur to them, even if the face-to-face session is focusing on something else. It also allows people to formulate and express a thought exactly the way they wish to. For those who rarely speak up in verbal discussions, *Today's Meet* allows them the chance to shape how the discussion evolves. Those who wish to make criticisms, ask hard questions, and introduce contentious ideas without fear of reprisal appreciate its anonymity. It also helps eliminate performance anxiety. In contrast to face-to-face discussions, the pressure to sound smart and highly informed is

lessened. And just like the *Chalk Talk* exercise described earlier, no one can domi-
nate the *Today's Meet* feed by raising their voice or drowning others out. So, for
anyone wanting to democratize classroom participation, this is a tool to consider.

Conclusion

Discussion has a bad reputation because of overuse and dreary familiarity. I am
embarrassed by the number of times I've used it purely because I imagined I
was supposed to. Growing up professionally in the field of adult education I was
told not to lecture but instead to create collaborative learning spaces in which
students' voices could be heard. Discussion was therefore my de facto mode of
teaching. As I moved into my career I monitored my use of lecturing to make
sure this didn't go on too long and that people would have the chance to talk. It
was almost a pedagogic bifurcation—'lecture bad (but sometimes unavoidable),
discussion good.'

But there is nothing inherently more creative in discussion than there is in
lecturing. Both can be done well or badly. Simply moving the chairs into a circle
and saying "we're going to hold a discussion" does not immediately democratize
or energize the classroom. Nor does it equalize power. Your power as facilitator, teacher, or leader still remains, as do the asymmetries of power relations and
dynamics between the learners. I have been in many discussion circles where it
looks as though contributions have been equalized but the facilitator uses his or
her power to lead the discussion to a predefined conclusion. By asking certain
questions, making eye contact with some and not with others, choosing to follow up some comments and ignoring others, and indicating what are 'good'
points, a facilitator can exercise power in a passive-aggressive way.

So it is hardly surprising if students display a marked reluctance, even hostility, to the process when they were burned by endless discussions that essentially were held only because the teacher thought that now it was necessary for
people to say something. The exercises reviewed in this chapter are all designed
to provide creative alternatives to the "now I've lectured so it's time to talk"
model. They use multiple modalities of communication, build in silence as an
intentional element of any conversational rhythm, and deliberately broaden the
amount of student participation. For me, a foundational reason to use discussion
is to provide as much of an engagement with democracy as is possible within a
classroom or organizational meeting. Just having people talking does not mean
democracy is at play. Indeed, discussions can easily replicate external power relations that are imported into the classroom whereby the most privileged and
confident in the external world exercise their privilege in the academy.

One final comment: introducing more creative modes of discussion into
classrooms will not be met with unalloyed joy by students who are comfortable with lecturing, or who sit back and stay silent in discussions knowing that
the articulate few that always speak will take the burden off quieter students'

shoulders. So expect resistance and suspicion when you first introduce these kinds of exercises and take it as a sign that you're doing something meaningful. Every classroom activity has advantages and drawbacks, and every new initiative will be opposed by some and welcomed by others. The point is to mix and match as many different forms of discussion so that people can see you're trying to work in ways designed to involve everyone in the class at some point.

Bibliography

Boal, A. 2002. *Games for actors and non-actors*. New York: Routledge.

Boal, A. 2006. *The aesthetics of the oppressed*. New York: Routledge.

Bohm, D. 1996. *On dialogue*. London: Routledge.

Butterwick, S. and Lawrence, R. 2009. Creating alternative realities: Arts-based approaches to transformative learning. In J. Mezirow & E. Taylor (Eds.), *Transformative learning in practice: Insights from community, workplace, and higher education*. San Francisco: Jossey-Bass, pp. 35–45.

Butterwick, S. and Selman, J. 2003. Deep listening in a feminist popular theater project: Upsetting the position of audience in participatory education. *Adult Education Quarterly*, Vol. 54, No. 1, pp. 7–22.

Cranton, P. 2009. From tradesperson to teacher: A transformative transition. In J. Mezirow & E. Taylor (Eds.), *Transformative learning in practice: Insights from community, workplace, and higher education*. San Francisco: Jossey-Bass, pp. 182–189.

Duffy, P. and Vettraino, E. (Eds.). 2010. *Youth and theater of the oppressed*. New York: Palgrave Macmillan.

Ganguly, S. 2010. *Jana Sanskriti: Forum theater and democracy in India*. New York: Routledge.

Grace, A. P. and Wells, K. 2007. Using Freirean pedagogy of just ire to inform critical social learning in arts-informed community education for sexual minorities. *Adult Education Quarterly*, Vol. 57, No. 2, pp. 95–114.

McNight, K. S. and Scruggs, M. 2008. *The second city guide to using improv in the classroom: Using improvisation to teach skills and boost learning*. San Francisco: Jossey-Bass.

Simpson, S. 2009. Raising awareness of transformation: Collage, creative expression, and transformation. In C. Hoggan, S. Simpson & H. Stuckey (Eds.), *Creative expression in transformative learning: Tools and techniques for educators of adults*. Malabar, FL: Krieger, pp. 75–101.

Smith, H. 2009. The Foxfire approach to student and community interaction. In L. Shumow (Ed.), *Promising practices for family and community involvement during high school*. Charlotte, NC: Information Age, pp. 47–61.

Snowber, C. 2010. Dance as a way of knowing. In R. L. Lawrence (Ed.), *Bodies of knowledge: Embodied learning in adult education*. San Francisco: Jossey-Bass, pp. 53–60.

Williams, H. S. 2010. Black mama sauce: Embodied transformative education. In B. Fisher-Yoshida, K. D. Geller & S. A. Schapiro (Eds.), *Innovations in transformative learning theory*. New York: Peter Lang, pp. 269–286.

11

DEVELOPING CREATIVE COMPETENCIES THROUGH IMPROVISATION—LIVING MUSICALLY

Robert Kaplan

Living Musically is an approach, using improvisation as a model or metaphor, to understand the world and live well in it. This way of thinking assumes that our lives are essentially unscripted improvisations and our ability to listen, be aware of, and respond effectively to relationships is central to our ability to live responsibly. This chapter presents tools that establish improvisation as a mode of creative inquiry and communication that can be used as an intentional practice, both individually and within groups.

Part of our self-awareness as human beings is built upon rhythm and movement, of which Flatischler (1992) writes:

> Our life in this world begins with the first breath. This, and the cutting of the umbilical cord, is a step toward rhythmic autonomy . . . In breathing we . . . encounter the co-existence of letting be and taking action—the two states whose interaction is an essential part of rhythm and music.
>
> *(p. 95)*

Our breathing ties us to the movement of time, and discovering our personal rhythm can serve to facilitate all listening—auditory listening, visual listening, and somatic listening. The theories and approaches presented here are a result of the author's experiences in music and dance improvisation, two-dimensional design, performance, and teaching. Interactive relationships inherent in music serve as the foundation for this approach. By devising frameworks to "play" within, we create a space to facilitate dialogues as a means of advancing ideas, working together, learning through experience, and experiencing directly. The frameworks presented draw on musical elements that include basic human capacities of breath, pulse, time, and the ability to perceive patterns, as well as gradations of texture, tension, nuance, and expression as part of a larger field of relationships. In this piece, music is used as a model or archetype of all basic modes of communication and humans living together; prior musical or artistic training is not necessary.

The process begins within each individual and progresses into simple relationships and ultimately to collective group ensemble play—developing the ability to communicate beyond words through sound, simple movement, and visual and spatial relationships. There is interplay between critical thinking and creative thinking as analytical, intellectual, and reasoning skill sets combine with intuitive and embodied sensory abilities for exploring new modes of communication and interaction, always with the potential to extend into other aspects of one's life. Common orienting concepts such as listening, focus, spontaneity, imagination, and collaboration weave through three stages for building an improvisational practice:

1. Awareness of self (mindful focus, being present)
2. Bridging beyond self
3. Creative interaction.

This chapter presents these three stages as part of a template that can be applied to oneself and/or to collaborative group-work. The template is flexible as one's awareness cycles through different stages of the practice, merging self-awareness in a continuous state of bridging out, beyond oneself into creative interaction with a medium, an idea, or with others (see Figure 11.1).

> The process of creating music as a shared experience helps us to integrate its meaning into the concept of who we are and how we relate to others. It also helps us find a way of relating that satisfies our own personal needs and yet adjusts to the objective circumstances of the world around us.
>
> *(Leite, 2003, n.p.)*

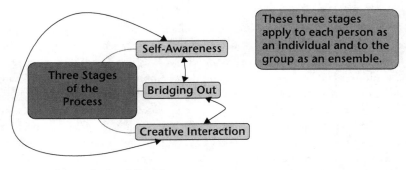

FIGURE 11.1 Improvisational Practice

When broken down, this approach to the practice of improvisation looks like the practice of being humane. It emphasizes shared responsibility in community, facilitates ways to negotiate differences, and aids in the development of listening skills, all of which contribute to shifts of awareness from the self to the group, and back.

Getting Started

Nachmanovitch (1990) writes that all creative acts are forms of play, which is the starting place of creativity in the human growth cycle and one of the great primal life functions. Without play, learning and evolution are impossible (p. 42). According to Ackerman (1999), "Because we think of play as the opposite of seriousness, we don't notice that it governs most of society—political games, in-law games, money games, love games, advertising games, to list only a few spheres where gamesmanship is rampant" (p. 11). One could add war games to the list. The spirit of play is central to this work, and the play inherently demands focus, or the need to keep one's eye on the ball as the playing unfolds. But what is the "ball"? What is the context of the play and how is it structured in higher education?

The "ball" is Viola Spolin's (1983) metaphor for the point of concentration, or point of focus. Spolin, America's most recognized pioneer in theatre games, taught that narrowing our focus in this way facilitates the *game* as it unfolds in real time. Without the "ball"—focus—there is no game. Focus is what engages and sustains an ongoing and evolving activity, keeping it alive in the present moment. Structuring a simple *score* creates limitations and conditions for things to happen. Each improvisational score establishes a language—a set of parameters or a field of focus—within which to play. Scores are like consonants, or frameworks, that are brought to life by vowels. David Abram (1996) describes how the ancient Hebrew language is comprised of consonants only, no vowels. It is our breath that shapes the consonants into vowels that form the meaning of the words (p. 242). The instructor and students' inquiry are the "vowels" that bring the concepts to life, shaping them into stories with their own interpretation and relationship to the shared human experience of rhythm, time, and communication. Keep in mind that a score can be many things, from a list you follow at the grocery store to a plan for an approach you will take in a job interview. "Performance" is shaped by one's ability to navigate the linear construct of time with the fluidity of water. Figure 11.2 shows a four-step process for building simple scores.

1. A simple seed idea defines parameters with one or two rules for engagement.
2. Play requires a willingness to experiment while letting go of judgment. It evolves through repetition, sustained focus, and working through ambiguity.
3. Reflection and discussion of the action, choices, and resultant relationships may bring up questions, suggestions for modifying the approach, and connections to other ideas or contexts.
4. Steps 3 and 4 are repeated as the inquiry deepens.

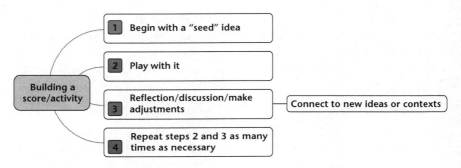

FIGURE 11.2 Foundational Practice

Defining parameters for shaping one's ideas helps provide form and content to spontaneous, intuitive interactions. Traditional musical syntax is built upon pitch, harmony, and rhythm, which narrow the realm of possibility for non-musicians. The theorist Leonard Meyer presents a series of *non-syntactic* parameters that expand the musical language to include a variety of textures. These extend contextual applications beyond traditional music into other aspects of life and can be used as basic building blocks. They include *density* (the amount of activity from dense to sparse), *dynamics* (in music this refers to varying degrees of loudness; in non-musical contexts it is the amount of energy or force used), *duration* (how long sounds are sustained), *range* (high or low range of pitch, or levels of height), *basic pulse patterns, flow,* and *silence* (Sarath, 2010).

Organization is further achieved through imitation or repetition, changing the tone color (timbre), fragmentation (deconstructing or breaking something into smaller parts), or retrograde (doing something in reverse from end to beginning). Using these parameters as tools for shaping ideas makes it easier to narrow one's focus and play with specific elements of an idea. "Technique itself springs from play, because we can acquire technique only by the practice of practice, by persistently experimenting and playing with our tools and testing their limits and resistances" (Nachmanovitch, 1990, p. 42).

This idea of practicing practice may sound odd, although when you break down the approach to deep practice, as Daniel Coyle does in *The Talent Code*, the steps are fairly straightforward. Essentially the skills are to (1) absorb the whole idea, or overview; (2) break it into chunks; (3) slow it down; and (4) repeat it. Musicians, dancers, and athletes apply these techniques in their practice (Coyle, 2009). The guitarist/composer David Torn[1] (personal communication, August 20, 2015) was describing how, when learning pieces as a kid, he would break the musical ideas apart using them as springboards for creating something new, leaving the written piece completely and constructing his own extemporaneous exploration. His folks never knew he was not "practicing" the music; but he actually was, in a deeper way, getting lost in the process by taking the new ideas into different directions. Torn was learning the written music by digesting the language and playing with it, illustrating Nachmanovitch's (1990) point of view, that improvisatory play is at the heart of creative activity—it is one of the great primal life functions and our brain's favorite way of learning and maneuvering (p. 42). Establishing and sustaining one's focus facilitates the shaping of ideas in a conversational realm, whether done as an individual activity or with others. This ability to maintain focus facilitates awareness of how everything may become a significant part of a larger field of relationships.

Awareness of Self—Focus

Self-awareness and listening are critical first steps for improvisation and ultimately for creative expression. It is about *being* in time. According to Perloff and Junkerman (1994), the composer John Cage viewed this as learning how to "inhabit oneself, to live in the depth of connection that is one's person" (p. 204), focusing, narrowing, and sustaining one's attention. The approach involves contemplative as well as more informal or pedestrian approaches to being—listening; establishing a personal relational space in which we are grounded, settled in the present and able to observe without judgment—observing with all senses, both internally and externally. Students learn to be more fully present in the classroom, meaning they are able to focus and sustain attention on evolving relationships, being respectful and responsible in relationships.

A contemplative approach to cultivating awareness and focus is through breath and body/mind awareness. Attuning to breathing ties us to the present moment. Always bringing our attention back to the breath when our mind wanders establishes a sense of being grounded, as if standing on a solid bridge with our thoughts, past, present, and future, all flowing down the river under the bridge. Jon Kabat-Zinn (2005) writes how breathing is fundamental to life:

> It is just happening . . . we usually don't pay attention to it unless we are choking or drowning, have allergies or a cold. But imagine resting in an awareness of breathing. To do so requires first that we feel the breath and afford it a place in the field of awareness, which is always changing in terms of what the mind or the body or the world offers up to divert and distract our attention. We might be able to feel the breath, but in the next moment, it is forgotten in favor of something else. The aiming is here, but there is no sustaining. So we have to aim over and over again. Coming back, coming back, coming back to the breath over and over again.
>
> *(pp. 75–76)*

Breath meditation is a contemplative practice that can be integrated into an informal or pedestrian practice by using the breath to observe the sensations in the body. This process of body/mind scanning[2] starts with observing the natural flow of our breathing, allowing the exhalation to drop further into the abdomen without force, observing the gentle turnaround into the inhalation. To begin, we allow the inhalation to only go to the top of the abdomen, hold for three counts and turn back into an exhalation. We then repeat this, again without forcing anything. Then we allow the inhalation to extend to the middle of our chest, hold for three counts, then exhale, holding at the base for three counts before inhaling again. This is repeated, then repeated again with the inhale extending to the top of the chest and held for three counts before exhaling. Observations and sensations in all body parts: torso, shoulders, neck, hips and lower back, tongue and jaw, elbows, eyes and forehead, hands, fingers, feet, and toes continually invite tension to release through exhalations. We end by returning to normal breathing, continuing to observe for a couple of minutes before finishing.

There is portability to this practice; we have an open invitation to apply any of these skills at any time—we just have to remember to remind ourselves to remember to remind ourselves to remember. One dance student was having difficulty staying balanced while performing a movement combination. Having learned this technique in an earlier class she remembered to "check-in" with a quick body/mind scan in the time of two breath cycles. Two things were revealed: that she was holding her breath while dancing, and that her right arm was tensing up at her shoulder. This observation helped her remember to breathe more freely, which opened her torso-arms-shoulder-neck and reduced her balance problem. Feeling one's breath, fusing with it and following it leads to new ways of shaping explorations. Breath becomes a primary element of discovery and an integral element in which unconscious physical acts are made conscious to further students' understanding of their physical interaction with the environment, and each other (Sellers-Young, 2002). It also forms the foundation upon which we are able to monitor and sustain attention.

Exercise 1: 60-Second Sound Score

For many, improvising with sounds can be overwhelming, as the "instrument" may be foreign or separate from our normal way of being, even when using our voice as an instrument. A 60-Second Sound Score contextualizes how we may transfer these techniques to other modes of interaction. The seed idea is painting with sound on a canvas of silence. Remembering Spolin's (1983) analogy—without the "ball" there is no game—we shift our focus from the breath to the *silence* of a 60-second window of time and the single sound we get to place in that window. Bringing the subjective experience into the objective realm is achieved by listening to recorded performances of this score while observing the language of sound shaping silence through time/space.

The 60-Second Sound Score is to be done with a group of five or more people:

1. Each person has a single, sustained, ringing sound to use only once.
2. Each person's focus is on the silence—the 60-second empty space into which they will place their one and only sound.

3. Players listen intently to the silence, making a choice of where, when, and how loud to approach their sound.

When listening to the recording of this one-minute piece, performers tend to first listen self-consciously for their one sound. Repeated listening facilitates objectivity, separating ourselves from our "sound" as "me," changing our relationship to the experience, setting up a new self-awareness in relation to time and space. In this case the silence is a foundation upon which we watch/listen, maintaining an intuitive stance for our entry into the sound-space. Repeated experiences such as this facilitate the ability to be in a heightened state of personal awareness, while opening that awareness to include others.

Listening activities such as this have caused many students to reconsider their habitual behavior of putting headphones on as soon as they step outside. As their awareness of soundscapes becomes sensitized they become curious about the symphony of sounds in the world around them. The unconventional products/artifacts (recordings of creative activities) become catalysts for students examining their personal listening habits, and their sense of aural and environmental space.

Exercise 2: Right Before Our Ears[3]—The Other

The seed idea is to listen (with headphones) to a short, challenging piece of music once a day for at least ten minutes each day for a week. Turn all phones off and do not allow anyone or anything to disrupt your attention.

Students are directed to:

- Write what you observe without editing. What are you hearing? How do you react to what you hear? Write about what you see/hear before you. Try to continue to describe it as faithfully as possible. Just write—don't overthink about what you're writing. Write whatever it is you can see/hear, and also whatever is in and on your mind. Write about what distracts you, too. And what it is like to bring your attention back to your subject. This is an exercise, but most importantly, it is *your* exercise. Be honest; do it as outlined here.

As students post this assignment nightly for a week, the instructor corresponds with comments each night allowing for direct assessment and documentation of students' progress, providing opportunities to help redirect habitual behavior—their reaction to something that was very different. Many students tend to begin repeating themselves after day 3, needing prompting from the instructor on how to listen to hear new things, or to hear in new ways. Some students were very challenged to get past their initial repulsion to the music.[4]

By carefully establishing a one-on-one online relationship with each student, over the course of a week most made a transformation and were able to "see" beyond their personal bias by identifying specific instruments to follow, listening to two instruments in relation to each other, determining what was causing the reaction they were experiencing, listening to how the range of highs and lows in pitch play out over the course of the short piece, or noticing how moving while listening made it easier. One student's final observation points to a larger issue:

> The music we have listened to thus far in the class has been unfamiliar and sometimes hard to listen to. The fear and discomfort we feel when confronted by "the other" in music is very similar to the fear and discomfort caused by "the other" in society, such as communities of people that we don't interact with often . . . how easy it is to ignore things or people that I am unfamiliar with and scared of.

This online exchange between instructor and student culminated in a class discussion about how we react in similar ways in different contexts, like social situations. The discussion touched upon assumptions we make such as racial profiling, what happens when we make assumptions and what are they based on, and what our responsibility is in this process. It became clear that the associations we bring to something are more a result of our own imagination rather than what is actually in front of us, and how important it is to become aware of what we are in relationship with, learning as much as we can about "the other."

Exercise 3: Drawing Conversations—Visual Listening

Another way to practice listening to our intuitive "voice," or inner impulse, is through drawing conversations: a my-turn/your-turn exchange where marks on a page replace spoken language.

*   The seed idea, or purpose, is to observe the point of intuitive impulse, observing the moment when you are looking at the design and something *tells* you what needs to come next. You *act* on that impulse by adding your line gesture(s), or marks, to the page: working on seeing beyond judgment and incorporating mistakes.

This score is to be done in pairs with a blank piece of paper serving as an empty, *silent* space. Using a pen, both people take turns marking the page. One person begins with a mark or line gesture; the other person responds in relation to the first mark. There are no mistakes as each mark is something on which the next person will build. Limiting our language to markings on paper invites us to "hear" the markings, as the pens become the instrument for expression and we develop visual listening. The aim is for the "person" to disappear as line gestures on the page begin to "speak," reshaping the space into a new form. A language is established through four main concepts: (1) nothing exists by itself, but in relation to what it is next to; (2) opposites generate maximum tensions; (3) variety stimulates the eye; and (4) repetition serves to unify and balance diverse elements. Abstract forms, shapes, lines, tones, and colors have a visual energy that radiates like heat waves in space and seem to have a life of their own. They interact with one another, creating tensions that communicate to the viewer without representing something from nature (Kaplan, 1998, p. 86). These concepts are shaped into visual conversations using the non-syntactic techniques mentioned earlier. The visual relationships unfolding through this score are much like relationships that we make in improvised music, but they unfold more slowly.

The conversation continues back and forth until the drawing is "done." The "finished" drawing is then analyzed, observing the use of space, quality of lines and shapes, repeating patterns, and so forth. The design is described using as many adjectives as possible. Then immediately, another drawing conversation begins, with the specific intention of creating contrast—whatever that means—based on the previous discussion. Looking at the evolving design, our actions are guided by the impulse to create a contrast to the first drawing, bypassing analytical pre-planning. When that drawing is complete, both drawings are compared, observing how contrasts were achieved, or not. "Drawing Conversations" is the first activity in a sequence that continues into a solo "doodle" project that offers opportunities to play with all aspects of improvisational practice alone, at any time. This two-dimensional design project is then extended into a three-dimensional collage, and eventually into a performance project.

Many students use the solo iteration of this doodle project as a way to relax, where it becomes a contemplative activity. Someone once presented their final solo doodle saying that they had so much homework to complete but all they wanted to do was this assignment. So they drew for two hours before doing the rest of their homework, which then seemed to get done effortlessly. This activity helped one first-year undergraduate student develop a deeper understanding of how to listen and shape ideas in another modality.

> The drawing conversation was an eye-opener . . . there are so many different ways to communicate. At first my partner and I were talking and drawing, but as the drawing became more detailed the talking stopped. I realized that objects and instruments are not meant to be "mastered" or totally controlled, but to be *linked* with. As dancers we are taught that our body is our instrument and we must learn to control and master it. It had never occurred to me to *listen* to my body and become *one* with it. Mastering and becoming one with something are two completely different things.

For this student, visual listening and interacting through two-dimensional spatial design was a portal into the improvisational process. They *became* the process, being grasped by an idea, getting swallowed up in time; the outside world disappears except for the world one is creating. Hours can go by feeling like minutes, tapping into a state much like Csikszentmihalyi's description of flow (1990).

Exercise 4a: Chaos to Unity Part One

Chaos to Unity is a warm-up score that follows an arc through each of the three stages of building an improvisational practice. Part One illustrates the first stage of the practice, Awareness of Self. It allows each person to focus internally on their personal relational space by connecting with their breath cycles. Part Two illustrates the second stage, Bridging Out, which focuses on peripheral awareness by bringing the breath cycles into sound, then into movement, gradually opening the awareness to the movement of the whole group's cycles while maintaining one's personal focus. The transition into Part Three illustrates the third stage, Creative Interaction. It begins with walking and leads to entrainment, establishing a group pulse, which is used for ensemble rhythmic play. Once the structure is learned, people are able to move through the full three-section score at their own pace, culminating in a rhythmic jam.

The seed idea for Part One of this score is to help students become fully present: first establishing one's personal awareness, then gradually expanding one's peripheral awareness to include others. A leader gives cues for the progression of the activity until the participants learn the score. The leader is also improvising, listening to the group, and sensing the right time to move the structure forward. This phase of the warm-up takes at least five minutes.

1. Begin by establishing personal, relational space by observing the flow of breath.
2. Leader's cue: bring individual breath cycles into an audible rhythm by snapping or clapping at the point at which the inhalation turns around into an exhalation. It starts to sound like kernels of popcorn, highlighting our similarities (we're all breathing) and our differences (we breathe in our own rhythmic cycles).
3. Leader's cue: take a step at the turnaround point of the breath. The rhythm is visible in the room, looking like a slow-motion, stop-action film with everyone moving at different times. While each person's focus is primarily internal, they are peripherally aware of the others, first through the snapping sounds, and now through the incremental traveling.
4. Leader's cue: the group begins walking through the full duration of the exhalation, stopping in stillness for the inhalation, opening awareness even more as we travel and negotiate with other bodies through the space.
5. Leader cue: invite everyone to notice others traveling in the same duration, and to "flock" with them—walking together as a group. The random patterns of people walking gradually begins to reshape into groups traveling

and stopping together, suggesting that as we expand our awareness out, we open ourselves to entrainment: synchronization of two or more rhythmic cycles. Flocking continues until one's natural breath patterns become stressed. Then they break away to follow their own breath rhythm.

6. Leader's cue: invite the group to walk naturally through the space, breathing normally, observing the kinesthetic flow of weaving in and out of one another with a heightened awareness of their interrelationships.

Student comments illustrate formative connections to autonomy and personal agency and a merging of who we are as individuals with what we know. One student writes, "The only way we were able to build order out of chaos was through our ability to listen [with all our senses] and adapt to each other." Another writes:

> listening to breath makes rhythm so much easier to understand and work with. It also makes a lot of sense. Breath is itself a rhythm . . . breath may just create a habit and skill for listening to rhythm and feeling it more clearly.

This student's reflection is supported by Lefebvre's (2004) view of our ability to listen first to our body and learn from it in order to appreciate and understand external rhythms. He writes, "The rhythm analyst . . . listens—and first to his body; he learns rhythm from it, in order consequently to appreciate external rhythms" (p. 19).

The process of facilitating awareness begins within oneself and is further defined as we are in relationship with others and the environment. Moving further into the practice of improvisation, we see that cycling back around to self-awareness is an ongoing part of the whole process that deepens and evolves with each new experience.

Bridging Beyond Self

The second stage of improvisational practice builds on the ability to maintain a sense of self-awareness while bridging beyond our own relational space engaging with others, playing in the space between us. In his book *Improvisation, Creativity, and Consciousness*, Ed Sarath presents the idea that "jazz's improvisation-based process scope renders it a uniquely powerful tributary that flows not only into the overarching musical ocean but the broader oceans of creativity and consciousness" (2013, pp. 3–4). He suggests that this can be a template that can inspire and inform self-transcending movement not only in other musical genres but wide-ranging fields in and beyond the arts (Sarath, 2013). The template Sarath speaks of echoes the Living Musically template mentioned early in the chapter, incorporating three learning approaches that constitute contemplative pedagogy:

first-, second-, and third-person practices. The discussion in the previous section focused primarily on first-person approaches: guiding one's internal, subjective awareness while working with imagery, somatics, and mindfulness practices. We also engage in third-person inquiry (outside us), which is more objective, analytical, and theoretical. But it is through improvisation that we engage in second-person approaches (between us) to explore ideas, bringing a whole new way of knowing to the experience (Gunnlaugson, 2009).

Exercise 4b: Chaos to Unity Part Two

The seed idea for Part Two of Chaos to Unity is the bridge from first person, subjective, to second person, intersubjective, relationships. Students make choices based on an unfolding field of relationships, where one's personal agency creates connections between knowledge, practice, and learning.

We resume the warm-up with everyone walking through the whole space, weaving in and out at one's own pace, breathing naturally.

1. To break up the monotony the leader calls out cues: walk twice as fast; twice as fast again; now super-slow-motion, and so forth, changing things up.
2. Once returning and settling back into a normal walking pace the leader invites the group to listen to each other's footfalls—the leader senses when the time is right for the next cue.
3. Listening continues, and without forcing anything, participants observe how long it takes for everyone to naturally fall into step.

Often, at this point, without being prompted, the group slowly reshapes their path into a circle or oval as they are listening to each other's footsteps. This transition period can be challenging for some who are used to imposing their will on a situation, or others who are ready to follow, bringing up each individual's relationship to *being in time*. There are instances when the group comes together very quickly, others where it slowly transitions into entrainment, and others where it becomes an extended battle of wills before someone prevails. In one instance someone was uncomfortable walking as quickly as the group, and they chose a slower gait. Although this person thought they were remaining independent, it turned out their steps were exactly twice as slow as the others, which is actually still agreeing and falling into step. "Life adapts and changes in this way, without an inherent, permanent hierarchy, with flexibility and radical adaptation to the moment and relationships with what is around it, now" (M. Montesano, personal communication, November, 2014). The transition from pedestrian walking to entrainment brings up many issues for different people as they are negotiating their actions in relation to others through time. Participants' patience is tested as they listen without forcing change, allowing a group mind to become established. A relevant passage from number 15 in the *Tao Te Ching* captures the essence of this: "Do you have the patience to wait / till your mud settles and the water is clear? / Can you remain unmoving / till the right action arises by itself?"

This simple warm-up structure inevitably brings up many questions. For example, one non-arts student writes about the "gray areas" and how things are not simply black or white:

> My question lies in the line between individuality and cooperation. How much must one sacrifice of themselves for the greater good of their group? How much will the group sacrifice to stay true to its constituent parts? Although there may not be finite answers to these questions, I look forward to exploring this gray area.

The understanding that things are not simply right or wrong opens the door for having nuanced experiences and discussion of the inner discernment of difference. We are moving from single states of awareness to the direct perception of differences and similarities. Playing in the gray areas between autonomy and community, holding a contradiction rather than resolving it, helps us practice sustaining contradictions.

Another student writes:

> Some of my peers and I discussed our own stubbornness in the walking exercise, choosing to stick to our own paces rather than conforming to the group. After the first day, one person said that in the end, everyone joined his pace, although it may be that he adjusted his pace just a slight amount and didn't realize it—I felt the same way, and I must remember to account for my own human error. This give-and-take between self and group corresponds to real life tensions between the individual and society.

The student's reflection also points out that reality is often resistant to simple resolution. As the Lebanese-French writer Amin Maalouf (as cited in Zajonc, 2006) has put it, "it is precisely through the irreconcilable complexities of our lives that our identity emerges. When we deny that complexity, as a society we quickly decompose into warring ethnic and religious factions vying for dominance" (p. 6).

Creative Interaction

Creative interaction is the final stage of this practice, where we are merged with the object(s) of our attention, listening with all our senses, engaged in an unfolding experience: letting go, constantly shedding thoughts or ideas that are not palpable in the moment. We practice through repetition, focus, use of the body, and awareness of self.[5] We have seen how all sound, movement, and markings have the ability to be used as basic means of communication or aesthetic expression—we imitate, contrast, elaborate, or fragment ideas, and play with silence-stillness-empty space. Remembering universally that nothing exists by itself but in relation to what it is next to, and that opposites generate maximum tensions, playing with two contrasting ideas can promote clarity, as we strive to communicate as clearly as possible. By practicing creative interaction we begin to see/hear/feel/taste/intuit our reality as something more than habitual existence: experiencing things as if for the first time, going from the ordinary to the *extra*ordinary, seeing the poetics in each moment.

Exercise 4c: Chaos to Unity Part Three

The seed idea for Part Three of the warm-up score consists of playing together with a common pulse, having a group rhythmic conversation, and finding an ending. We resume the score as the group has fallen into step with everyone walking to the same "beat." As this happens there is a major shift in the room, as all extraneous steps are gone and the unison footfalls pulse through the space. Out of this unison people are free to gradually "play" with the rhythm by clapping, snapping, vocalizing, stomping, and changing their foot patterns: listening to the pulse, imitating patterns heard from across the room, adding contrasting sounds or rhythms. This is a spontaneous group rhythmic conversation where awareness is seamlessly shifting from the group to the self and back; where people are negotiating through sound. Endings are perhaps the most challenging aspects of improvised music, particularly in open structures such as this. At first the instructor can cue the group to gradually find an ending; through intense listening the exercise eventually will come to a close. Through discussion and repetition of the score, or by creating new scores, we become aware of subtle cues and possibilities that increase our ability to be receptive of others, sense possibilities, and act as a group to achieve a common goal (Sarath, 2010).

This process is a synthesis of critical, creative, and integrative learning approaches that require us to find a balance between facts and the way we relate to facts. An engineering major made a connection between this practice and particle physics:

> The universe is universally made of the same material (homogeneous) and appears the same from every direction (isotropic). To this end, I have begun to perceive myself as but a small component of the whole. The periodic table of elements which culminate my being, are the same materials utilized throughout all of space and time. With this vantage point, disappearing is actually an amazing experience because it simply means looking beyond yourself and noticing all that is around you. My flow state is now easier to access because I notice everything that's around me all the time.

I can now start to switch between my reasoned knowledge and intuitive knowledge by simply acknowledging my existence in relation to the universe and letting myself enter a flow state, where my inner critic is silent and listening.

Using improvisation to facilitate integrative learning increases opportunities for students to build across the curriculum by making connections among ideas and experiences. It also allows for the transfer of learning to new, complex situations within and beyond the campus into everyday life. Another student wrote:

I compared growing in my improvisational practice to learning a new language. I have to manipulate, form connections, and really try to see beneath the surface of the meaning. In order to embody a concept I need to creatively interact with it. The group dynamics within a score changed every time we did it showing the growth as a class as well as individuals, and our increased capability to bridge beyond the self and towards others.

Over time students grow and understand how this is a flexible practice—flexible to different personal approaches and different situations. It is also an ongoing practice that often gets messy and confusing, as life often does. But the tools remain relevant. When asked to reflect on the process seven years later, a former graduate student wrote, "I find myself listening more to my subconscious thoughts and intuition and realizing their credence and importance."

Conclusion

While a course like this can be a valuable one-of-a-kind experience, the learning deepens and expands when woven through a curriculum, as in project-based curricula or instances where somatic, contemplative, or mindfulness practices are an essential part of curricula.[6] Creative learning should know no borders, and the Living Musically approach can serve as a thread that weaves through each year of a curriculum connecting concepts with lived experience. Students report that it allows them to consider, and reconsider, concepts more deeply—concepts that they either thought they understood, or had previously dismissed as simple or shallow, only to find new levels of connection and understanding.

In order to realize the benefits of the integrative and contemplative pedagogies that include first-, second-, and third-person practices, one must decrease the amount of material covered to allow time for deeper experiences. Therefore, what is gained and lost in bringing a greater emphasis on creativity to higher education? What is lost is the amount of information students learn, the breadth of information. However, there is something gained in achieving greater depth of understanding that extends into breadth in a different way. Palmer talks about how it was not until he appropriated the history of the Holocaust as a lens to scrutinize his own life story that he realized the foundations for his own moral response to such evil.

> We need to understand why a large percentage of the people who oversaw the murder of six million Jews had doctoral degrees from some of the "great" universities of the era. We need to understand how integrative forms of teaching and learning can mitigate against educational travesties and tragedies such as this.
>
> *(Palmer, Zajonc & Scribner, 2010, p. 32)*

Integrative and contemplative pedagogies such as Living Musically provide opportunities for students to connect deeply with concepts, integrating them into the heart of their personal lived experience, thus achieving a breadth of understanding in the application of knowledge. Palmer continues:

> Giving students knowledge as power over the world while failing to help them gain the kind of self-knowledge that gives them power over themselves is a recipe for danger—and we are living today with the proof of that claim in every realm of life from economics to religion. We need to stop releasing our students into the wild without systematically challenging them to take an inner as well as outer journey. Integrative education can help us do just that.
>
> *(Palmer et al., 2010, p. 49)*

How do we promote creative practices such as Living Musically through the wider university community? Many universities have incredible transdisciplinary collaborations between sciences and arts, sustainability and arts, health-wellness and arts, community-based and socially embedded programs, as well as an ever-growing number of courses that incorporate creativity and creative learning strategies. But what happens in between the projects, in between the courses? Is it possible to create an atmosphere of creative play for faculty members to engage with other faculty across disciplines in interdisciplinary labs that support the practice of improvisation as a catalyst for dialogue? Labs that allow faculty members to share approaches through participatory experiences can stimulate new pedagogical approaches, new collaborations, and new ways of engaging with habitual material.

> Creative people feed off the energy of others; they excel when challenged and forced to confront and incorporate other perspectives and approaches; and they depend on the support and encouragement of allies and colleagues when trying out new and often risky ideas.
>
> *(Tepper, 2004, p. B7)*

Most faculty members cringe at the thought of taking on more responsibility. The idea being proposed here is based upon Tepper's vision of the creative campus and Palmer's transformation conversations on campus.[7] While dialogue and conversations are invaluable, the labs that have been conducted at Arizona State University (ASU) show promise, as they give participants an opportunity to explore and play with ideas and frameworks with colleagues through varied modes of dialogue, different ways of knowing. Pairs of faculty members lead the sessions from different improvisational disciplines. The labs are small, transdisciplinary structured explorations and discussions of creativity and mindfulness, designed to contribute to the well-being of the faculty and university community. This open-ended, non-goal-oriented approach is an essential form of exploration and can become a fertile field of resources for curricular development and research over time. As Palmer writes:

> This kind of collegiality is not easily achieved, but neither is it impossible. The faculty I know who have invested themselves in such relationships report better learning outcomes for students and, equally important, new energy for their own academic lives.
>
> *(Palmer et al., 2010, p. 40)*

Daniel Nagrin (1994) writes that if one of the many definitions or uses of art is a "rehearsal for the life one fears, hopes, expects to live, and if one believes we are living in a swiftly changing environment, then the art form of improvisation becomes an exercise in attuning to an uncertain existence" in a rapidly changing world (p. x). It is in this larger context that the practice of improvisation can potentially facilitate a diplomatic role of uniting people. However, language itself can be a stumbling block. Each school or community has a culture that responds to certain ideas or words in unique ways. The I-Word and other words can trigger negative or positive reactions. As Labaree (2013) puts it:

> Maybe improvisation, or the I-word, as I choose to call it, causes no problems in your musical life. In my own, it is the source of daily dissonance, a major player in an often unacknowledged tug of war of meanings, musical politics, and practice within my immediate musical community . . . for example, "improvisatory" functions as a marker for what is free, irrational, or otherwise unexplainable in musical experience.
>
> *(p. 1)*

As stated on the Critical Studies in Improvisation (CSI) website:

> improvisation [itself] is a contested term. Its cultural significance is in dispute in both the academy and in the broader public understanding. [CSI] seeks to reveal the complex structures of improvisational practices and to develop an enriched understanding of the social, political, and cultural functions those practices play.
>
> *(Critical Studies in Improvisation, n.d.)*

Musical, movement, and other forms of improvisation are profoundly collaborative creative processes in which participants must *always* be listening, ready to change direction or modify their point of view in an instant, aware of themselves and their responsibility in relationship with others, while working together, free of judgment, to create a collective whole. This way of being in the world with others is a model worth striving for, as it engages learners in sustained, active, and experiential modalities that can effect deeper changes for new ways of making meaning. A Living Musically vision is a campus community where improvisational practice is established in all areas of learning, teaching, and research; building a community around the investigation and practice of approaches to transdisciplinary improvisation; and sharing these with faculty, students, staff, administrators, and other communities.

Notes

1. David Torn is an American composer, guitarist, and music producer. He is known for the organic blending/manipulation of electronic and acoustic instruments and performance techniques that have an atmospheric or textural quality and effect (https://en.wikipedia.org/wiki/David_Torn).
2. This practice is common in various somatic disciplines such as yoga, tai chi, the Feldenkrais Method and the Alexander Technique, body mind centering, ideokinesis, as well as in mindfulness practices.
3. Adapted from an activity, Right Before Your Eyes, by Joanna Ziegler, as her mentee at the Contemplative Pedagogy Summer Session held at Smith College through the Center for Contemplative Mind in Society, 2008. See Dustin and Zeigler (2007), pp. 154–157.
4. Students listened to the fourth movement, "Presto," of the *Chamber Concerto for 13 Instrumentalists* (1969–70) by Gyorgy Ligeti. It is 3:36 long.
5. The idea of repetition, focus, use of body, and awareness of self was something I learned from Joanna Ziegler, as her mentee at the Contemplative Pedagogy Summer Session, 2008.
6. This is the case in the dance curriculum in the School of Film, Dance and Theatre at ASU. This spiral approach helps students synthesize concepts and practices from different classes during three of their four years in the curriculum.
7. The concept of transformative conversations is central to the work of the Center for Courage & Renewal (http://www.couragerenewal.org). A brief summary of the ideas behind the Center's work can be found in a document titled "Foundations of the Circle of Trust® Approach," available at http://www.couragerenewal.org/about/foundations. For a detailed exploration of those ideas, see Parker J. Palmer, *A Hidden Wholeness: The Journey Toward an Undivided Life* (San Francisco: Jossey-Bass, 2004).

Bibliography

Abram, D. (1996). *The spell of the sensuous: Perception and language in a more-than-human world* (p. 242). New York: Pantheon Books.
Ackerman, D. (1999). *Deep play* (p. 11). New York: Random House.
Coyle, D. (2009). *The talent code: Unlocking the secret of skill in maths, art, music, sport, and just about everything else* (pp. 74–94). New York: Random House.
Critical Studies in Improvisation. (n.d.). *Focus and scope.* Retrieved from http://www.criticalimprov.com/about/editorialPolicies#focusAndScope

Csikszentmihalyi, M. (1990). *Flow: The psychology of optimal experience.* New York: Harper & Row.

Dustin, C. A. & Zeigler, J. E. (2007). *Practicing mortality: Art, philosophy, and contemplative seeing* (pp. 154–157). New York, NY: Palgrave Macmillan.

Flatischler, R. (1992). *The forgotten power of rhythm: Taketina* (p. 95). Mendocino, CA: LifeRhythm.

Gunnlaugson, O. (2009). Establishing second-person forms of contemplative education: An inquiry into four conceptions of intersubjectivity. *Integral Review, 5*(1), 25–50. Retrieved from http://integral-review.org/documents/Gunnlaugson,%20Intersubjectivity%20Vol.%205,%20No.%201.pdf

Kabat-Zinn, J. PhD. (2005). *Coming to our senses: Healing ourselves and the world through mindfulness* (pp. 75–76). New York: Hyperion.

Kaplan, S. (1998). Reflections of a teacher/artist. *The Journal of Nassau Community College Devoted to Arts, Letters, and Sciences, 7*(4), 86–88.

Labaree, R. (2013). Living with the I-word: Improvisation and its alternates. *Critical Studies in Improvisation / Études Critiques En Improvisation, 9*(2), n.p. Retrieved from http://www.criticalimprov.com/article/view/2204

Lao, T. & Mitchell, S. (1988). *Tao te ching: A new English version.* New York: Harper & Row.

Lefebvre, H. (2004). *Rhythmanalysis: Space, time, and everyday life* (p. 19). London: Continuum.

Leite, T. (2003). Music, metaphor and "being with the other." *Voices: A World Forum for Music Therapy, 3*(2), n.p. Retrieved November 21, 2015, from https://voices.no/index.php/voices/rt/printerFriendly/125/101

Nachmanovitch, S. (1990). *Free play: Improvisation in life and art* (p. 42). New York: Penguin Putnam.

Nagrin, D. (1994). *Dance and the specific image: Improvisation* (p. x). Pittsburgh, PA: University of Pittsburgh Press.

Palmer, P. J., Zajonc, A., & Scribner, M. (2010). *The heart of higher education: A call to renewal: Transforming the academy through collegial conversations* (pp. viii–ix). San Francisco: Jossey-Bass.

Perloff, M. & Junkerman, C. (1994). *John Cage: Composed in America* (p. 204). Chicago: University of Chicago Press.

Sarath, E. (2010). *Music theory through improvisation: A new approach to musicianship training* (pp. 1–7). New York: Routledge.

Sarath, E. (2013). *Improvisation, creativity, and consciousness: Jazz as integral template for music, education, and society* (pp. 3–4). Albany: State University of New York Press.

Sellers-Young, B. (2002). Breath, perception, and action: The body and critical thinking. *Consciousness, Literature and the Arts, 3*(2), n.p. Retrieved September 30, 2015, from https://blackboard.lincoln.ac.uk/bbcswebdav/users/dmeyerdinkgrafe/archive/sellers.html

Spolin, V. (1983). *Improvisation for the theater: A handbook of teaching and directing techniques* (C. Sills & P. Sills, Eds.). Evanston, IL: Northwestern University Press.

Tepper, Steven J. (2004). The creative campus: Who's no. 1? *The Chronicle of Higher Education, 51*(6), B6–B8. Retrieved from http://www.vanderbilt.edu/curbcenter/cms-wp/wp-content/uploads/Creative-Campus-Chronicle-w-Cover.pdf

Zajonc, A. (2006). Cognitive-affective connections in teaching and learning: The relationship between love and knowledge. *Journal of Cognitive Affective Learning, 3*(1), 1–9. Retrieved from http://www.arthurzajonc.org/uploads/JCAL%20Love%20and%20Knowledge%20paper.pdf

12

REALIZING THE POTENTIAL FOR CREATIVITY IN TEACHING AND LEARNING

Lorraine Stefani

Introduction

Creative learning occurs when learners are encouraged to 'think outside of the box' and offer the world new knowledge. If the purpose of a university level education is to develop the skills of critical and creative thinking, this in turn means that teachers and facilitators must also appreciate the need to relinquish control and be responsive and receptive to new ideas, new ways of thinking. To equip learners to navigate their future careers in an increasingly complex world, we need to look beyond established knowledge and be proactive in identifying issues of future relevance as well as focusing our energies on solving current problems. In essence this requires a fulsome realization of a paradigm shift from transactional to transformational learning. A critical question regarding this premise is: how can teachers or facilitators of student learning be encouraged and supported in developing, designing and delivering a creative learning environment? In turn this leads to the question of whose responsibility it is to affect paradigm change which could have profound effects on the student learning experience, a shift in thinking about the nature of knowledge in the 21st century, and a strong focus for teaching and learning on what is not known rather than what is easily accessible information?

The level of expertise within the university community in diverse fields of study uniquely qualifies higher education institutions to strive toward being a step ahead of the times. This notion underpins much of our research endeavours. In 1990 Ernest Boyer's seminal work on the Scholarship of Teaching and Learning (SOTL) was published. A key premise of SOTL is to enhance and augment learning among and between individual learners by investigating the many features of discipline specific expertise and best pedagogical practice (McKinney, 2006). Until recently, however, making meaningful changes to our time-honoured approaches to learning, teaching and assessment in such a way that we encourage and value creative thoughts and ideas has been resisted. Part of the problem may be that our established pedagogical approaches feel safe. How would we assess creative ideas, for example? How would we know that creative ideas were 'right'? How could we challenge ideas that stray from our orthodox valuing of what is 'known' rather than what is unknown?

Within universities, faculty work within a constrained and relatively controlled environment and paradoxically, while higher education institutions are creators of new knowledge through their research endeavours, not all facilitators of learning apply the same level of creative thinking and knowledge generation in the classroom. To effect change in this regard means we must support and develop teachers and facilitators, enable them to change their behaviours, shift their beliefs and empower them in such a way that they have the courage to be creative in their teaching and facilitation of learning. However to be successful in this, we first need to understand what creativity and creative pedagogies might look like. We need to understand the 'big picture' regarding the current constraints and the culture of higher education in the 21st century, and we need to exploit the potential for academic development and developers to take the lead in enabling the design, development and delivery of a higher education curriculum for creative learning.

This chapter offers an exploration of what creativity and creative learning might mean, the existing challenges regarding shifting paradigms in learning and teaching, the changing learning landscape and the potential role of academic development and developers in effecting transformation in learning and teaching. The chapter will end with a radical thought on bringing the tools of research into the domain of learning and teaching for the purpose of promoting creative learning in all of our classrooms.

Creativity in Learning

> Creativity should be a central part of what you do with learners to motivate them and better promote lifelong learning.
>
> *Andrei Aleinikov (2013, p. 327)*

> Creativity is imaginative activity fashioned so as to produce outcomes that are both original and of value.
>
> *(NACCCE, 1999, p. 30)*

The many exciting examples of creative learning and teaching throughout the chapters of this book are testimony to the idea that creative learning is occurring across many disciplines in many different higher education institutions across the globe. However, it is still considered in some way 'special' to be teaching for *creative learning*, and we must ask ourselves why this is the case. One answer to the question may be that many of us don't quite understand what it means.

Many countries perceive a need for higher education to play a profound role in contributing to a socially responsible (in the sense of critically aware rather than just compliant) citizenry (Kreber, 2009). It has often been stated both in the popular press and in scholarly works by educational philosophers such as Barnett, for example, in his books *Beyond All Reason: Living With Ideology in the University* (2003) and *Thinking and Rethinking the University* (2014) that we are living in an age of super-complexity. Climate change, for example, although it has its detractors, is without doubt creating significant challenges affecting geographical locales in different ways, with water and food shortages becoming a pressing issue for large swathes of our global population. Wars appear to be becoming more intractable, and the political will to intervene in meaningful ways comes secondary to the arms race which provides billions of dollars and jobs for those dedicated to continued production of the biggest and best weapons of mass destruction. The migration of millions of displaced people who risk their lives to escape war and persecution and then become refugees, asylum seekers and illegal immigrants presents huge humanitarian crises.

Our students and graduates and society in general face these and other unprecedented highly complex problems, often termed 'wicked problems' (Australian Public Services Commission [APSC], 2007). Tackling wicked problems is an evolving art, requiring thinking that is capable of grasping the big picture, and broader, more collaborative and creative approaches. And yet, in recent times there has been something of a capture of the purpose of higher education such that the current mantra is that it should serve the needs of the labour market (Stefani, 2014), but whose labour market would that be? Barnett (2003) argues that universities have slipped into the habit of disregarding social problems. Albeit some universities have in the last decade established public (even global) health departments and introduced development economics courses, in general we tend to spend considerable time and energy developing technology with applications for the military, but less time contemplating strategies for peace; we put significant effort into streamlining industrial processes, but we put less effort into alleviating the effects of industrial waste; we have thrown ourselves headlong into the advancement of medicine, but we forget the public health risk that occurs when a large segment of the population lacks basic access to care.

The Challenges to Creative Learning

There is a desire for creativity in learning as stated by, for example, internationally recognized leaders in the development of creativity, innovation and human resources, by the Australian Public Service Commission and the New Zealand Ministry of Business, Innovation and Employment. There are many great learning innovations often driven by passionate individuals in the learning and teaching enterprise, but paradoxically there is also a sense that in the current environment there is more of a risk-averse culture while universities focus on chasing each other up the league tables. Conformity and conservatism have become the new norm, and as a consequence faculty, interested in their own career prospects, may shy away from innovative and creative learning and teaching strategies for fear of poor evaluations from students unaccustomed to being challenged in new ways. We will not achieve the conditions for creative learning to flourish until we explore the barriers and consider the enablers to meaningful, sustainable shifts in the learning paradigm.

In the 21st century, higher education institutions should be providing an education that does not only serve the needs of the labour market but also equips graduates with a sound basis for contributing to society in many different ways. Striving toward providing society with innovative services that build on expertise in education and research is the very essence and major strength of higher education. Nevertheless we face many challenges in designing, developing and delivering a curriculum that equips graduates with the ability to critique major wicked problems, to apply their knowledge and skills in an interdisciplinary way, to transcend intercultural differences and to become active, engaged global citizens.

There is much comment in the higher education literature relating to the purpose of a university education in the 21st century. Quite possibly this is no different from questions posed during previous centuries. Some of the more recently advocated functions of universities as expressed by Boulton and Lucas, for example (2008, para. 30), include entrepreneurialism, managerial capacity, leadership, teamwork, adaptability and the effective application of technical skills. However, surely the very nature of a university education is rooted in intellectual and critical engagement with significant questions stimulated through active enquiry within individual disciplines and across disciplines (Kreber, 2010). Stated in slightly different terms but with the same overarching point being made:

> Never was the need greater for people who can combine their thinking, knowledge, capabilities and values in imaginative ways: to work with complexity to create wealth and prosperity, to tackle social and environmental problems to enrich cultures, and enhance their own development and wellbeing. Universities and higher education institutions surely have a vital role to play in the development and nurturing of creative thinkers for more creative societies.
>
> *(Jackson, 2013, p. 17)*

To effectively realize their critical role in shaping the world's future, higher education institutions need to foster a climate and culture in which creative learning *and teaching* are promoted, supported and valued; a culture that allows experimentation, new ideas, even failure—for what is failure if not an opportunity to learn?

Higher education institutions need to develop and nurture the creativity of all staff involved in the enterprise of learning and teaching and show courageous leadership in promoting creativity which inevitably entails a level of risk. It is no longer enough to teach students all that we know. Rather it is time to explore, innovate and enable the co-creation of new knowledge. A report by the European Universities Association (EUA) titled *Creativity in Higher Education* (2007) identified as key factors for fostering human potential for creativity in higher education: employing a variety of settings in which diverse roles are assigned to both students and teachers, and encouraging the learning community to question established ideas, to go beyond conventional knowledge and to strive toward originality.

In a lecture for the Glion Institute for Higher Education in 2000, J. J. Duderstadt, president emeritus of the University of Michigan, suggested that American higher education has become what, in the business world, would be called a mature enterprise: increasingly risk-averse, at times self-satisfied, and unduly expensive. Higher education is, he suggests, an enterprise that has yet to address the fundamental issues of how academic programs and institutions must be transformed to serve the changing educational needs of a knowledge economy. It has yet to successfully confront the impact of globalization, rapidly evolving technologies, an increasingly diverse and aging population, and an evolving marketplace characterized by new needs and new paradigms. He also suggested that the rapid increase in the price of a college education, driven in part by cost-shifting from tax support to tuition in public institutions, by inefficiency and stagnant productivity gains, and by unbridled competition for the best students, faculty, resources and reputations, is undermining public confidence in higher education (Duderstadt, 2000). Interestingly, through the chapters in a recent edited book by Sarah Pickard (2014) titled *Higher Education in the UK and the US: Converging University Models in a Global Academic World*, very similar points are being made about the state of higher education in the UK. The *Creativity in Higher Education* report produced by the EUA (2007) had this to say regarding quality assurance:

> Quality mechanisms set boundaries and indicate what is appreciated and valued in higher education and what is not. They reflect value systems, which have to be monitored to ensure that they mirror the institution's ethical and strategic choices. Quality processes *have the potential to strengthen creativity and innovation* if they are geared towards enhancement and focus on the capacity to change as a way to incorporate a future dimension. However, *they can also have highly detrimental effects* if they stress conformity over risk-taking, are oriented towards the past rather than the future and develop into burdensome bureaucracies.
>
> *(p. 32, emphases added)*

Some would argue that burdensome bureaucracies are exactly what quality mechanisms have become leading to increased compliance and risk aversion. The recent indication by the UK government of the introduction of a Teaching

Excellence Framework as a parallel to the Research Excellence Framework does not necessarily bode well for creativity in learning and teaching. The UK education minister is proposing a Teacher Excellence Framework (TEF) to be underpinned by an external assessment process undertaken from within the existing Higher Education landscape. The idea behind this is to re-assure fee-paying students and employers that teaching excellence is guaranteed (THES, 2015). This might be considered a move guaranteed to ensure that creativity in learning and teaching will actually be discouraged for fear that innovative approaches to learning and teaching will not 'fit' with the inevitable metrics approach to 'judging' teaching excellence. In a further cynical approach to 'regulating' the UK higher education sector, the UK government suggests that universities able to show that they offer *high-quality teaching* will be allowed to increase tuition fees in line with inflation from 2017–18! It is perhaps too tempting to consider that excellence in teaching is not the real goal of government, but rather the issue is that the more students pay, the less the government is required to fund higher education. What might be considered to qualify as 'high quality teaching' must also be a cause for concern. Surely the issue should be 'high quality learning' fit for purpose in the 21st century.

Swimming Against the Tide: Exploiting the Potential for Creative Learning

When we raise the issue of creative learning, do we mean creative thinking? Are we proposing that students learn to look at problems or situations from a fresh perspective that might well suggest unorthodox solutions? Do we mean we should be developing *creative pedagogies*? Andrei Aleinikov defined the concept of a 'creative pedagogy' as an approach to creative teaching to promote creative learning (1989). While his published work makes for difficult reading, essentially he posited that what a creative pedagogy means is that the learner is no longer an 'object' of pedagogy but rather becomes a creator of new knowledge in the field being taught. This suggests the generation of new ideas and learning from what doesn't work as well as from what does. This is the premise from which Jackson (2013) draws out four key issues relating to creative learning. The first of these relates to drawing inspiration from one's academic discipline. The discipline plays a profound role in the lives of academics and it is very likely that one's academic discipline exerts a strong influence on how we teach and how we value students' learning (Kreber, 2009, p. 19). Trowler (2009) gives further backing to this notion when he argues that faculty feel strongly that their discipline plays perhaps the most significant role in university pedagogy. A question to ask ourselves is, how do we capitalize on this to support and promote creative thinking? Jackson (2013) asks what it means to be a creative engineer, doctor, historian, teacher or any other practitioner in a discipline. He provides evidence that in eight disciplines surveyed, academics share similar perceptions of what being creative means in their discipline. Research carried out by Reid and Petocz (2010) with students and university lecturers asserts that different discipline areas generate views of creativity that are related to the domain of study and the role played by particular individuals in the pedagogical process. Clearly some lecturers inspire creativity more than others and this is an area requiring attention in academic development strategies.

In his second premise for supporting creative learning, Jackson (2013) argues for pedagogies and activities that include co-curricular experiences and opportunities that engage learners with the unfamiliar, complex, perplexing and unpredictable, to encourage them to take risks. The critical issue is that learners and learning should not be penalized for taking on the challenge even if the outcomes or solutions are unorthodox! Preparing and supporting students to think creatively requires us to transform the classroom into a creative and flexible learning environment that allows learners to innovate, create, take risks and think imaginatively. To achieve this there is a need to develop teachers such that they too have the confidence to take risks to allow creativity to flourish, and it requires significant changes to our assessment strategies such that we consider the learning process not just the product, and that we learn from our students by encouraging peer learning and peer assessment. Much has been written about the shift from the 'sage on the stage' transmitter of knowledge approach to teaching to the 'guide on the side facilitator of learning' (e.g., Stefani and Nicol, 1997; Jarvis, 2006) and changing pedagogies as a consequence of the digital age (e.g., Beetham and Sharpe, 2007; Laurillard, 2012). Jackson (2013) offers us a new option for the teacher of the 21st century which he calls the 'meddler-in-the-middle' whom he describes as an 'involved co-learner/co-producer in the learning process.' He suggests that students' creativity is best served by teachers who are 'meddlers' and 'facilitators.' Can we support teachers to become these meddlers-in-the-middle who can encourage and support co-curricular authentic learning opportunities for all students? Can we help expose our students to the wicked problems which truly exist, not just the sanitized version of problems which we have already solved?

Introducing a Learning Ecology

John Seely Brown wrote an article in 2000 titled *Growing Up Digital: How the Web Changes Work, Education and the Ways People Learn.* In this article he introduced the idea of a 'learning ecology.' He described the learning ecology as an open, complex, adaptive system comprising elements that are dynamic and interdependent: an environment in which to learn. In the context of the digital world, the concept can be further interpreted as a collection of overlapping virtual communities of interest cross-pollinating with each other, constantly evolving and self-organizing. What renders the idea of ecology so enticing is its power, its adaptability to new contexts and its diversity. The idea of the learning ecology requires the creation and delivery of a learning environment that presents a diversity of learning options to the students. This environment then provides students with opportunities to learn through models and methods that best support their needs, interests and personal situations.

Becvar (2007) further elaborates on the concept of the learning ecology, drawing on the work of Brown and Duguid (2000) with a particular focus on social learning. Students can be formed into learning teams for collaborative activities or self-organize into discussion groups where students explore learning topics. The instructional design and content elements that form a learning ecology are often dynamic and interdependent. The learning environment should enable structural elements designed as small highly relevant reusable learning objects to be reorganized into a variety of pedagogical models. This dynamic reorganization of content into different pedagogical models creates a learning system that is adaptable to varying student needs. The challenge in developing a learning ecology is to define and create an environment that balances the many resources and methods people may apply to learning. In this environment, the learner is not an 'object' of pedagogy but rather a creator of pedagogies and new knowledge.

These ideas were considered radical at the time of writing. However in his third idea relating to creative learning, Jackson (2013) refreshes the concept of the 'personal learning ecology.' He suggests that we need to encourage learners, as part of their higher education experience, to develop their own learning ecologies rather than always having learning outcomes, content and learning process imposed upon them. He likens this idea to our informal, authentic learning experiences—that is to say, the processes we develop in particular contexts to problem solve, to bring together different resources for learning, development and achievement. This is another aspect of learning and teaching that academic developers can support. It is not beyond academics in whatever discipline base to develop authentic learning scenarios and support students in the art of working in teams to take on the challenge. This is happening in pockets of the higher education terrain but is not necessarily the norm. Often faculty need support to manage new learning, teaching and assessment strategies, to manage the introduction of new and more creative pedagogies.

A relatively recent development which changes the ecology of learning is the idea of the 'flipped classroom.' At the most simplistic level, the flipped classroom is a pedagogical model in which the typical lecture and homework elements of a course are reversed. Short video lectures are viewed by students at home before the class session while in-class time is devoted to exercises, projects or discussions. Made popular by Eric Mazur (2009), the real benefit of the flipped classroom is that students (ideally) are doing the lower levels of cognitive work (gaining knowledge and comprehension) outside of class and focusing on higher forms of cognitive work (application, analysis, synthesis and/or evaluation) in class. In a flipped classroom that is facilitated well, students are motivated and incentivized to do some preparatory work outside of formal class time, deeper discussion occurs in class, correction of misconceptions takes place, support in organizing knowledge and instant feedback make for a different quality of learning experience. Research informs us that this metacognitive approach to instruction can help students take control of their own learning by defining their learning goals and monitoring their progress in achieving them (Bransford, Brown and Cocking, 2000, p. 18). Even more sophisticated levels of learning can occur in the flipped classroom when students are provided with real-life authentic challenges, and the facilitators have the courage to cope even when they don't have all the answers! In such learning situations the ecology is transformed, authentic learning is promoted and creativity can flourish.

The idea of the flipped classroom also aligns well with Jackson's fourth suggestion for developing creativity (Jackson, 2013), which is the adoption of a lifewide concept of education, a lifewide curriculum, which embraces all the spaces and places for learning, personal development and self-actualization.

The Role of Academic Development in Transforming Learning and Teaching

At the start of their careers, not all faculty understand the complexity of teaching or facilitating learning. Fortunately, in many countries there has been an increased emphasis on providing development opportunities relating to learning and teaching and even an expectation of completion of accredited programmes focused on learning and teaching enhancement. Provision of such programmes and other development opportunities and interventions has largely been the domain of academic development centres. Different universities in different countries have different titles and nomenclature for these centres and indeed for their agendas. It is not within the scope of this chapter to detail the history of academic development, but in general developers can legitimately claim to be engaged in a project to improve the quality and status of university teaching and to enhance the student learning experience (Stefani and Elton, 2002; Prebble et al., 2004; Buckridge, 2008; Kreber 2010). However, it may be time to suggest that academic development needs to change with the times. Our agenda needs to be explicitly transformative as opposed to more compliant. We need to articulate our vision of the student learning experience in the 21st century, and influence policy to move teaching and learning forward and provide the necessary purposeful development framework.

In the complex world in which we live, educators need to focus on enabling learners to become more imaginative, intuitive, critically reflective of assumptions and more creative in their problem solving or problem identification. Academic developers working in partnership with teachers within and across different disciplinary landscapes can show leadership in enabling the development of a transformative and creative curriculum. There is a wealth of resources to enable academic developers, including a significant body of research and scholarship relating to academic development—a multitude of local, national and international conferences and seminars. Prominence is given to teaching excellence awards in many universities, which requires presentation of a portfolio of classroom practice and teaching philosophy. There are professional bodies such as the Staff and Educational Development Association (SEDA) UK, the Higher Education Academy (UK), the Office of Learning and Teaching (OLT) Australia, Ako Aotearoa (National Centre for Tertiary Teaching Excellence) New Zealand, the Society for Teaching and Learning in Higher Education (STLHE) Canada. The Higher Education Teaching and Learning Association, through its journals and books, reaches out to a global community of academics, and there are many other professional bodies dedicated to the enhancement of learning and teaching, leading change in higher education and the professionalization of teaching. And yet there are still demands for improvement and enhancement and better student learning outcomes from governments around the world! We surely must ask what is going wrong, and why is academic development not making the critical impact necessary to transform learning and teaching to fit the needs and challenges of the 21st century?

As with many disciplines and professions or 'academic tribes' (Becher, 1989), academic development and developers have a tendency to talk to themselves and write for themselves in journals that most academic staff within their discipline are not accessing. While the reasons for this are understandable, with academic developers being as much subject to research and publishing pressures as faculty in any other discipline, the challenging issue is that much of the scholarship of academic development does not become embedded into learning and teaching policy and practice applicable across the whole of institutions.

To draw on some examples of innovation and creativity in the classroom described earlier such as authentic, co-curricular learning opportunities, the knowledge generation potential of the flipped classroom, the social learning opportunities afforded by technology, a critical stumbling block for effecting meaningful change is our inflexibility regarding assessment of student learning. In general, assessment of student learning is limited to that which is easy to assess. This often means assessing little more than content knowledge and understanding. What our assessment regimes often fail to determine are the less tangible higher cognitive skills that are required to equip graduates for a complex world. We tend to have as a mantra that our higher education learning and teaching strategies equip learners with critical thinking skills, but paradoxically we may lack the expertise to assess higher level critical thinking skills.

Academic developers themselves may need to become more creative in their thinking and in their approaches to supporting faculty across all disciplines to provide transformative learning and assessment experiences. To this end, academic developers could exploit the nature of different disciplines, the research approaches taken by engineers, scientists, historians and indeed all disciplines.

Research in itself is a 'creative act': it is the development of ideas and products that are original and useful; it is the examination and/or combination of existing facts, ideas and theories in original and useful ways; it is studious inquiry or examination of facts, revision of accepted theories or laws in light of new facts or practical application of such new or revised theories or laws. It might even be suggested that research is the way you educate yourself. These current interpretations or definitions of research seem to fit well with the idea of a transformative learning experience. Research is not about reiterating the old; it is about searching for new knowledge, new ideas. Exploring the scalability of research projects and bringing a research-oriented learning paradigm into the classroom could also contribute to increasing awareness of interdisciplinary research for the next generation of faculty. Authentic learning opportunities and the wicked challenges we face today require multidisciplinary and interdisciplinary approaches. The solutions to complex problems quite possibly lie in the 'liminal' spaces, the boundaries or thresholds of different academic discipline domains.

A research thesis or dissertation is not assessed through ranking or grading; it is assessed or judged by peers in the field, it is assessed by questioning how 'conclusions' were arrived at, by questioning the research methodology or approach. Given the spotlight in universities is generally on research productivity, a legitimate question is, why are we not applying our research active mindsets and skill sets to our teaching? Why is the classroom not more of a research laboratory with assessment strategies commensurate with the ways in which we judge research outputs?

Of course the argument can be made that with large classes these ideas are impractical, particularly when it comes to assessment of student learning. However the new approaches that would be required include collaborative peer, self and tutor assessment, for example (Stefani, 1994; Falchikov, 2005), portfolio approaches to personal and professional development (Stefani, Mason and Pegler, 2007). Assessment in inquiry-based learning paradigms in different disciplines is an ongoing process and requires that students demonstrate their understanding through explanation, interpretation and application. Examples of assessment within the inquiry-based learning paradigm which is not dissimilar to the suggested research-oriented approach to learning are already out there in the literature (e.g., Blessinger and Carfora, 2014), in published conference proceedings and in teaching excellence award portfolios. Academics already know how they judge research outputs. What is required now of academic developers is to exploit academics' creativity within their discipline and persuade them to use these techniques in learning, teaching and assessment; to enable everyone to flip their classroom and have confidence in their own critical thinking skills to find new solutions and creative ideas and to help learners to challenge taken-for-granted knowledge. Consideration needs to be given to curriculum design for the university of the 21st century. Chaos in the classroom is not what is being advocated, rather the approaches we have traditionally used are being questioned and challenged. What are the curriculum design frameworks we should use in the 21st century? Who are the key stakeholders in the process? New models for curriculum design are required that are responsive to changing student profiles and the pervasive influence of technologies. Authentic co-curricular learning experiences are required to support the development of graduates equipped with more than their chosen discipline-based knowledge.

To exploit the idea of personal learning ecologies and the power of technology, we could ask our students how they should be assessed, how they would like to learn, how they set their learning goals. This would perhaps be throwing down the gauntlet to our learners, or perhaps it would be liberating them and would be inviting and valuing their creative responses to the ever more complex challenges of the 21st century.

Bibliography

Ako Aotearoa, National Centre for Tertiary Teaching Excellence (NZ). https://akoaote aroa.ac.nz (Retrieved 10 August 2015).

Aleinikov, A. G. (1989) On Creative Pedagogy. *Higher Education Bulletin* 12, 29–34 cited in Aleinikov, A. (2013) Creative Pedagogy. *Encyclopaedia of Creativity, Invention, Innovation, and Entrepreneurship.* Springer, New York, p. 327.

Australian Public Services Commission (APSC). (2007) Building Capability: A Framework for Managing Learning and Development in the APS. http://apsc.gov.au (Retrieved 23 November 2015).

Barnett, R. (2003) *Beyond All Reason: Living With Ideology in the University.* SRHE/Open University Press, Buckingham, UK and Philadelphia.

Barnett, R. (2014) *Thinking and Rethinking the University.* SRHE/Open University Press, Buckingham, UK.

Becher, T. (1989) *Academic Tribes and Territories.* SRHE and Open University Press, Buckingham.

Becvar, L. A. (2007) *Investigation of the Evolving Dynamics of a Learning Ecology.* PhD Thesis, University of California, San Diego, pp. 5–8. http://hci.ucsd.edu/amaya/Dissertation_ Becvar.pdf (Retrieved 31 August 2015).

Beetham, H. and Sharpe, R. (2007) *Rethinking Pedagogy for a Digital Age: Designing and Delivering E-Learning.* London and New York: Routledge.

Blessinger, P. and Carfora, J. (2014) *Inquiry-Based Learning for Faculty and Institutional Development: A Conceptual and Practical Resource for Educators.* Bingley, UK: Emerald Group.

Boulton, G. and Lucas, C. (2008) *What Are Universities For?* League of European Research Universities, LERU Office, Leuven, Belgium.

Boyer, E. L. (1990) *Scholarship Reconsidered: Priorities of the Professoriate.* Carnegie Foundation for the Advancement of Teaching, Princeton, NJ.

Bransford, J. D., Brown, A. L. and Cocking, R. R. (2000) *How People Learn: Brain, Mind, Experience and School.* National Academy Press, Washington, DC.

Brown, J. S. (2000) Growing Up Digital: How the Web Changes Work, Education and the Ways People Learn. *Change*, March–April, pp. 11–20.

Brown, J. S. and Duguid, P. (2000) Knowledge and Organization: A Social-Practice Perspective. *Organization Science*, 12(2), 198–213.

Buckridge, M. (2008) Teaching Portfolios: Their Role in Teaching and Learning Policy. *International Journal for Academic Development*, 13 (2) pp. 117–127.

Duderstadt, J. J. (2000) *The Future of the Research University in the Digital Age*. Proceedings of the Glion III Conference, 31 May 2001, Glion, Switzerland.

European Universities Association. (2007) *Report on the EUA Creativity in Higher Education Project*. http://www.eua.be/activities-services/publications/eua-reports-studies-and-occasional-papers.aspx (Retrieved 16 August 2015).

Falchikov, N. (2005) *Improving Assessment through Student Involvement: Practical Solutions for Aiding Learning in Higher and Further Education*. Routledge, London and New York.

Higher Education Academy, UK. http://www.hea.ac.uk/ (Retrieved 17 September 2015).

Higher Education Teaching and Learning Association (HETL). http://hetl.org (Retrieved 23 November 2015).

Jackson, N. J. (2013) The Concept of Learning Ecologies. In N. J. Jackson & G. B. Cooper (Eds.), *Lifewide Learning, Education and Personal Development*. E-book, Chapter A5. http://www.lifewidebook.co.uk/conceptual.html (Retrieved 10 September 2015).

Jarvis, P. (Ed.) (2006) *The Theory and Practice of Teaching* (2nd ed.). Routledge, London and New York.

Kreber, C. (Ed.) (2009) *The University and Its Disciplines: Teaching and Learning Within and Beyond Disciplinary Boundaries*. Routledge, New York.

Kreber, C. (2010) Demonstrating Fitness for Purpose: Phronesis and Authenticity as Overarching Purposes. In L. Stefani (Ed.), *Evaluating the Effectiveness of Academic Development: Principles and Practice*. Routledge, New York and London, pp. 45–58.

Laurillard, D. (2012) *Teaching as a Design Science: Building Pedagogical Patterns for Learning and Technology*. Routledge, London and New York.

Mazur, E. (2009) Farewell, Lecture? *Science*, 323, pp. 50–51.

McKinney, K. (2006) Attitudinal and Structural Factors Contributing to the Challenges in the Work of the Scholarship of Teaching and Learning. *New Directions for Institutional Research*, 129 (Summer), pp. 37–50.

National Advisory Committee on Creative and Cultural Education (NACCCE). (1999) *All Our Futures: Creativity, Culture and Education*. DFEE, London.

Office of Learning and Teaching (Australia). http://www.olt.gov.au (Retrieved 20 November 2015).

Pickard, S. (Ed.) (2014) *Higher Education in the UK and US: Converging University Models in a Global Academic World*. Brill, Leiden and Boston.

Prebble, T., Hargreaves, H., Leach, L., Naidoo, K., Suddaby, G. and Zepke, N. (2004) *Impact of Student Support Services and Academic Development Programmes on Student Outcomes in Undergraduate Tertiary Study: A Synthesis of the Research*. http://www.educationcounts.govt.nz/Publications/tertiary_education/5519 (Retrieved 31 August 2015).

Reid, A. and Petocz, P. (2010) Diverse Views of Creativity for Learning. In Claus Nygaard, Clive Holtham & Nigel Courtney (Eds.), *Teaching Creativity—Creativity in Teaching*. Oxfordshire: Libri, pp. 103–120.

Society for Teaching and Learning in Higher Education (Canada). http://www.stlhe.ca (Retrieved 23 November 2015).

Staff and Educational Development Association (UK). http://seda.ac.uk (Retrieved 20 November 2015).

Stefani, L.A.J. (1994) Peer, Self and Tutor Assessment: Relative Reliabilities. *Assessment in Higher Education*, 19 (1) pp. 69–75.

Stefani, L. (2014) A Case Study of the Land of the Long White Cloud. In P. Blessinger & J. P. Anchan (Eds.), *Democratizing Higher Education: International Comparative Perspectives*. Routledge, New York and London, pp. 111–124.

Stefani, L. and Elton, L. (2002) Continuous Professional Development of Academic Teachers through Self-Initiated Learning. *Assessment and Evaluation in Higher Education*, 27 (1), pp. 117–129.

Stefani, L., Mason, R. and Pegler, C. (2007) *The Educational Potential of E-Portfolios: Supporting Personal Development and Reflective Learning*. Routledge, London and New York.

Stefani, L. and Nicol, D. (1997) From Teacher to Facilitator of Collaborative Learning. In S. Armstrong, G. Thompson & S. Brown (Eds.), *Facing Up to Radical Changes in Universities and Colleges*. Kogan Page, London, pp. 131–140.

THES, Times Higher Education. (1 July, 2015) *Jo Johnson Unveils Teaching REF Plans*. https://www.timeshighereducation.co.uk/news/jo-johnson-unveils-teaching-ref-plans (Retrieved 31 August 2015).

Trowler, P. (2009) Beyond Epistemological Essentialism: Academic Tribes in the 21st Century. In C. Kreber (Ed.), *The University and Its Disciplines: Teaching and Learning Within and Beyond Disciplinary Boundaries*. Routledge, London and New York.

PART IV

Conclusion

13

THE FUTURE OF CREATIVE LEARNING

Linda S. Watts and Patrick Blessinger

With the contributors' perspectives regarding creative learning in mind, what synthesis of the implications of this work might emerge? As a provisional conclusion—for creativity is nothing unless it remains open-ended—this chapter will reflect on the nature of creativity and explore the immediacy of creative learning to the current moment in higher education. Based upon those considerations, we will enumerate ten principles that seem compatible with the best-so-far practices affirmed within this book. We will then examine what challenges such experiences pose for instructors. Next, we will discuss what difficulties creative learning practices pose to institutions of higher education, and weigh what would be involved in approaching colleges and universities to function ever more fully as creative learning environments. Finally, we will identify some reasonable next steps in promoting creative learning within 21st-century higher education.

What, Then, Is Creative Learning?

With regard to learning, Plutarch asserts,

> For the mind does not require filling like a bottle, but rather, like wood, it only requires kindling to create in it an impulse to think independently and an ardent desire for the truth.
>
> *(Babbitt, 1927, 255–256)*

We might think of creative learning as the fanning of that vital flame, whether accomplished by efforts from the student, the instructor, the learning environment or, in the best scenarios, a combination of the three. Through passionate curiosity, active engagement, and open-ended inquiry, instructors and students together create an atmosphere in which inquiry and passion for learning produces unconventional perspectives, new questions, innovative research, imaginative findings, and changed outlooks.

Is Creativity a Gift?

For many years, the discourse in education surrounding creativity tended to perceive and portray it as something rare, even anomalous as a phenomenon. Within such a framework, it would seem that only a small subset within any student population possesses distinctive attributes associated with creativity. Often, such a paradigm conflated creativity with high intelligence, regarding both as rarities reserved for an elite population of 'gifted and talented' students. Not only does such a model of creativity imply that creativity is an exceptional occurrence, it also suggests that it is a property inborn in individuals. Within that view, educational settings might at most address the needs of such extraordinary students to work at an appropriate challenge level within their schooling.

Among the unfortunate (and likely unintended) consequences of such a definition of creativity is the notion that just as high intelligence is supposed relatively uncommon, so is creative ability in students. As a result, the tendency within education has been to reinforce such a bifurcation between creativity's haves and have-nots. If creativity is envisioned as a personal attribute reserved for the few, then it proves of little consequence to the way most students learn. At best, it is a consideration in delivery of instruction for those unusual students who are categorized as creative.

At the opposite end of the spectrum from the 'genius theory' about creativity— which essentially arises from the historical period of Romanticism—is the notion that not only does every individual have creative potential, but also deserves the opportunity to cultivate that ability through higher education (Davis and Arend, 2013, 119). One of the premises of this collection is that *all* students function as creative learners and possess creative potential. While that creative turn may manifest itself in different ways, extents, and circumstances, every individual learner benefits from an educational setting that attends to the needs and benefits of such creativity through thoughtful instruction. *If all students possess the potential for creativity, then teachers do well to consider how their instructional objectives, curricular designs, learning assessments, and institutional structures reflect that fact.*

Is Creativity a Choice?

As distinct from the exceptionalism argument regarding creativity, we might suggest that creativity is a virtue on which any learner may advance. In that sense, creativity may be an intentional act, or choice, on the part of both instructors and students. Where innovation is a value, and when multiple possibilities may be entertained in company, learners are more inclined to tap into their creative energies. In other words, within a customary model of education as information transmission and content retention, there is little incentive—or even rationale—for a student to produce fresh perspectives or arrive at new possibilities. In fact, where students perceive college learning as a routine procedure with one correct method and a stable, finite, and universally correct result, they have a substantial disincentive for personal interpretation or novel approach. *In a situation where unexpected responses are valued, however, students are both more disposed and more incentivized to engage learning creatively.*

Is Creativity a Skill or Behavior?

As distinct from those who posit creativity as an inborn property of select individuals, another perspective approaches creativity as an activity in which anyone may engage. Within such a framework, the emphasis is on configuring instruction in such a way that students are afforded opportunities not only to express their creativity, but also to develop, direct, and take greater ownership of it. In other words, all students need rehearsal in exercising creative thinking and creative production of knowledge. On these terms, creativity may be regarded as a skill to be exercised, rather like a muscle that needs motion to maintain its tone, build its control, and increase its strength.

This perspective allows that creativity is, like other academic abilities, something that flourishes with time, practice, and patience. If education is engaged as more than the transfer of information, or something else, then such opportunities to summon creativity and marshal it for enhanced learning become a priority. For this reason, there is sound basis for instructional designs in higher education that invite students to do more than accumulate information and display content mastery. Such things, while necessary conditions for intellectual development, are of limited use without a sense of how to bring that knowledge to bear on actual issues, problems, or questions. *Increasingly, stakeholders in higher education (from students to employers) are less interested in what graduates know than in what they can do with what they know.*

Is Creativity a Practice?

Not long ago, it became fashionable in higher education to cast the engaged relationship between instructors and students as chiefly the act of shared knowledge production. Rather than receiving an education passively, students were participating in creating knowledge. And while knowledge is undeniably valuable to a learner and serves as the foundation for higher order learning, it is not sufficient in itself. In other words, knowledge creation is a necessary condition for learning but not a sufficient one. As Albert Einstein is credited (perhaps erroneously) with saying, "Any fool can know. The point is to understand." Creative learning is neither the receipt nor the relay of knowledge by a student, but rather the process by which new insights take shape and/or find application. *Based upon the case studies and conceptualizations of creative learning included within this book, it might make most sense to say that creative learning is a context-sensitive capacity for contending with complexity that anyone might cultivate given the proper conditions.*

How Might Educators Promote Creative Learning?

It is daunting to set forward advice on a topic such as creativity in higher education. There is, first of all, the question of definition. Even if we work toward a shared understanding of what creativity involves, it is no small matter to address ways in which, or strategies by which, we might increase its role in the design, delivery, and results of college and university instruction (Robinson, 2011; Nygaard et al., 2012; Sweet and Carpenter, 2013). Furthermore, there may be important differences among embracing creativity, fostering creative expression, and promoting creative learning.

Almost fifty years ago, Nevitt Sanford contended: "If the disposition to creativity embodies such traits as independent thinking, openness to experience, and breadth of view, then we are talking about something that can be developed or at least encouraged in college" (Heist, 1967, 98). Nonetheless, the notion of education for creativity continues to prove contentious, with some continuing to maintain that creativity cannot be taught. *Whether or not one believes that creativity can be taught, there is good reason to suppose that creativity can—and should—be tapped more effectively in the context of higher education.*

Why Is It Crucial to the Current Moment?

In this historical moment, there are considerable pressures on and within the academy that are calling for higher education to reexamine its assumptions and revamp its practices. Some of these pressures, though, function as counterforces against the movement toward making colleges and universities ever more creative learning environments.

A few examples may suffice to summon this paradox. As promising as the Information Age may be for broadening access to higher education, the brisk proclivities of digital technology may sometimes work against reflection, and the persistence of a digital divide still constrains inclusion. An era of public accountability challenges higher education to prove the impacts of its instruction, while at the same time placing a disproportionate emphasis on those results easiest to measure rather than those most profound in the lived world of learners. A business model applied to higher education offers ways to make tertiary education more efficient with its stewardship of resources, but it may not always follow that such interventions make it more effective or equitable for learners. Still, one might argue that *under current circumstances in higher education, particularly the rapid changes in funding and framing, colleges and universities have few if any alternatives to engaging creative learning as means to transform higher education to address existing and emerging needs.* To do so, we must find productive ways of engaging and transcending the paradox.

What Best-So-Far Practices Do These Chapters Identify?

As editors, our selection of contributors for this anthology reflects our shared conviction that creative learning transcends individual capacities, disciplinary constraints, national boundaries, and institutional barriers. Chapter authors include individuals who lead campus-level or field-inclusive efforts to improve postsecondary teaching and learning, especially as they pertain to promoting creativity. Their instructional areas range widely, with representation of such curricular areas as education, policy/leadership, fashion/design, performance studies, philosophy/general education, mathematics, film-theatre/dance, and marine studies. Taken together, their chapters offer readers both case studies in effective practice and insightful chapters about creative learning. All authors agree that creativity can be learned and enhanced by anyone, given the right motivation and the right environment. Therefore, *we argue that creative learning is, in large part, intentional, and as such may be cultivated by learners, stimulated by teachers, fostered through curriculum and learning activities, and promoted by institutions of higher learning.*

It is both hazardous and unhelpful to pretend that creative learning can be reduced solely to instructional procedures. As Parker Palmer has indicated in *The Courage to Teach: Exploring the Inner Landscape of a Teacher's Life*, we err if we rely too much on our techniques, as if mistaking the apparatus of education for its attainments. He writes: "Technique is what teachers use until the real teacher arrives" (Palmer, 1998, 5).

Although it would run contrary to the very nature of creative learning to propose a particular protocol for its enhancement throughout higher education, it may nonetheless be possible to articulate ten guiding principles that appear to accompany creative learning and to characterize environments hospitable to creative learning practices.

Principle #1: Playfulness

Higher education has a long-standing reputation, whether favorably or unfavorably so, for being serious. While it is vital to approach higher education with a sense of seriousness of purpose, we need not always take ourselves so seriously, particularly if our shared purpose is prompting creative learning. As many scholars included within this book indicate, some of the most timely investigations of creative learning seek to engage the digital world, in which distinctions between formal and informal learning, public and private learning, and academic and social endeavors become ever more blurred. Because digitally mediated activities tend to bring our various identities and social worlds into contact with one another, it may be additionally important to adopt a more playful approach to creative learning. Whether directly utilizing platforms such as gaming or social media, instruction that engages this digital sensibility as a feature rather than a flaw may prove useful in promoting creative learning experiences.

For example, in her contribution to this book, Alison James directs attention to the power of play within higher education. Whether discussing the educational use of LEGO® SERIOUS PLAY® or other three-dimensional modalities, James deems play 'the partner of creative learning.' It not only supports the construction of new forms, but it also helps students travel to new cognitive and conceptual fields of action in their learning.

Where students form an appreciation for the generative and flexible energy of play, they become more disposed to try unfamiliar methods, explore hunches, and pursue possibilities for creative learning.

Principle #2: Improvisation

Another recurring image across this book's chapters involves the relevance of the theatrical concept of improvisation to creative learning. In one sense, this notion of improvisation underscores the sense in which creative learning does not typically follow a preset protocol. Rather, it remains a somewhat unpredictable process in which learners may make unexpected choices, employ unconventional strategies, revise their approaches based upon findings, and explore multiple (often simultaneous) possibilities. It is only when students contend with unstructured and open-ended inquiries that they can develop some of the crucial abilities for creative learners.

Kanta Kochhar-Lindgren's international arts-research projects offer a case in point. Her innovative theatre and dance projects help higher education instructors reimagine the way collaboration can speak constructively to lived-world challenges. For instance, her work on water offers a model of how common concerns in the world can lead to common ground through practice-as-research transnational partnerships.

Similarly, Lorraine Stefani's chapter on "Realizing the Potential for Creativity in Teaching and Learning" identifies the importance of both new partnerships and new media in higher education. For example, she stresses the value of thoughtful coordination of curriculum and co-curriculum in promoting creative learning on campus. Further, she urges educators to consider the role of emerging technologies in students' personal learning ecologies.

When students cultivate their comfort with the unscripted nature of creative learning activities, they become more adept at developing adaptive strategies and formulating imaginative responses.

Principle #3: Rhythm

It is intriguing how frequently the book contributors here, along with other scholars of creative learning, invoke the musical concept of rhythm to describe the shared experience of productive immersion in a shared task.

Robert Kaplan suggests that movement, and in particular, rhythm, is integral to both our self-awareness (personal rhythm) and our creative connections to others (shared rhythm). He challenges educators to embrace the ways in which breath and body/mind awareness can promote contemplative practice and creative interaction. Such attunements are particularly helpful to development of transferable skills, such as articulation, active listening, and collaboration.

In characterizing the psychology of optimal experience, Mihaly Csikszentmihalyi set forward the concept of 'flow.' " 'Flow,' [he explains] is the way people describe their state of mind when consciousness is harmoniously ordered, and they want to pursue whatever they are doing for its own sake" (Csikszentmihalyi, 1990, 6). Like Csikszentmihalyi's notion of 'flow,' the idea of rhythm suggests the sense in which *creative learning asks students to embrace an experience that is engulfing, and further asks them to consider how collaboration could be approached as a mutual experience of activity purposefully synchronized over a duration in time.*

Principle #4: Resourcefulness/Innovation

Dancer/choreographer Twyla Tharp once described innovation in this way: "In essence, you are giving yourself permission to daydream during working hours." The capacity for wonder and the freedom to dream with one's eyes open both prove important to the development of creative learning across subject areas and levels of study.

Fredricka Reisman's discussion of graduate students enrolled within an online program in creativity and innovation suggests how students can bridge between their academic and professional lives, and in so doing become ever more creatively engaged learners. She also advances some thoughts about how such innovative learning in higher education may be thoughtfully assessed using new models and instruments. That is, student learning assessment needs to align explicitly with expectations for creative learning. (Treffinger et al., 2002; Kaufman et al., 2008; Fleith et al., 2014)

As several contributors to this book have established, *creative learning is significantly more likely to occur in a setting where students give themselves, and are afforded by peers and instructors, permission to muse, speculate, and even daydream.*

Principle #5: Risk-Readiness

In "A Plea for Intellectual Risk-Taking," novelist Erika Duncan makes a case for the value of experimentation to intellectual growth (Duncan, 1984, 195). That is, in one's learning journey, a student can either become risk-averse or risk-ready.

The risk-averse student may succeed in higher education, but largely through reinforcement of prior learning and repetition of prior performances. They make the learning environment, and its outcomes, predictable by avoiding taking chances. By the same token, however, they make their educational progress more shallow and their products more conventional.

Other students, often by prioritizing increased sophistication in capacities achieved over highest possible grades awarded, develop the ability to view a learning task from unexpected vantage points with unforeseen and welcome results. These risk-ready students have come to value the role of trial within learning; further, they recognize that digressions and mistakes may prove momentary setbacks, but often enough yield deeper learning and more profound growth. As author Aniekee Tochukwu once put it, "Problems contain the seeds of our glory." Creative learners value experimentation, tolerate ambiguity, thrive on collaboration, and persist in contending with a complex task or problem.

As a case in point, consider Nives Dolšak and Cinnamon Hillyard's work with first-year undergraduates. Their project offers a persuasive example of how active learning strategies can help students experience creative learning through immersion in scenarios. They challenge students to build trust within groups, forge efficacious collaborative relationships, and realize new levels of cooperation (and its accompanying rewards).

Those willing to remain venturesome within their educational development are much more likely to uncover new strategies and devise creative solutions.

Principle #6: Resilience

For many years, educators interested in creativity sought to identify factors that would assist them in measuring a student's creative potential. As Robert Sternberg and others have noted, however, this process of identification only becomes more difficult as students participate in schooling. As students attend school and mature, they tend to display increased signs of intellectual conformity (Beghetto and Kaufman, 2010, 412). The more schooling completed, the more likely a student will be inclined to follow a well-worn path, however imperfect, to a task's execution.

A student who expects to perform flawlessly in a new activity on their first attempt is easily thwarted. By contrast, learners who give themselves time and room to grow are apt to improve over time. They cultivate confidence within themselves by adopting the premise that a task they find difficult at first will respond to consistent effort over time. They recognize that a complicated and even strange problem stands to teach them more than a simple and familiar one. They understand that instructors who challenge them to do their best work in the face of such problems do so in order to raise the level of their students' learning. Students' ability to rally when faced with hardships, whether within the classroom or without, is crucial to their long-term effectiveness as creative learners.

As Gina Rae Foster's work suggests, a student's demonstrated attributes in responding to untoward or adverse conditions proves a salient factor in their prospects for creative learning. Among these properties, she highlights the importance of capacity, community, flexibility, and stability. Such abilities/ resources are crucial to persistence and performance in higher education, as student success studies indicate. Apart from the difficulties of pursuing advanced degrees, college and university students come to the experience with a stress load and, often enough, residual trauma from prior life and work experiences. Once matriculated, such students face new or additional challenges for growth. In particular, Foster identifies the role such resilience plays within students' abilities to engage in critical thinking, goal-setting and assessment, time management, communication, and creative problem solving.

When students engage their work with a sense of agency in a learning environment where they receive both challenge and support for its encounter, they are more disposed toward creative learning.

Principle #7: Responsiveness

Deep and humane discussions are crucial to many forms of creative learning in higher education. These rich experiences prove especially challenging to sustain when topics are controversial, views conflict, and class size is large. While most students are accustomed to conversations, most are really a "succession of monologues," as critic Stephen Bonnycastle observes (1996, 5). True dialogue means much more than just talk; it is instead a subtle and mutual process. Dialogue involves a set of values to which participants freely dedicate themselves. It also relies upon some key practices, such as listening, encouraging, balancing, asking, explaining, and compromising. Students often undervalue dialogues because they are risky, unpredictable, and remind us that knowledge is neither perfect nor permanent. As with most any human practice, we can also cultivate dialogue.

Thomas F. Beech, of the Fetzer Institute, an organization whose mission is to "foster awareness of the power of love and forgiveness in the emerging global community," has characterized this need for responsiveness in terms of listening. He writes,

> When I can't—or don't—listen, I shut out external voices and shut down internally as well. If I listen deeply enough, however, I hear not only new ideas and valuable information but also hopes and dreams, joys and sorrows. I hear what is not said as well as what is spoken. I hear people the way they want to be heard, the way they hear themselves. I hear *them*. This kind of listening involves more than my ears. It engages my eyes, my body language, and most of all my heart.
>
> *(Beech quoted in Intrator, 2005, 82)*

Stephen Brookfield's piece on reenvisioning strategies for classroom-based discussion offers several ways to open up dialogue, deepen listening, and make ever more purposeful conversations among learners. In the ways he invites students to inhabit silence productively, to visualize or dramatize discussion, and to engage in embodied practice, Brookfield helps students explore richer, more intricate forms of classroom contact, connection, and co-creation.

In part because creative learning so frequently relies on effective communication with others, it is important for students to build their abilities to conduct, and be guided by, meaningful spoken exchanges that can proceed toward new avenues of shared understanding.

Principle #8: Reflective Practice

The higher education student's experience often seems headlong, with few if any embedded opportunities to consolidate, integrate, or synthesize learning. Most educators, however find such 'serial learning' both limited and limiting. On the importance of reflection, author Dawna Markova once declared,

> What brings us to wisdom is using our consciousness to reflect on our thinking. It doesn't just happen to us as we grow older. We can choose to 'quest' ourselves forward. We can search for the larger questions that lead us beyond *either* and *or*. These evocative questions challenge how we think, how we diminish ourselves and fragment the world. They can cleave open the habits of mind that enslave us.
>
> *(Markova quoted in Intrator, 2005, 63)*

In other words, students cultivate wisdom through sincerity in posing big questions and forthrightness in reflecting on their findings.

Linda S. Watts's course on contemplative practices for the helping professions, incorporating as it does mindfulness practices such as meditation, photography, guided visualization, and reflective writing, hinges on the notion that metacognition is as important for the graduate of higher education as for its students. By taking such an approach to creative learning, students simultaneously cultivate central practices within many professions, including observation, description, narrative, commentary, advocacy, and intervention.

Creative learners recognize that and how reflection is importantly a tripartite practice, involving one's ability to look back (retrospective), look within (introspective), and look ahead (prospective).

Principle #9: Reciprocity

Although much of higher education continues to be calibrated to an individualist and entrepreneurial model of learning, in which students compete both directly and indirectly, creative learning becomes more plausible in an atmosphere where students can readily see that their destinies, in both learning and life, are intertwined. As early as 1967, figures such as Donald W. MacKinnon attempted to shift the focus on creativity in higher education from identifying creative individuals to investing in creative collectives (Heist, 1967, 1–20). Subsequent developments in higher education, such as community-based learning, call for respectful and reciprocal learning not only with one's student peers, but also with one's community partners.

David Giles and Clare McCarty, through their discussion of phenomenological strategies for instruction, encourage us to keep in mind "a relational foundation to educational endeavor in Higher Education." They call for their students to inhabit the creative space of 'between' while learning in partnership with others. In this way, learners develop such sensibilities as tact, resoluteness, and moral judgment.

Creative learning environments help students grow in terms of valuable and lifelong areas of excellence including empathy, responsibility, and ethical conduct.

Principle #10: Irreverence

There is also a sense in which creative learners must hold in tension their regard for the learners who came before them and their need to challenge the accuracy, sufficiency, and continued relevance of previous knowledge. In this regard, and in the words of physicist Richard Feynman, creative learners may be urged to "study hard what interests you the most in the most undisciplined, irreverent and original manner possible" (Feynman, 2005, 206). To engage in creative learning, one must be prepared to ask tough questions both of oneself and others. Such questioning is necessary not for purposes of competition, but rather to join and contribute to an ongoing academic and social discourse that may demand refinements, whether large or small.

Gray Kochhar-Lindgren's work with the Common Core at the University of Hong Kong represents a hope-inspiring case for 'whole-person education' that positions learners to see traditionally separated bodies of knowledge and fields of endeavor through their interplay. He writes, "Creative learning, in this context, is an interactive multiscalar practice that actively constructs connections between sites, questions, capacities, materials, methods, and experiences that, incrementally shaping collective and individual dispositions, creates a tendency *toward*."

Creative learning directs students to the possibilities of the thresholds between, and interstices among, conventionally divided areas of inquiry.

What Challenges Does Creative Learning Pose for Instructors?

For those who might be overwhelmed by the prospect of reconfiguring higher education to promote creative learning, we would simply suggest that such changes need not be entire and instant to prove beneficial to learners. Rather, the difference can be implemented in increments or by degrees. Often, this means examining a course design and looking for places where a student activity, assignment, or experience can be made more inviting for the purposes of creative learning. In other words, we recognize that, for a host of sound reasons, instructors must balance competing demands for content coverage, course sequencing, skill scaffolding, and the like. Still, there may be moments where a given prompt can offer students a chance for open-ended inquiry, inventive thinking, or creative problem solving.

Take, for example, one of the challenges Linda faces in teaching courses devoted to the study of literature. Students in humanities courses, particularly those enrolled for purposes of satisfying degree distribution requirements, may think that they are in such a course to become 'well-rounded' individuals or to develop 'appreciation' for the arts. While these are understandable assumptions, particularly based upon the usual rhetoric surrounding general education programs, their tendency is to render students passive spectators in their own learning. That is, they approach the course as if their purpose is to become better audience members for the creative efforts of others.

Where this is the case, it can be difficult for students to sense the immediacy of learning or to express internal motivation to excel. Sometimes, however, a fairly modest shift in orientation on a given assignment can begin to address this difficulty and help students engage more authentically in creative learning. For instance, in a course on "Literature of the Civil Rights Movement," students simultaneously learned the history of the social movement and studied examples of literary expression emerging from, and/or chronicling, the movement (such as Alice Walker's *Meridian* and Toni Cade Bambara's *The Salt Eaters*). As one of their culminating activities for the course, the challenge for students became to think carefully about the gaps in currently available civil rights literature. The core of the prompt read as follows:

> Your central objective within this assignment is to 'pitch' an idea for a critically needed new work of civil rights literature. The idea you advance must (1) feature at least one African American female participant in the Civil Rights struggle; (2) illuminate the meanings and realities of the Civil Rights Movement in the United States; (3) detail a plan for the literary work and articulate a rationale for its specific manner of literary treatment; and (4) articulate both the work's audience and the work's historical significance and cultural impact. Your work should take the form of an original poster, which you will be required to research, develop, and present at a campus-based poster session.

Linda asked class members to shift their perspectives—from respondents to civil rights literature to advocates for it—by arguing for a specific work that we urgently need but do not yet have.

In completing this assignment students could not remain consumers of litera-ture. Rather, they had to think of themselves as proponents, and in some cases authors, of urgently needed literary works on a given topic. In so doing, they gained a measure of control over their approach to the assignment (choice), they got the chance to argue on their own terms (voice), and they were pushed to think beyond existing literature to imagine a need and develop a proposal for a literary work that would speak to that need (vision). In this way, students used their knowledge of existing civil rights history and civil rights literature as a means by which to question what is missing, imagine what could be beneficial, and argue for what is most immediately needed by today's (and perhaps tomor-row's) readers.

As this small example suggests, *any instructional move that entrusts to students the work of pursuing meaningful, difficult-to-resolve questions can contribute to creative learn-ing in a course and help build a creative learning environment on a campus.*

What Would It Take for Colleges and Universities to Function as Creative Learning Communities?

It stands to reason that if we, as educators, expect our students to engage learning as a transformative process, we must require the same of ourselves as instructors. In order for higher education to become ever more hospitable to making its sites function as creative learning environments, we must be willing to acknowledge that such a goal might require some structural and institutional changes for col-leges and universities.

One such level of structural change involves the curriculum in higher educa-tion. While the postsecondary curriculum is always undergoing revision, it is generally additive or subtractive rather than revolutionary in nature. This fact makes educators who are committed to creative learning come to grips with the problem of precedent. As Csikszentmihalyi puts it, "Schools teach how to answer, not to question" (quoted in Jackson et al., 2006, xix). How can we reinvest in higher education, imbuing it with the verve and promise of creative learning?

Next there are the challenges of accountability currently facing higher educa-tion. Central among these is the assessment of student learning in colleges and universities. According to Norman Jackson, the way we approach student learn-ing assessment in itself often constrains or even discourages creative learning in higher education. He writes,

> Creativity is inhibited by predictive outcome-based course designs, which set out what students will be expected to have learned with no room for unanticipated or student-determined outcomes. Assessment tasks and assessment criteria which limit the possibilities of students' responses are also significant inhibitors of students' and teachers' creativity.
>
> *(Jackson et al., 2006, 4)*

As educators, we must seek balance in assessment, forming clear and mutual expectations for a creative learning experience while avoiding too formulaic and prescriptive methods for its evaluation.

In addition, it is time to look anew at the manner in which we calculate faculty instructional load and conduct collegial review of instruction. Both processes need to reckon in substantive ways the factors involved in delivering participatory, transformative learning experiences. Further, higher education must take care to ensure thoughtful review of faculty performance in conducting high-impact practices, which may prove more elusive to document. Student learning in such cases is often subtle, various, and longitudinal in nature (Kuh, 2008).

Finally, if creative learning is to thrive in higher education, it must become prominent during key moments in institutional decision-making, such as shared governance, strategic planning, and budgeting. For instance, most colleges and universities need to invest more consistently and shrewdly in professional development opportunities for higher education faculty and staff if they are to become ever more robust agents of creative learning at the course, unit, and institutional levels.

What Are Reasonable Next Steps in Pursuing Creative Learning?

Whether out of conviction or of necessity, recent higher education has gravitated toward new experiences for its students and new outcomes for its graduates. Increasingly, institutions lay claim to serving as environments for profound learning. It is tempting to be a little skeptical about these purported paradigm shifts. At Linda's current campus, for example, the mission and vision speak of transformational learning. More than once, when uncomfortable with the hubris of such declarations, she has quipped that "our students are transformed by the experience of study; now they are dreadful, but in a whole new way." While we believe wholeheartedly in learning as a transformative process, we remain uneasy about it as a marketing claim to our prospective students or an implied warrant of merchantability with regard to our graduates. It is too easy to fall into hyperbole. Creative learning must be understood as a vital component of quality higher education.

To accomplish this end, educators must revisit the relationship between *criticality* and *creativity* in postsecondary education. Traditionally, many people have regarded creativity as a personality characteristic. According to this view, within a family or a classroom, a given individual may distinguish herself or himself on the basis of a disposition or perceived inclination toward creativity. Frequently, this determination relies upon a rather limited notion of creativity as the province of particular domains, usually aesthetic ones. On these terms, the creative individual emerges as one who gravitates toward artistic endeavors and excels in them. Within such a system, there is an implicit division of labor in which some individuals contribute the critical thinking, with distinct others providing the creative thinking.

In the context of debates regarding general education programs for under-graduates, for example, it is often the case that colleges and universities empha-size the role of critical thinking within their curriculum. Indeed, it is the rare higher education instructor who does not suppose that they are engaged in mak-ing their students better critical thinkers. There is much less consensus, however, regarding the elements of critical thinking. Most favor a definition that features a willingness to examine assertions, an ability to analyze truth claims, a skill for posing and pursuing questions that help build understanding, and inform result-ing judgment and action. In short, critical thinking in higher education tends to be cast as an analytical process.

Some colleges and universities have begun to explore the possibility that anal-ysis alone is not sufficient for our students and graduates. In addition to criti-cal thinking, learners need to be engaged in creative thinking. Some describe critical thinking as a convergent process, while creative thinking is a divergent process (Cropley, 2001, 1–2).

A few higher education institutions have even posited that the current his-torical moment in time demands that learners blend or bridge these forms of thinking. The notion is that any complex problem requires more than a deft explication; it also needs active engagement and generative energy such that a constructive response may follow. (An analogy in the practice of medicine may prove clarifying here. A physician not only needs formal training to diagnose a health condition, but also the ability to select, communicate, and make com-pelling a treatment plan for the patient. Otherwise, the diagnosis offers little benefit.)

There is no essential reason why creative learning activities need to be reserved for just a subset of learners narrowed by field in higher education. Like-wise, creativity and criticality need not be juxtaposed (or perhaps even sharply distinguished from one another). After all, the qualities that underlie critical thinking (articulated in 1987 by the National Council for Excellence in Critical Thinking as "clarity, accuracy, precision, consistency, relevance, sound evidence, good reasons, depth, breadth, and fairness") and those associated with creative thinking (expressed by Training Requirements and Nursing Skills for Mobility in Health Care [TRaNSforM] as "open-mindedness, flexibility and adaptabil-ity") are hardly discrete. *The properties of critical thinking and creative thinking are overlapping and complementary strengths, and each set of attributes contributes to forming and maintaining a creative learning environment.*

In other words, one who has command of information may be educated, but only one who is agile, venturesome, and ethical in its use may be wise. When higher education places too much importance on information transfer, it runs the risk of leaving learners far short of wisdom in the exercise or application of their education.

We might further assert that creative learning is a capacity that only grows in importance when considering the 21st-century learning priorities for higher education (Pellegrino and Hilton, 2012; Sweet and Carpenter, 2013; Bass and Eynon, 2016).

Twenty-first century learners need . . .

- Content, but they need equally to connect that content to consequences. They need to be willing to take intellectual risks to arrive at fresh insights, devise unconventional solutions, or generate previously unrealized alternatives.
- Information, but they need equally to accompany that information with the web of meaning that comes only from context.
- Practical skills, but they need equally to consider the implications of their use.
- To function as independent and efficacious individuals, but they need equally to establish and grow their abilities as collaborators.
- To think for themselves and function as self-regulated learners, but they need equally to contribute to, and benefit from, productive communication and dialogue with others.
- To pursue advanced understandings of a field of study, but they need equally to see that area of knowledge in its complex relationship to other fields of inquiry.
- To make thoughtful use of emerging technologies including social media, but they need equally to value and cultivate the aptitudes necessary to effective live, face-to-face interaction with peers in the exploration of a subject or topic.
- To remain open to unconventional possibilities in higher education learning, but they need equally to be prepared to pursue those options that prove genuinely innovative in their potential relevance and value to the human condition (thereby avoiding novelty for its own sake).

Conclusion

Progressive educator Myles Horton once commented, "I think that if I had to put a finger on what I consider a good education, a good radical education, it wouldn't be anything about methods or techniques. It would be loving people first" (Horton et al., 1990, 118). As students strive to become better learners, better professionals, and better global citizens, creative learning may well be the force that helps them do so while simultaneously holding them true to their even more basic calling: the work of becoming more fully human.

Earlier in this chapter, we referenced Parker Palmer on the insufficiency of technique in evoking what good instruction is, does, or makes possible. He emphasizes:

Technique is what teachers use until the real teacher arrives, and we need to find as many ways as possible to help that teacher show up. But if we want to develop the identity and integrity that good teaching requires, we must do something alien to academic culture: we must talk to each other about our inner lives—risky stuff in a profession that fears the personal and seeks safety in the technical, the distant, the abstract.

(Palmer, 1997, 18)

Not only does Palmer's distinction between technique and teaching prove apt, but it also underscores the sense in which educators must be brave if the goal is both to engage in and to elicit transformational learning (Taylor and Cranton, 2012). For just as Palmer speaks of the 'courage to teach,' *we must find the courage to learn, the courage to challenge, and the courage to involve others in change, both personal and collective.*

When interviewing college faculty about their best instructional practices, researcher Ken Bain asked them, "Is your course like a journey, a parable, a game, a museum, a romance, a concerto, an Aristotelian tragedy, an obstacle course, one or all or some of the above?" (Bain, 2004, 186). The modes and metaphors informing creative learning in higher education are manifold. This book's account of creative learning as it might ideally apply to higher education suggests that the very definition of the term has varied widely, shifted rapidly, and often become a flash point for controversy. In the same way, it may be expected that the current discourse regarding creativity will continue to evolve, changing our sense of creative learning as a phenomenon, and informing our understanding of its meanings within higher education. We believe the pedagogy advanced within and across the chapters of this book points toward compelling ways in which creative learning may prove a portent, signaling promising developments for addressing crucial needs within higher education.

Bibliography

Babbitt, F. C., ed. (1927). *Plutarch: Moralia*, Vol. I. Cambridge: Harvard University Press.

Bain, K. (2004). *What the Best College Teachers Do*. Cambridge: Harvard University Press.

Bambara, T. (1980). *The Salt Eaters*. New York: Random House.

Bass, R., and Eynon, B. (2016). *Open and Integrative: Designing Liberal Education for the New Digital Ecosystem*. Washington, DC: AAC&U.

Beech, Thomas F. (2005). "The Courage to Learn." In S. M. Intrator (Ed.), *Living the Questions: Essays Inspired by the Work and Life of Parker J. Palmer* (pp. 82–87). San Francisco: Jossey-Bass.

Beghetto, R., and Kaufman, J. (2010). *Nurturing Creativity in the Classroom*. Cambridge: Cambridge University Press.

Bonnycastle, S. (1996). *In Search of Authority: An Introductory Guide to Literary Theory*. Peterborough, ON: Broadview Press.

Cropley, A. J. (2001). *Creativity in Education and Learning: A Guide for Teachers and Educators*. London: Kegan Paul.

Csikszentmihalyi, M. (1990). *Flow: The Psychology of Optimal Experience: Steps Toward Enhancing the Quality of Life*. New York: Harper Perennial.

Davis, J. R., and Arend, B. D. (2013). *Facilitating Seven Ways of Learning: A Resource for More Purposeful, Effective, and Enjoyable College Teaching.* Sterling, VA: Stylus.

Duncan, E. (1984). "A Plea for Intellectual Risk-Taking." In *Unless Soul Clap Its Hands: Portraits and Passages* (pp. 193–206). New York: Schocken Books.

Feynman, R. (2005). *Perfectly Reasonable Deviations from the Beaten Track: The Letters of Richard P. Feynman.* New York: Basic Books.

Fleith, D., Bruno-Faria, M., and Alancar, E. (2014). *Theory and Practice of Creativity Measurement.* Waco, TX: Prufrock Press.

Heist, P. (1967). *Education for Creativity: A Modern Myth?* Berkeley: Center for Research and Development in Higher Education, University of California, Berkeley.

Horton, M., Bell, B., Gaventa, J., and Peters, J. M. (1990). *We Make the Road by Walking: Conversations on Education and Social Change.* Philadelphia: Temple University Press.

Intrator, S. M. (2005). *Living the Questions: Essays Inspired by the Work and Life of Parker J. Palmer.* San Francisco: Jossey-Bass.

Jackson, N., Oliver, M., Shaw, M., and Wisdom, J. (2006). *Developing Creativity in Higher Education.* London: Routledge.

Kaufman, J. C., Plucker, J., and Baer, J. (2008). *Essentials of Creativity Assessment.* Hoboken, NJ: Wiley.

Kuh, G. (2008). *High-Impact Practices: What They Are, Who Has Access to Them, and Why They Matter.* Washington, DC: AAC&U.

Markova, D. (2005). "Thinking Ourselves Home: The Cultivation of Wisdom." In S. M. Intrator (Ed.), *Living the Questions: Essays Inspired by the Work and Life of Parker J. Palmer* (pp. 60–71). San Francisco: Jossey-Bass.

National Council for Excellence in Critical Thinking. (1987). "Defining Critical Thinking." Retrieved from http://www.criticalthinking.org/pages/defining-critical-thinking/766

Nygaard, C., Courtney, N., and Holtham, C. (2012). *Teaching Creativity—Creativity in Teaching* (Learning in Higher Education Series). Oxfordshire: Libri.

Palmer, P. (Nov/Dec 1997) "The Heart of a Teacher, Integrity and Identity in Teaching." *Change Magazine,* 29(6): 14–21.

Palmer, P. (1998). *The Courage to Teach: Exploring the Inner Landscape of a Teacher's Life.* San Francisco: Jossey-Bass.

Pellegrino, J. W., and Hilton, M. L. (Eds.). (2012). *Education for Life and Work: Developing Transferable Knowledge and Skills in the 21st Century.* Washington, DC: National Research Council of the National Academies/National Academies Press.

Robinson, K. (2011). *Out of Our Minds: Learning to be Creative.* Capstone.

Sweet, C., and Carpenter, R. (2013). *Teaching Applied Creative Thinking: A New Pedagogy for the 21st Century.* Stillwater, OK: New Forums Press.

Taylor, E. W., and Cranton, P. (2012) *Handbook of Transformative Learning: Theory, Research, and Practice.* San Francisco: Jossey-Bass.

TRaNSforM. (2016)."Working Definition of Creative Thinking." Retrieved from http://www.transformnursing.eu/transform/working-definitions/creative-thinking.aspx

Treffinger, D. J., Young, G. C., Selby, E. C., and Shepardson, C. (2002). *Assessing Creativity: A Guide for Educators.* Storrs, CT: National Research Center on the Gifted and Talented.

Walker, A. (1976). *Meridian.* New York: Washington Square Press.

ABOUT THE CONTRIBUTORS

The Editors

Patrick Blessinger is the Founder, Executive Director, and Chief Research Scientist of the International Higher Education Teaching and Learning Association (HETL) and an Adjunct Associate Professor in the School of Education at St. John's University (New York City). Dr. Blessinger is the editor-in-chief of two international academic journals and two international book series on higher education.

Linda S. Watts is Professor of American Studies and Co-director of the Project for Interdisciplinary Pedagogy in the School of Interdisciplinary Arts and Sciences at the University of Washington, Bothell.

The Contributing Authors

Stephen Brookfield is the John Ireland Endowed Chair at the University of St. Thomas in Minneapolis-St. Paul. He has taught for forty-five years in community, adult, and higher education in Britain, Canada, and the United States and has authored, edited, or co-authored eighteen books, six of which have won the Cyril O. Houle World Award for Literature in Adult Education. Informed by European critical theory and American pragmatism, he is engaged in the experimental pursuit of beautiful consequences and interested in learning about, and helping others fight against, ideological manipulation. His work within and outside higher education focuses on teaching critical thinking, democratizing the classroom, and understanding the responsible use of teacher power. To accomplish these projects he uses primarily discussion-based exercises and activities. He runs workshops around the world and gives away his exercises and techniques for free at http://www.stephenbrookfield.com.

Nives Dolšak is Professor at the School of Marine and Environmental Affairs, University of Washington, Seattle. She is also a Visiting Professor at the Faculty of Economics, University of Ljubljana, Slovenia. She has co-edited two volumes, *The Drama of the Commons* (National Academy of Sciences Press, 2002) and *The Commons in the New Millennium: Challenges and Adaptation* (MIT Press, 2003). Her other work examines political and economic factors impacting global climate change mitigation at local, state, and national levels; linkages between commercial interests, voting, and bilateral environmental aid allocation; the role of social capital in environmental policy; and diffusion of market-based environmental policy instruments. She serves on the Science Panel of Puget Sound Partnership.

Gina Rae Foster currently directs the Lehman Teaching & Learning Commons at Lehman College/CUNY in the Bronx, New York, and chairs both the International Higher Education Teaching & Learning Association's Anthology Editorial Advisory Board and the CUNY Center for Teaching & Learning Directors Council. Her faculty positions include acting as Poet-in-Residence and Marina Tsvetaeva Fellow in Poetics for the European Graduate School's division of Philosophy, Art, and Critical Thought and as Professor in the Institute for Critical Philosophy at the Global Center for Advanced Studies. Dr. Foster's recent books include *heart speech this* (2009), *Beautiful Laceration* (2012), and *Lyric Dwelling: The Art and Ethics of Invitation and Occupation* (2012), all published by Atropos Press. She serves on the editorial boards for the *Journal for Meaning Centered Education* and the *International Higher Education Teaching and Learning Review.* A graduate of Pomona College in Claremont, California, Dr. Foster holds a DPhil in Philosophy, Art, and Critical Thought from the European Graduate School; an MFA in Creative Writing from the University of Oregon; and an MA in Religion from Vanderbilt University. Dr. Foster is certified in International Trauma Studies through the International Trauma Studies Program affiliated with Columbia University.

David Giles is Professor and Dean of the School of Education, Flinders University, South Australia. David has taught in primary schools, secondary schools, teachers' colleges, colleges of education, and in four public universities and one independent tertiary college across New Zealand and Australia. He currently teaches in pre-service teacher education, educational leadership and management, and higher education. His preferred research approaches are hermeneutic phenomenology and appreciative inquiry, approaches that open the ontological and life-centric nature of everyday educational experiences. From earlier research on the teacher-student relationship in higher education, David's research now explores the relational nature of pedagogy, organizational culture, and leadership. These research inquiries have led to his phenomenological construction of "relational leadership" and the co-construction of postgraduate educational leadership and management programs with colleagues. A recurring theme in his work and practice is that relational and moral imperatives for education are essential to our praxis.

Cinnamon Hillyard is Associate Professor of Mathematics in the School of Interdisciplinary Arts and Sciences at the University of Washington, Bothell, where she teaches mathematics, statistics, and interdisciplinary research courses. Her research focuses on how people use quantitative information to make decisions and how undergraduate education can foster the development of quantitative literacy. She collaborates with the Carnegie Foundation for the Advancement of Teaching, where she has led multiple initiatives around the Quantway program including developing curriculum, working with a network of faculty to implement the curriculum, and studying its effectiveness across campuses nationwide. She has also held leadership positions in the National Numeracy Network and Math Association of America's working group on Quantitative Literacy.

Norman Jackson is Emeritus Professor at the University of Surrey, a Fellow of the Royal Society of Arts, and founder of two social educational enterprises, "Lifewide Education" and "Creative Academic." His views of learning in higher education have been shaped by the diverse perspectives he has enjoyed over a long career in teaching; research; quality assurance; policy-making; professional, educational, and organizational development; system-wide brokerage; and as a writer and thought leader. His interest in creativity in higher education began in 2000, when he led the UK-wide imaginative curriculum network for the Higher Education Academy. To find out more about his work on creativity in higher education, visit http://www.creativeacademic.uk/.

Alison James is Associate Dean, Learning and Teaching, at the London College of Fashion. She is also a National Teaching Fellow (2014) and Principal Fellow of the Higher Education Academy. Alison has taught, researched, and written extensively on creative and multisensory approaches to learning, personal and professional development (PPD), and play in higher education (HE). She is co-author, with Professor Stephen Brookfield, of *Engaging Imagination: Helping Students Become Creative and Reflective Thinkers* (Jossey-Bass, 2014). Alison is an accredited LEGO® SERIOUS PLAY® facilitator and has worked in Europe as well as the UK. She works extensively with LEGO at the University of the Arts, London, and in external collaborations and is co-founder of the LEGO in HE network. She has won a University of the Arts London Excellent Teaching Award for using LEGO SERIOUS PLAY to enhance student learning and staff and educational development.

Robert Kaplan is a multi-instrumentalist performer and composer—piano, guitar, electronics, and percussion. He has worked as a composer, teacher, and musician in dance since 1976, having taught and performed at major national and international dance festivals since 1980—Regional Dance American's Craft of Choreography Conferences, Bates Dance Festival, and American Dance Festival. His book, *Rhythmic Training for Dancers*, CD-ROM: *An Interactive Guide to Music for Dancers*, and accompanying Instructor's Guide were published internationally by Human Kinetics, Inc. (2002). Over seventy of his scores for choreography have been performed throughout the United States, Europe, Asia, and Mexico. Trained as a classical pianist, Kaplan has always improvised, including stints in improvisation-based groups with guitarist and composer/producer David Torn, multi-percussionist/composer Geoffrey Gordon, and composer and saxophonist Thomas Chapin. Kaplan is a Professor and the Music Director for Dance in the School of Film, Dance, and Theatre at Arizona State University. He is currently facilitating the I.D.E.A. Impulse Initiative, building a community around the research and practice of improvisation across disciplines.

Gray Kochhar-Lindgren is Professor and Director of the Common Core at the University of Hong Kong. Prior to this position, he served as the Associate Vice Chancellor for Undergraduate Learning and Professor of Interdisciplinary Arts & Sciences at the University of Washington, Bothell, where he oversaw, among other programs, community-based learning and research, global initiatives, and the Student Success Center. With a PhD in Interdisciplinary Studies from Emory University, Gray is the author of *Narcissus Transformed* (Penn State University Press, 1993); *Starting Time* (White Cloud Press, 1995); *TechnoLogics* (SUNY Press, 2004); *Night Café* (EyeCorner Press, 2010); *Philosophy, Art, and the Specters of Jacques Derrida* (Cambria Press, 2011); and *Kant in Hong Kong: Walking, Thinking, and the City* (EyeCorner Press, 2014). The recipient of two teaching awards, he has taught in Switzerland, Germany, and the United States, and in 2009–10 served as a Fulbright Scholar in General Education at the Hong Kong America Center and the University of Hong Kong, where he taught in both philosophy and comparative literature. Currently, he is working on projects on philosophy in the streets; the transdisciplinary university; and art, politics, and education in Hong Kong.

Kanta Kochhar-Lindgren, an artist and performance studies scholar, directs *Folded Paper Dance and Theatre*. Her current art project, *Touching Cities* (Hong Kong, Singapore, Kochi), focuses on the relationships between dance, cultural heritage, memory, disability, water, and urban experience. Her written scholarship includes topics such as water and performance, translation and embodiment, disability and performance, transnational avant-garde Asian performance, and experiments in creative learning in international higher education.

Clare McCarty is currently Senior Lecturer in the School of Education at Flinders University in South Australia. Her early degrees were attained in London at King's College and the Institute of Education; her PhD was awarded by the University of Technology, Sydney. As a longtime secondary school teacher, Clare's pedagogical practice was transformative, and in her present role she specializes in creativity in education. While at Flinders University she has received a Faculty Excellence in Teaching Award and three vice chancellor's grants to enhance the pastoral and pedagogical experience of a large cohort of first year students. She has also been appointed Director of First Year Studies and has twice been elected as a member of the Flinders University Council.

Fredricka Reisman, PhD, is Professor and Founding Director of Drexel University's School of Education. She is Director of the Drexel-Torrance Center for Creativity and Innovation, and creator of the online Creativity and Innovation master's and EdD programs. She served as Professor and Chair of the Division of Elementary Education at the University of Georgia; as an elementary, middle, and high school mathematics teacher in New York State; and as a mathematics education instructor at Syracuse University. She is author of several books on subjects that include diagnostic teaching, teaching mathematics to children with special needs, and elementary and mathematics education pedagogy. She has co-authored a trilogy of books with world-renowned creativity scholar and researcher, E. Paul Torrance, on teaching mathematics creatively. She also co-authored (with David Tanner, formerly Chief Innovation Officer at DuPont) *Creativity as a Bridge Between Education and Industry: Fostering New Innovations* (CreateSpace, 2014), available from Amazon.com. She and her co-authors created a free Apple app (downloadable via iTunes), the Reisman Diagnostic Creativity Assessment (RDCA), which taps eleven creativity research-based factors. Dr. Reisman was awarded the 2002 David Tanner Champion of Creativity Award by the American Creativity Association (ACA) and is currently completing her fourth year as ACA president.

Lorraine Stefani is Professor of Higher Education Strategic Engagement at the University of Auckland (UoA), New Zealand. She is involved in many strategic higher education initiatives including President of HETL; member of the Royal New Zealand College of General Practitioners Education Advisory Board; and former member of the Inaugural Board of Directors for Ako Aotearoa (New Zealand National Centre for Tertiary Teaching Excellence). She is a Senior Fellow of the Staff and Educational Development Association (UK) and a Senior Fellow of the Higher Education Academy (UK). She is a member of several other professional bodies including the International Leadership Association and the Higher Education Research and Development Society Australasia (HERDSA). Lorraine has published widely on a range of contemporary issues in higher education and is a frequent keynote speaker at international conferences.

INDEX

interdisciplinary learning 7
International Red Cross 125
intuitive "voice" 184
iPad app 17
iPhone app 17
irreverence 223
iterative processes 48
iTunes 17

Jackson, N. J. 201–2, 203, 204
James, Alison 120, 124
Jansen, Sen 41
Jesmes, Jebin 41
Jewell, Paul 76

Kabat-Zinn, Jon 181
Kane, P. 124
Kant, Immanuel 62
Kaplan, Robert 219
Kerala 40, 41
Klein, Gary 144
knowing 108
knowledge 6, 10
Kochhar-Lindgren, Gray 223
Kochhar-Lindgren, Kanta 41, 218
Kreuzer, Paul 147
Kristiansen, Per 128

Laban Movement Analysis 46–7
Laban, Rudolf 46
language 72, 193
lateral thinking 29
Lawrence, R. 171
learning: creativity in 197–8; diagnostic
    learning 20–1; formal learning systems
    6; innovation pedagogy and 19–20;
    role of academic development in
    transforming 204–7; self-initiated
    learning 19; supporting 202; traditional
    modes of 121; transforming 34; see also
    creative learning
learning-centered practices 11
learning ecology 202–4
learning objectives 100–2
learning relationship 106–7
learning spaces, meaningful and engaged
    67, 71–6, 79–80
LEGO SERIOUS PLAY 119, 123; creative
    learning and 125–35; use in corporate
    settings 126; use in higher education
    contexts 126; workshop 126–8, 130–2
Lehman College/CUNY 141–2, 146, 147
Levinas, Emmanuel 93
listening 181–2, 183

Living Musically: awareness of self/
    focus 181–2; background 177–9;
    benefits 191–4; bridging beyond self
    187–8; Chaos to Unity exercise 186–91;
    creative interaction 189–90; Drawing
    Conversations exercise 184–6; exercises
    182–91; getting started 179–81; Right
    Before Our Ears exercise 183–4;
    60-Second Sound Score exercise 182–3
Lucas, C. 199
*Lyric Dwelling: The Art & Ethics of
    Invitation & Occupation* (Foster) 149

MacKinnon, Donald W. 223
Maguire, Emma 77
Markova, Dawna 222
Mazur, Eric 203–4
McCarty, Clare 223
McTighe, Jay 99
"meddlers" 202
mental rehearsal 35
mentoring 145
Meyer, Leonard 180
Mills, C. W. 54–5
mindfulness: assignment prompt 102–3;
    assignment responses on student
    writing 103–8; course planning
    calendar 111–17; course syllabus 100–2;
    earthly aspirations course objective
    101–2; humanistic content course
    objective 100; interaction with higher
    education 108–10; learning objectives
    100–2; literary cluster 103; lofty
    aspirations course objective 101; specific
    skills course objective 100; translatable
    abilities course objective 100
Mississippi River 40, 41
Mitchell, Nora 108
m-learning 23
mobile computing 23
Montgomery College 167
multidisciplinary learning 7
multimedia 23
musicalizing discussion 168–9

Naake, Joan 167
Nachmanovitch, S. 179
Nagrin, Daniel 193
National Aeronautics and Space
    Administration (NASA) 125
National Council for Excellence in
    Critical Thinking 227
natural creativity 6
natural sciences 58

41–2; doorway as key signature of 44; overview 39–41; as type of participatory choreographies 40–1, 46–51
water stories 40
Web 2.0 x
Web 3.0 x
Wells, K. 166
"whole-person education" 59–60

wicked problems 198
Wiggins, Grant 99
Williams, H. S. 171
Willingham, Daniel T. 139, 140–1, 148
Wilson, Frank 125

Yeats, W. B. 59

"zone of proximal development" 141